S
THE COVENANTS,
AND THE PROPHESIES

HANS WILLER LAALE

THE SEED, THE COVENANTS, AND THE PROPHESIES
Copyright © 2017 by Hans Willer Laale

All rights reserved. Neither this publication nor any part of this publication may be reproduced or transmitted in any form or by any means, electronic or mechanical, including photocopying, recording or any information storage and retrieval system, without permission in writing from the author.

Unless otherwise indicated, all scripture taken from the Holy Bible, American Standard Version, which is in the public domain. Scripture marked (NKJV) taken from the New King James Version®. Copyright © 1982 by Thomas Nelson. Used by permission. All rights reserved.

Printed in Canada

ISBN: 978-1-4866-1502-5

Word Alive Press
131 Cordite Road, Winnipeg, MB R3W 1S1
www.wordalivepress.ca

Cataloguing in Publication may be obtained through Library and Archives Canada

Contents

Acknowledgements v
Preface vii
Introduction ix

History, Part One: Old Testament

1. The Pre-Patriarchal Period 3
2. The Patriarchal Period 11
3. The Pre-Monarchic Period 21
4. The United Kingdom 33
5. The Divided Kingdom 45
6. The Intertestamental Period 103

History, Part Two: New Testament

7. The Church Age 111
8. Day of the Lord 129

Part Three: Prophecies Fulfilled

9. The Prophesies of the Old Testament 137
10. Prophecies in Genesis 141
11. Prophecies in Exodus 147
12. Prophesies in Numbers 149
13. Prophesies in Deuteronomy 151
14. Prophesies in Joshua 155
15. Prophesies in Judges 157
16. Prophesies in Job 159
17. Prophesies in Psalms 161
18. Prophesies in Proverbs 193

19.	Prophesies in Isaiah	195
20.	Prophesies in Jeremiah	227
21.	Prophesies in Ezekiel	233
22.	Prophesies in Daniel	235
23.	Prophesies in Hosea	241
24.	Prophesies of Joel	245
25.	Prophesies of Amos	247
26.	Prophesies in Obadiah	249
27.	Prophesies in Jonah (Jonas)	251
28.	Prophesies in Micah	253
29.	Prophesies in Nahum	255
30.	Prophesies in Habakkuk	257
31.	Prophesies in Zephaniah	259
32.	Prophesies in Haggai	261
33.	Prophesies in Zechariah	263
34.	Prophesies in Malachi	271

Acknowledgements

This book is dedicated to my brother Bent Jorgen Laale. May the good Lord watch over him and bless him for the duration of his pilgrimage. I also extend my most sincere thanks to friends and colleagues for their encouragement, unreserved support, suggestions and advise. Special thanks is owed to Word Alive Press for their professionalism.

Above, all, thanks be to God for providing me with direction and good health throughout the writing

Preface

Remember the former things of old: for I am God, and there is none else; I am God, and there is none like me; declaring the end from the beginning, and from ancient times things that are not yet done; saying, My counsel shall stand, and I will do all my pleasure; calling a ravenous bird from the east, the man of my counsel from a far country; yea, I have spoken, I will also bring it to pass; I have purposed, I will also do it.

—Isaiah 46:9–11

Introduction

No language is sufficient to express the origin, the dignity, even the substance and nature of the preexisting Son of God, for who has known the Father, but the Son, and no one can know the Son fully, but the Father alone, by whom He was begotten.[1]

The preexisting Son of God

> *who, existing in the form of God, counted not the being on an equality with God a thing to be grasped, but emptied himself, taking the form of a servant, being made in the likeness of men; and being found in fashion as a man, he humbled himself, becoming obedient even unto death, yea, the death of the cross.*
> —Philippians 2:6–8

Thus He fulfilled the eternal plan of salvation for the redemption of fallen humanity.

The purpose of this book is to inspire interest in those who believe, and in those who do not, that an eternal, redemptive, and divine plan has been unfolded by the holy prophets of God in the Old Testament and fulfilled in the New Testament. The covenant concept establishes God's redemptive relationship to man in all periods of man's history. It provides a central unifying principle for understanding the whole of Scripture, and defines the unique relationship between God and man: *"And I will walk among you, and will be your God, and ye shall be my people"* (Leviticus 26:12). Information is interconnected to provide an abbreviated history of the people and rulers of Israel, their relationships to God, to one another, and to the surrounding superpowers Egypt, Aram-Syria, Assyria, Babylon, Persia,

---

1 C. F. Cruse, I. Boyle. The Ecclesiastical History of Eusebius Pamphilus (Baker Book House, Grand Rapids, Michigan, 1971), I.II.15–16.

Greece and Rome. Pendulous chronologies and unsolved chronological problems regarding the reigns of kings make it necessary at times to resort to conjecture, and some conclusions drawn may seem tentative. The emphasis throughout has been to provide an overview from a literal biblical perspective of God's unique plan of salvation for the human race. Unless otherwise indicated Scriptures are taken from the American Standard Version (ASV).[2] Events are liberally documented with excerpts and explanatory footnotes dealing with a variety of matters covering a wide range of time occasionally filled with lacunae hungering like empty spaces in a puzzle to be filled. The contents is designed for students and laymen interested in acquiring an understanding of the inter-connectedness of the Old and New Testaments. It is hoped that this abridged history of Israel and Judah, woven into the unfolding historical fabric of ancient, medieval, and modern political and religious conflicts, will stimulate interest in God's word, elicit dialogue, and provide readers with a fair measure of enjoyment as well as spiritual direction.

The book is held together by a thin thread, the Seed of the woman (Genesis 3:15), that on wings of prophesy makes its way throughout the Old Testament to find fulfillment in the New Testament. Seen from afar the "Seed of the woman" initially is perceived indistinctly, but as revelations are made by God's inspired holy prophets over time, a detailed portrait emerges of Jesus Christ the incarnate Word of God, in His all-embracing fullness. The book is arranged chronologically into pre-historical and historical periods: Pre-Patriarchal Period, Patriarchal Period, Pre-Monarchic Period, United Kingdom Period, Divided Kingdom Period, Inter- Testamental Period, the Church Age, the Day of the Lord, and the Prophesies Fulfilled.

---

[2] The author of the book adheres to the biblical principle of divine authorship of the plenary and verbal inspiration of the original autographs. The author also accepts full responsibility for any errors of interpretation made by him.

History
Part I
Old Testament

Chapter One

THE PRE-PATRIARCHAL PERIOD[3]

In the beginning God created the heavens and the earth.

—Genesis 1:1

In six days he created *ex nihilo* everything that He had made, and it was very good. Having made everything He had made, God on the sixth day of creation said:

Let us make man in our image, after our likeness: and let them have dominion over the fish of the sea, and over the birds of the heavens, and over the cattle, and over all the earth, and over every creeping thing that creepeth upon the earth. And God created man in his own image, in the image of God created he him; male and female created he them.

—Genesis 1:26–27[4]

God commanded and they were created. Being bearers of God's image and endowed with thought, knowledge, action, and freedom of will, Adam and Eve in their initial innocence were deceived by the serpent, elsewhere called the Devil and Satan, the prince of this world, the god of this world, the adversary, and the spirit that now works in the children of disobedience. Trusting the serpent, in opposition to God's holy standard of righteousness, they transgressed the Edenic covenant. Irresistibly they were drawn by desire to eat the fruit of the forbidden Tree of the Knowledge of Good and Evil, and when desire was conceived it gave

---

3   For the chronology from Moses to Joshua see Eusebius. Preparation for the Gospel (Baker Book House, Grand Rapids, Michigan, 1981), Part 2, Book X, Chapter XIV, p.539.

4   The two words "Us" and "Our" introduces God as a plurality (compound unity, tri-unity) consisting of God the Father, God the Son, and God the Holy Spirit (Genesis 1:26; 11:7). The account of the creation of Eve is given in Genesis 2:21–23.

birth to sin, and sin brought forth the corruption of human nature and spiritual death. The image of God's imparted righteousness and holiness in man was broken, and man became estranged from God. Since sin by its nature is hateful to a righteous God, and merits just punishment, Adam and Eve were expelled from the Garden of Eden. God also placed cherubim at the east of the garden, and a flaming sword which turned every way to guard the way to the Tree of Life.[5] An unconditional Covenant of Grace was then introduced by God whereby the promised Seed of the woman in time would redeem sinful humanity from the fall's curse, and crush Satan's head. Through Adam and Eve sin thus entered the world, and spiritual death through sin spread to all men, even over those who had not sinned according to the likeness of the transgression of Adam.[6] Moreover, sin marred the entire creation for the Apostle Paul writes:

> *For we know that the whole creation groaneth and travaileth in pain together until now. And not only so, but ourselves also, who have the first-fruits of the Spirit, even we ourselves groan within ourselves, waiting for our adoption, to wit, the redemption of our body.*
>
> —Romans 8:22–23

The fall of Adam made necessary a Redeemer who, as a Second Adam, and quickening spirit, would in time expiate the cumulative sins of mankind by offering himself as a sin-offering in our stead, and restore what the first Adam had lost. The Apostle Paul writes that the redemptive plan was purposed in the mind of God before the foundation of the world, and before time began:

> *Blessed be the God and Father of our Lord Jesus Christ, who hath blessed us with every spiritual blessing in the heavenly places in Christ: even as he chose us in him before the foundation of the world, that we should be holy and without blemish before him in love: having foreordained us unto adoption as sons through Jesus Christ unto himself, according to the good pleasure of his will, to the praise of the glory of his grace, which he freely bestowed on us in the Beloved…*
>
> —Ephesians 1:3–6

---

[5] Genesis 3:24.

[6] The prophet Hosea refers to the transgression of Adam as a "transgression of the Edenic covenant." (Hosea 6:7).

The Pre-Patriarchal Period

The plan to rescue man from the curse was first revealed in a garden eastward in Eden when God rebuked Satan the old serpent, and said:

I will put enmity between thee and the woman, and between thy seed and her seed: he shall bruise thy head, and thou shalt bruise his heel.

—Genesis 3:15[7]

The "Seed of the woman" carried with it the unconditional guaranteed promise of a future redeemer, and the prophesies concerning Him yet to be incrementally revealed over time as the Word of God was breathed into chosen prophets of God, and enlarged. The prophetic promises, foretelling the facts of Christ's incarnation, ministry, doctrine, death, resurrection and ascension, like a golden cord of grace and truth running through the entire contents of the Old Testament, have their fulfillment in the New Testament Messiah, the "Seed of the woman." The promises are anticipatory and preparatory in that they prefigure things to come in the New Testament. Thus since the days of Abel the expectations concerning the coming of the Messiah, and the work He was foreordained to accomplish on earth, as the promised "Seed of the woman," were kept alive by faith from generation to generation in the hearts and minds of god-fearing Jews. However, not all had faith, for:

The life of men, in ancient times, was not in a position to receive the doctrine of Christ in the all-comprehensive fulness of its wisdom and its virtue.[8]

Now Adam knew his wife, and she gave birth to righteous Abel and unrighteous Cain who killed his brother. Then Adam again knew his wife and she bore a son named Seth. To Seth also there was born a son called Enosh (Gr. Enos), and for a while men began to call upon the name of the Lord. After Enosh came Cainan, Mahalaleel, Jared and the prophet Enoch [a type of Christ] of whom it is said that

---

[7] The bruising of "His heel" prophetically pictures Messiah's future sufferings. The bruising of "his head" was accomplished when Satan was defeated by the death and resurrection of Jesus Christ. *"To this end was the Son of God manifested, that he might destroy the works of the devil"* (1 John 3:8), and *"that through death he might bring to nought him that had the power of death, that is, the devil; and might deliver all them who through fear of death were all their lifetime subject to bondage"* (Hebrews 2:14–15).

[8] C. F. Cruse and I. Boyle. The Ecclesiastical History of Eusebius Pamphilus (Baker Book House, Grand Rapids, Michigan, 1971), I. II.18.

he *"walked with God: and he was not; for God took him"* (Genesis 5:24). After Enoch came Methusaleh, Lamech and Noah, a just man perfect in his generations. Alienation from God was catastrophic, for by the time of Noah, the son of Lamech, the Lord saw that the wickedness of man was great in the earth, and that every intent of the thoughts of his heart was only evil continuously, and the Lord in righteous indignation said, *"I will destroy man whom I have created from the face of the ground... for it repenteth me that I have made them"* (Genesis 6:7).[9]

True to God's command Noah, the son of Lamech, *"prepared an ark [made of gopherwood] to the saving of his house; through which he condemned the world, and became heir of the righteousness which is according to faith"* (Hebrews 11:7; see also Genesis 6:14–16). God established His covenant with Noah, his sons, his wife, and his son's wives, and their descendants, thus preserving the human race so that the promised Seed of the woman in the fulness of time might be born (Genesis 6:18; 9:9–11). Exceedingly provoked by the evil He saw, God sent a great flood. The deluge swept away all flesh in whose nostrils was the breath of the spirit of life, and only Noah, and his sons Ham, Shem and Japheth and their wives were preserved in the ark. From them the human race was repopulated. With them God established the Noarhic Covenant promising never again to destroy the earth as long as His sign, a rainbow, would appear in the clouds above (Genesis 9:11–17). The deluge, however, did not eradicate the potential for evil in the hearts of men, for ancient Enoch, the seventh from Adam, of whom it is said that he had this testimony that he pleased God, he seeing far ahead of his own time and beyond the time of God's covenant promise to Noah to the last days, prophesied that at the end of days the Lord would judge all ungodly sinners:

> *And behold! He comes with ten thousands of His holy ones, to execute judgment upon all, and to destroy all the ungodly: And to convict all flesh of all the works of their ungodliness which they have ungodly committed, and of all the hard things which ungodly sinners have spoken against Him.*
> —The Book of Enoch I:9[10]

---

9 *"And God said unto Noah, The end of all flesh is come before me; for the earth is filled with violence through them; and, behold, I will destroy them with the earth"* (Genesis 6:13).

10 R. H. Charles., tr. The Book of Enoch I:9 (Mineola, New York: Dover Publications, Inc., 2007), 32 (a republication of the Society for Promoting Christian Knowledge, London 1917. Originally published by Canon Charles at Clarendon Press, Oxford in 1893. Enoch divides biblical history into periods called weeks.

The end-time prophesy of Enoch, repeated almost verbatim by the prophet Jude in the New Testament Epistle of Jude, significantly refers to the Second Coming or advent of the Lord at the last day, and to the execution of judgment on the ungodly:

And to these also Enoch, the seventh from Adam, prophesied, saying, Behold, the Lord came with ten thousands of his holy ones, to execute judgment upon all, and to convict all the ungodly of all their works of ungodliness which they have ungodly wrought, and of all the hard things which ungodly sinners have spoken against him.
—Jude 14–15

The Apostles Matthew and Luke in general terms compare the behavior of mankind before the time of Noah to mankind's behavior at the Second Coming of the Son of Man:

And as were the days of Noah, so shall be the coming of the Son of man. For as in those days which were before the flood they were eating and drinking, marrying and giving in marriage, until the day that Noah entered into the ark, and they knew not until the flood came, and took them all away; so shall be the coming of the Son of man... Watch therefore: for ye know not on what day your Lord cometh.
—Matthew 24:37–39, 42
(see also Luke 17:26, 30)

The Apostle Paul is more precise, for to young Timothy, his *"true child in faith"* (1 Timothy 1:2), he writes:

But know this, that in the last days grievous times shall come. For men shall be lovers of self, lovers of money, boastful, haughty, railers, disobedient to parents, unthankful, unholy, without natural affection, implacable, slanderers, without self-control, fierce, no lovers of good, traitors, headstrong, puffed up, lovers of pleasure rather than lovers of God; holding a form of godliness, but having denied the power thereof: from these also turn away... For the time will come when they will not endure the sound doctrine; but, having itching ears, will heap to themselves teachers after their own lusts; and will turn away their ears from the truth, and turn aside unto fables.
—2 Timothy 3:1–5, 4:3–4
(see also Revelation 21:8)

Even at the very end of days when God will send His angel to destroy mankind with plagues - even then, writes the Apostle John, the un-reformable and un-redeemable will refuse to repent of their evil works:

> *And the rest of mankind, who were not killed with these plagues, repented not of the works of their hands, that they should not worship demons, and the idols of gold, and of silver, and of brass, and of stone, and of wood; which can neither see, nor hear, nor walk: and they repented not of their murders, nor of their sorceries, nor of their fornication, nor of their thefts.*
> —Revelation 9:20–21

Continuing the Apostle John adds:

> *And men were scorched with great heat: and they blasphemed the name of God who hath the power over these plagues; and they repented not to give him glory... and they blasphemed the God of heaven because of their pains and their sores; and they repented not of their works.*
> —Revelation 16:9, 11

Despite the goodness, forbearance and longsuffering of God towards sinners, for He takes no pleasure in the death of the wicked (Ezekiel 33:11), nor is He willing that any should perish (2 Peter 3:9), such reprobate souls who have no fear of God before their eyes, who care not about the consequences of their ungodly actions, and do not like to retain God in their knowledge, will never repent.[11] They treasure to themselves divine wrath, and on the appointed Day of Judgment they will be accounted unrighteous by a judicial act of a holy and righteous God faithful to the balanced application of His attributes, for He has appointed a day in the which He will judge the world in righteousness (Revelation 20:11–15). As pondered by the writer of The Epistle to the Hebrews:

---

[11] By contrast to the ungodly, the apostle Paul lists the virtues cultivated by the godly: *"But the fruit of the Spirit is love, joy, peace, longsuffering, kindness, goodness, faithfulness, 23 meekness, self-control"* (Galatians 5:22–23). In Exodus the Lord God is proclaimed to be *"merciful and gracious, slow to anger, and abundant in lovingkindness and truth; keeping lovingkindness for thousands, forgiving iniquity and transgression and sin; and that will by no means clear the guilty, visiting the iniquity of the fathers upon the children, and upon the children's children, upon the third and upon the fourth generation"* (Exodus 34:6–7).

...how much sorer punishment, think ye, shall he be judged worthy, who hath trodden under foot the Son of God, and hath counted the blood of the covenant wherewith he was sanctified an unholy thing, and hath done despite unto the Spirit of grace?

—Hebrews 10:29

By contrast, Abel, Enoch and Noah at the dawn of history all became heirs of the righteousness which is according to faith, for it is recorded:

By faith Abel offered unto God a more excellent sacrifice than Cain, through which he had witness borne to him that he was righteous, God bearing witness in respect of his gifts: and through it he being dead yet speaketh. By faith Enoch was translated that he should not see death; and he was not found, because God translated him: for he hath had witness borne to him that before his translation he had been well-pleasing unto God... By faith Noah, being warned of God concerning things not seen as yet, moved with godly fear, prepared an ark to the saving of his house; through which he condemned the world, and became heir of the righteousness which is according to faith.

—Hebrews 11:4–5, 7

The same author, presumably the Apostle Paul, writes that *"without faith it is impossible to be well-pleasing unto him, for he that cometh to God must believe that he is, and that he is a rewarder of them that seek after him"* (Hebrews 11:6). So, throughout the history of the Jews and Gentiles a godly remnant, of whom the world is not worthy, have obtained a good testimony through faith in the truthfulness of the divine testimony revealed to the Jews in ever increasing totality by the prophets over time. They all died in faith not having received the prophesied promises, but having seen them afar off, they were assured of them, and embraced them, and confessed that they were strangers and pilgrims on the earth (Hebrews 11:13,39). To them faith rested immediately on "Thus said the Lord."

Chapter Two
THE PATRIARCHAL PERIOD

Following the time of Noah and the "Great Flood" the prophesy of the promised Seed of the woman was passed along the godly line to Shem, the son of Noah, and after him to Arphaxad, Cainan, Sala, Eber, Peleg, Ragau, Saruch, Nahor, Terah, and to Abram (renamed Abraham), the son of Terah living in Haran. The Period of the Patriarchs, as presented in the books of Moses, is essentially a family history concentrating on the three patriarchs Abram (Abraham) (ca. 2166–1991 B.C.), Isaac (ca. 2066–1886 B.C.), Jacob (ca. 2006–1859 B.C.), and Jacob's twelve sons. For believing God's command Abraham left Ur of the Chaldees for Canaan, and for obeying God's command Abraham was accounted as if righteous, and became the recipient of an important covenant involving not only himself, but also his natural and spiritual posterity, a godly lineage through which the promised Seed of the woman would come.

> *And when Abram was ninety years old and nine, Jehovah appeared to Abram, and said unto him, I am God Almighty; walk before me, and be thou perfect. And I will make my covenant between me and thee, and will multiply thee exceedingly... As for me, behold, my covenant is with thee, and thou shalt be the father of a multitude of nations. Neither shall thy name any more be called Abram, but thy name shall be Abraham; for the father of a multitude of nations have I made thee. And I will make thee exceeding fruitful, and I will make nations of thee, and kings shall come out of thee. And I will establish my covenant between me and thee and thy seed after thee throughout their generations for an everlasting covenant, to be a God unto thee and to thy seed after thee. And I will give unto thee, and to thy seed after thee, the land of thy sojournings, all the land of Canaan, for an everlasting possession; and I will be their God.*
>
> —Genesis 17:1–2, 4–8

Abraham believed in the "Promised Seed," whose anticipated coming had been foretold centuries before to Adam and Eve. On hearing that God would make him a father of many nations Abraham asked the Lord God, "*O Lord Jehovah, what wilt thou give me, seeing I go childless, and he that shall be possessor of my house is Eliezer of Damascus?*" (Genesis 15:2) In reply, the word of the Lord came, saying:

> *This man [Eliezer] shall not be thine heir; but he that shall come forth out of thine own bowels shall be thine heir... Nay, but Sarah thy wife shall bear thee a son; and thou shalt call his name Isaac: and I will establish my covenant with him for an everlasting covenant for his seed after him.*
>
> —Genesis 15:4, 17:19

By this promise, God created a spiritual lineage through which the promised Seed of the woman would eventually come. Since the covenant also made mention of the land of Canaan as Abraham's everlasting possession, Abraham again asked, "*O Lord Jehovah, whereby shall I know that I shall inherit it?*" Answering, God said, "*Take me a heifer three years old, and a she-goat three years old, and a ram three years old, and turtle-dove, and a young pigeon*" (Genesis 15:8–9). The heifer, the goat and the ram were then cut in two down the middle, and each piece placed opposite the other, and it came to pass during the night that what appeared like a burning torch passed between the pieces.[12] In this manner God unilaterally and symbolically demonstrated that He, in the likeness of a burning torch, would never break His covenant with Abraham. It was a binding covenant between God and Abraham and his descendants forever, ratified by circumcision (Genesis 17:10–14).[13]

Various elements of God's covenant with Abraham occur again and again throughout Genesis:

> *...and I will make of thee a great nation, and I will bless thee, and make thy name great; and be thou a blessing: and I will bless them that bless thee, and him that curseth thee will I curse: and in thee shall all the families of the earth be blessed.*
>
> —Genesis 12:2–3

---

12 For the same ancient method of ratifying a covenant see Jeremiah 34:18,19.

13 Genesis 17:10–14. Long before Abraham received the command of circumcision he believed in the Lord, and the Lord accounted it to him for righteousness. (Romans 4:3; James 2:23). Jesus said, "*Verily, verily, I say unto you, Before Abraham was, I am*" (John 8:58).

> *Unto thy seed have I given this land, from the river of Egypt unto the great river, the river Euphrates...*
>
> —Genesis 15:18

> *...[I] will multiply thee exceedingly... for the father of a multitude of nations have I made thee. And I will make thee exceeding fruitful, and I will make nations of thee, and kings shall come out of thee.*
>
> —Genesis 17:2, 5–6

> *...Abraham shall surely become a great and mighty nation, and all the nations of the earth shall be blessed in him?*
>
> —Genesis 18:18

> *...and in thy seed shall all the nations of the earth be blessed; because thou hast obeyed my voice.*
>
> —Genesis 22:18

> *...and I will multiply thy seed as the stars of heaven, and will give unto thy seed all these lands; and in thy seed shall all the nations of the earth be blessed.*
>
> —Genesis 26:4

> and thy seed shall be as the dust of the earth, and thou shalt spread abroad to the west, and to the east, and to the north, and to the south: and in thee and in thy seed shall all the families of the earth be blessed.
>
> —Genesis 28:14

The faith of Abraham in God's covenant promises was severely put to the test when God commanded him to offer up his only son Isaac as a burnt offering:

> *Take now thy son, thine only son, whom thou lovest, even Isaac, and get thee into the land of Moriah; and offer him there for a burnt-offering upon one of the mountains which I will tell thee of.*
>
> —Genesis 22:2[14]

---

[14] Mount Moriah subsequently became the site of Solomon's temple in Jerusalem and the site of Calvary.

Arriving at the place of which God had told him, Isaac asked Abraham, *"Behold, the fire and the wood: but where is the lamb for a burnt offering?"* Abraham replied, *"God will provide himself the lamb for a burnt offering, my son..."* (Genesis 22:7–8) Then Abraham built an altar, placed wood in order, bound Isaac his son and laid him on the altar, upon the wood. But when he stretched out his hand and took the knife to slay his son, the Angel of the Lord called out from heaven and said, *"Lay not thy hand upon the lad, neither do thou anything unto him; for now I know that thou fearest God, seeing thou hast not withheld thy son, thine only son, from me"* (Genesis 22:12). Commenting on Abraham's obedience to God's command, one Bible teacher writes:

> "On Mount Moriah Jehovah was teaching Abraham what He Himself was prepared to provide. He was teaching the awful cost to Himself of the provision of the sacrifice for sin. Does it break your heart, Abraham, to give up, to slay, yes, by your own hand, as an innocent sacrifice, your well-beloved and only son? Then think of the awful and infinite cost to Me of what I am prepared to do for man. The thing that Abraham fore-shadowed on Mount Moriah was realized, accomplished, when God's Son upon the cross cried, 'It is finished.'"[15]

Having passed the test of faith God said, *"[A]nd in thy seed shall all the nations of the earth be blessed; because thou hast obeyed my voice"* (Genesis 22:18). The Abrahamic Covenant was a promise of salvation through the "Seed of the woman" to all mankind - to men of faith and obedience, to Jews and Gentiles alike, but in their order. The promised seed was not the nation of Israel, but Christ the Messiah who alone can and will yet fulfill all the promises made to Abraham.

> *Now to Abraham were the promises spoken, and to his seed. He saith not, And to seeds, as of many; but as of one, And to thy seed, which is Christ... And if ye are Christ's, then are ye Abraham's seed, heirs according to promise.*
> —Galatians 3:16, 29[16]

> *Wherein God, being minded to show more abundantly unto the heirs of the promise the immutability of his counsel, interposed with an oath; that by two*

---

15   N. Stone. Names of God (Moody Press, Chicago, 1944), p. 68; John 10:17–18.
16   Galations 3:8. This truth was also preached by the apostle Peter to the Jews and Gentiles alike on the day of Pentecost when the Holy Spirit of God was given to the disciples (Acts 3:25-26).

immutable things, in which it is impossible for God to lie, we may have a strong encouragement, who have fled for refuge to lay hold of the hope set before us: which we have as an anchor of the soul, a hope both sure and stedfast and entering into that which is within the veil; whither as a forerunner Jesus entered for us, having become a high priest for ever after the order of Melchizedek.

—Hebrews 6:17–20

Throughout his long life Abraham relied on God implicitly for guidance, and he trusted in God's temporal and spiritual promises. As stated by one commentator:

"A remnant of the sons of Abraham, that is Abraham's spiritual seed, continued to hold tightly to the promise of God through all of their national history."[17]

The Abrahamic covenant was renewed and reaffirmed first to Isaac (ca. 2066–1886 B.C.), the son of Abraham, and then to Jacob (ca. 2006–1859 B.C), the son of Isaac and Rebecca. Following the death of Sarah (Sarai) and then of Abraham, Isaac went to Abimelech the king of the Philistines in Gerar. There God appeared to Isaac in a dream and extended to him the covenant promises made earlier to Abraham, saying:

…sojourn in this land, and I will be with thee, and will bless thee; for unto thee, and unto thy seed, I will give all these lands, and I will establish the oath which I sware unto Abraham thy father; and I will multiply thy seed as the stars of heaven, and will give unto thy seed all these lands; and in thy seed shall all the nations of the earth be blessed; because that Abraham obeyed my voice, and kept my charge, my commandments, my statutes, and my laws.

—Genesis 26:3–5

Now God had given Isaac's wife Rebekah two sons Jacob and Esau. When Isaac was near death and about to pass on his blessing to Esau the firstborn, Esau in weakness sold his birthright as the firstborn to Jacob, who by deceit thus obtained the blessing. The birthright was the promise to which Esau was heir under the Abrahamic covenant. Fearing Esau's anger, Jacob fled to Rebekah's brother Laban

---

17   J. Tunstall. The Seed of the Woman. The Story of an Ancient Prophesy Fulfilled (AuthorHouse, Bloomington, IN, 2011), p. 126.

in Haran, and on the way he had a vision in which the Lord God reconfirmed the promises earlier given to Abraham and Isaac:

> *I am Jehovah, the God of Abraham thy father, and the God of Isaac: the land whereon thou liest, to thee will I give it, and to thy seed; and thy seed shall be as the dust of the earth, and thou shalt spread abroad to the west, and to the east, and to the north, and to the south: and in thee and in thy seed shall all the families of the earth be blessed. And, behold, I am with thee, and will keep thee whithersoever thou goest, and will bring thee again into this land; for I will not leave thee, until I have done that which I have spoken to thee of.*
> —Genesis 28:13–15

Jacob married Laban's two daughters Leah and Rachel, and in time he sired twelve sons and a daughter with Laban's two daughters and their maids (Genesis 35:23–26).[18] Following his eventual departure from Laban, and his reunion with Esau, Jacob had an encounter with an assailant (a type of the pre-incarnate Christ):

> *And he said, Thy name shall be called no more Jacob, but Israel: for thou hast striven with God and with men, and hast prevailed.*
> —Genesis 32:28

Jacob (Israel) thus became the father of the nation of Israel through his children. Now Joseph (ca. 1915–1805), the firstborn of Jacob's sons, was conspired against by his jealous brothers who sold him for twenty shekels of silver as a slave to a caravan of Ishmaelites on their way to Egypt. In Egypt he gained favor with Potiphar, the captain of Pharaoh's guard, who recommended him as a dream interpreter possibly to Pharaoh Senusret II (Sesostris II) (ca. 1880–1874 B.C. ?), or to Pharaoh Senusret III (Sesostris III ?) (ca. 1874–1855? B.C.) of the 12th Dynasty, for Joseph had correctly interpreted the dreams of Pharaoh's butler and baker who had been with him in Potiphar's prison. Pharaoh's dreams were interpreted by Joseph as representing seven years of plenty followed by seven years of famine. Pleased with the interpretation, Pharaoh raised Joseph to a position of prominence and power in the land, and during the years of abundance that followed,

---

18 Leah gave birth to six sons Reuben, the firstborn, Simeon, Levi, Judah, Issachar, Zebulun, and a daughter Dinah. Bilhar, Rachel's maidservant, gave birth to two sons Dan and Naphtali. Zilpah, Leah's maidservant, gave birth to two sons Gad and Asher, and Rachel gave birth first to Joseph and later to Benjamin.

Joseph collected and stored up reserves of grain for the anticipated famine (Genesis 39:1–47). Then when famine struck the region, Jacob (Israel) to avoid starvation was forced to send his sons to Egypt for grain. Joseph, however, made his half-brothers return to Canaan for his own brother Benjamin and his father Jacob (Israel) to whom God had spoken in a night vision saying:

I am God, the God of thy father: fear not to go down into Egypt; for I will there make of thee a great nation: I will go down with thee into Egypt; and I will also surely bring thee up again: and Joseph shall put his hand upon thine eyes.
—Genesis 46:3–4

Years later, when Jacob (Israel) was dying, he called for Joseph and said:

God Almighty appeared unto me at Luz in the land of Canaan, and blessed me, and said unto me, Behold, I will make thee fruitful, and multiply thee, and I will make of thee a company of peoples, and will give this land to thy seed after thee for an everlasting possession.
—Genesis 48:3–4

Jacob (Israel) then blessed Joseph's two sons Ephraim and Manasseh by his wife Aseneth, and gathering his remaining sons he told them what would befall them in the last days. His blessing on Judah, his fourth son, included a prophetic reference to the coming of Shiloh (a type of Christ):

The sceptre shall not depart from Judah, nor the ruler's staff from between his feet, until Shiloh come; and unto him shall the obedience of the peoples be.
—Genesis 49:10

The "scepter" representing Jewish authority was foretold to disappear following the birth and revelation of Shiloh, who as the prophesied Star out of Jacob should one day impose His rule with a rod of iron (Revelation 2:27). The Amorite sorcerer and diviner Balaam, son of Beor, a contemporary of Moses and Joshua, was hired by Balak, son of Zippor, to curse the children of Israel, but foreseeing the distant coming of Shiloh, the "Seed of the woman," he prophesied:

I see him, but not now; I behold him, but not nigh: there shall come forth a star out of Jacob, and a sceptre shall rise out of Israel, and shall smite through the corners of Moab, and break down all the sons of tumult... and out of Jacob shall one have dominion...

—Numbers 24:17, 19

As prophesied by the Apostle John in the Book of Revelation, Shiloh the Lion of the tribe of Judah and the Root of David, also referred to as a Lamb, will at the end of time appear as "the worthy One to open the scroll of judgments sealed with seven seals" (Revelation 5:2–14).

Having pronounced his blessing on Judah, Jacob (Israel) assured Joseph of divine help from the mighty God of Jacob (Israel) from whence is Messiah, the Shepherd and Stone of Israel:

Joseph is a fruitful bough, a fruitful bough by a fountain; his branches run over the wall. The archers have sorely grieved him, and shot at him, and persecuted him: but his bow abode in strength, and the arms of his hands were made strong, by the hands of the Mighty One of Jacob (from thence is the shepherd, the stone of Israel), even by the God of thy father, who shall help thee, and by the Almighty, who shall bless thee, with blessings of heaven above, blessings of the deep that coucheth beneath, blessings of the breasts, and of the womb. The blessings of thy father have prevailed above the blessings of my progenitors unto the utmost bound of the everlasting hills: they shall be on the head of Joseph, and on the crown of the head of him that was separate from his brethren.

—Genesis 49:22–26

Following the death and burial of Jacob (Israel), and then of Joseph, the Period of the Patriarchs came to an end.[19] Despite the many sins that men are prone to commit, the patriarchs from the time of Abraham to the death of Joseph, although prone to sin, all lived by faith.

Now the children of Israel remained in the land of Egypt for about four hundred years (ca. 1876–1446 B.C.) until a different Pharaoh, perhaps Amenemhat III (ca. 1855–1808 B.C.), the eldest son of Senusret III, arose who did not know Joseph. Fearing the multiplication and growing power of the twelve Hebrew tribes in Goshen, Pharaoh set cruel taskmasters over them and made them

---

19 Following the death of Joshua the bones of Joseph, which the children of Israel had brought up out of Egypt, were buried at Shechem, in the plot of ground which Jacob had bought from the sons of Hamor, the father of Shechem, for one hundred pieces of silver. (Josh. 24:32).

serve rigorously as slaves.[20] They were however not without hope, for the groans of the children of Israel in bondage were heard by God who remembered His covenants with Abraham, with Isaac (Israel), and with Jacob, that He would judge the nation whom they would serve, and would bring them out with great possessions in the fourth generation.

> *Know of a surety that thy seed shall be sojourners in a land that is not theirs, and shall serve them; and they shall afflict them four hundred years; and also that nation, whom they shall serve, will I judge: and afterward shall they come out with great substance.*
>
> —Genesis 15:13–14

When the children of Israel increased abundantly, and the land was filled with them, Pharaoh Amenhotep I (ca. 1525–1504 B.C. ?) in dread of the Israelites ordered two Hebrew midwives Shiphrah and Purah to drown the male Hebrew children in the River Nile. To save her newborn child from being killed, Jochebed, the wife of Amram of the house of Levi, entrusted Miriam, the sister of Moses and oldest daughter of Amram, to place the child in a basket by the river's edge where the child Moses was found possibly by Hatshepsut (ca. 1473–1458 B.C.) the daughter of Pharaoh Thutmose I (ca. 1504–1492 B.C.).[21] Pharaoh's daughter then instructed Miriam to bring Jochebed to care for her own child.

Years later, Moses now an adult, killed an Egyptian and fled from the face of Pharaoh to the land of Midian where he married Zipporah the daughter of Reuel a Midianite. Forty years he served Jethro, his father-in-law, who was a priest of Midian. During this time the Angel of the Lord [YHWH], identified as God the

---

[20] Possibly Pharaoh Ahmose I (Amosis I) (ca. 1550–1525 B.C.), or Pharaoh Amenhotep I (ca.1525–1504 B.C.) of the 18th Dynasty of Egypt. For approximate chronologies of the Egyptian Pharaohs see: http://en.wikipedia.org/wiki/list_of_pharaohs; as well as http//www.metmuseum.org/toah/hd/phar/hd_phar.htm;   http://www.touregypt.net/kings.htm. J. Forty. Ancient Egyptian Pharaohs (J. G. Press, 1998); Heilbrunn. Timetable of Art History. List of Rulers of Ancient Egypt and Nubia (http//:www.metmuseum.org/toah/hd/phar/hd_phar.htm). Pendulous chronologies based on the Palermo Stone, the Abydos Kinglist, the Turin Canon and Manetho should all be viewed with caution.

[21] According to the conjecture of one writer the daughter could have been Hatshepsut (ca. 1479–1473 B.C.)], the daughter of Pharaoh Thutmose I (ca. 1504–1492 B.C.) and granddaughter of Pharaoh Amenhotep I (ca.1525–1504 B.C). Hatshepsut married her half-brother Thutmose II (ca. 1492–1479 B.C.), and following his death she assumed the role of Pharaoh along with Thutmose III (ca. 1479–1425 B.C.). See: http://crossexamined.org/ancient-israel- myth-or-history-part-3c/.

"I AM" appeared in a flame of fire from the midst of a burning bush and commissioned Moses to deliver the people from the oppression of Pharaoh's taskmasters. God said, *"See, I have made thee as God to Pharaoh; and Aaron thy [younger] brother shall be thy prophet"* (Exodus 7:1). Returning to Egypt, Moses delivered God's message to Pharaoh: *"Jehovah, the God of the Hebrews, hath sent me unto thee, saying, Let my people go…'"* (Exodus 7:16) Thereafter, following ten encounters with Pharaoh's Magicians involving a variety of plagues, the last bringing death to the firstborn of the Egyptians, including an unnamed firstborn son possibly of Pharaoh Amenhotep II (ca. 1427–1400 B.C.), or Pharaoh Thutmose IV (ca. 1400–1390 B.C.), the Hebrew people were finally allowed to depart. Leaving they emptied Egypt, for the Lord gave the people favor in the sight of the Egyptians so that they granted them what they requested.

In preparation for the departure Moses formally inaugurated the Ordinance of the Passover. Addressing the congregation of Israel he instructed the people saying:

> *In the tenth day of this month they shall take to them every man a lamb, according to their fathers' houses, a lamb for a household: and if the household be too little for a lamb, then shall he and his neighbor next unto his house take one according to the number of the souls; according to every man's eating ye shall make your count for the lamb. Your lamb shall be without blemish, a male a year old: ye shall take it from the sheep, or from the goats: and ye shall keep it until the fourteenth day of the same month; and the whole assembly of the congregation of Israel shall kill it at even. And they shall take of the blood, and put it on the two side-posts and on the lintel, upon the houses wherein they shall eat it…. And the blood shall be to you for a token upon the houses where ye are: and when I see the blood, I will pass over you, and there shall no plague be upon you to destroy you, when I smite the land of Egypt… And ye shall observe this thing for an ordinance to thee and to thy sons for ever.*
>
> —Exodus 12:3–7, 13, 24

As the people departed the Angel of the Lord spared the firstborn in the houses of the Hebrews that were marked on the doorposts and lintel with the blood of a sacrificed lamb. The blood foreshadowed the atoning blood sacrifice for sin yet to be offered by Jesus Christ, the promised Seed of the woman, and our vicarious substitute on the day of His crucifixion.

Chapter Three
THE PRE-MONARCHIC PERIOD[22]

It came to pass around ca. 1446 B.C. that the Lord with a mighty hand and with an outstretched arm, with great terror and with signs and wonders, brought the children of Israel out of the land of Egypt. Following a hasty departure and deliverance from the Egyptian taskmasters at the Red Sea, where the Egyptian army perished, the Israelites set out on their long meandering journey in the Sinai wilderness in which they were strangers and pilgrims for forty-years. They were attacked by Esau's descendants the Amalekites, and having wandered through the desert they eventually arrived at the base of Mount Horeb (Mount Sinai) which burned with fire. There God appeared to Moses and the Israelites in a cloud, and made a conditional covenant with His people that included the Decalogue, or Ten Commandments, a summary of the immutable moral law and mirror of God's true righteousness. For forty days and forty nights God wrote on two tablets the words of the covenant which He commanded His people to obey. It was a conditional covenant of works known as the Mosaic Covenant.

> *I am Jehovah thy God, who brought thee out of the land of Egypt, out of the house of bondage. Thou shalt have no other gods before me.*
>
> *Thou shalt not make unto thee a graven image, nor any likeness of any thing that is in heaven above, or that is in the earth beneath, or that is in the water under the earth: thou shalt not bow down thyself unto them, nor serve them; for I Jehovah thy God am a jealous God, visiting the iniquity of the fathers upon the children, upon the third and upon the fourth generation of them that hate me, and showing lovingkindness unto thousands of them that love me and keep my commandments.*

---

[22] For the chronology from the Judges to the Priest Samuel see Eusebius. Preparation for the Gospel (Baker Book House, Grand Rapids, Michigan, 1981), Part 2, XIV, 539.

Thou shalt not take the name of Jehovah thy God in vain; for Jehovah will not hold him guiltless that taketh his name in vain.

Remember the sabbath day, to keep it holy. Six days shalt thou labor, and do all thy work; but the seventh day is a sabbath unto Jehovah thy God: in it thou shalt not do any work, thou, nor thy son, nor thy daughter, thy man-servant, nor thy maid-servant, nor thy cattle, nor thy stranger that is within thy gates: for in six days Jehovah made heaven and earth, the sea, and all that in them is, and rested the seventh day: wherefore Jehovah blessed the sabbath day, and hallowed it.

Honor thy father and thy mother, that thy days may be long in the land which Jehovah thy God giveth thee.

Thou shalt not kill.

Thou shalt not commit adultery.

Thou shalt not steal.

Thou shalt not bear false witness against thy neighbor.

Thou shalt not covet thy neighbor's house, thou shalt not covet thy neighbor's wife, nor his man-servant, nor his maid-servant, nor his ox, nor his ass, nor anything that is thy neighbor's.

—Exodus 20:2–17
(see also Deuteronomy 5:6–21)[23]

The Decalogue defines man's conduct to God, and man's conduct to man. God defines the standard, and the standard demands full compliance and obedience. It can not be added to, nor can anything be taken from it (Deuteronomy 4:2; 12:32; Proverbs 30:5–5; Ecclesiastes 3:14; Revelation 22:18–19). As stated by two Jewish scholars of ethics, God's standard:

> May be governed neither by the accepted notions of public opinion nor by the whims of the individual conscience. Moral values are not matters of subjective choice or personal preference. Right and wrong, good and evil are absolute values that transcend the capricious

---

23 To the Ten Commandments Moses added, *"[A]nd thou shalt love Jehovah thy God with all thy heart, and with all thy soul, and with all thy might"* (Deuteronomy 6:5). Jesus, paraphrasing Moses, said, *"[A]nd thou shalt love the Lord thy God with all thy heart, and with all thy soul, and with all thy mind, and with all thy strength. The second is this, Thou shalt love thy neighbor as thyself. There is none other commandment greater than these"* (Mark 12:29–31; see also Matthew 22:37–40).

variations of time, place, and environment as well as human intuition or expediency.[24]

The Mosaic law system established Israel as a distinct people and nation under theocratic rule, and has dominion over man as long as he lives.[25] In exchange for the loyalty and obedience of the people, God pledged to take the tribes of Israel, His special treasure, under His protection and theocratic rule, but for breaking the Mosaic covenant the people would bring upon themselves divine judgment.

Having received God's conditional covenant, which sinners are incapable of keeping for *"through the law cometh the knowledge of sin"* (Romans 3:20; see also 1 Timothy 1:9–10)—Moses took the Book of the Covenant and read it in the hearing of the people, and the people in unison responded, *"All Jehovah hath spoken will we do, and be obedient"* (Exodus 24:7). Then Moses took the blood of oxen, sprinkled it on the people, and said, *"Behold the blood of the covenant, which Jehovah hath made with you concerning all these words"* (Exodus 24:8). The blood of the sacrificed oxen pointed forward in time to the blood sacrifice to be made by Christ, the "Seed of the woman," in our behalf. God also instructed Moses to make a tabernacle according to the patterns of heavenly things shown to Moses on the mountain.

> *And let them make me a sanctuary, that I may dwell among them. According to all that I show thee, the pattern of the tabernacle, and the pattern of all the furniture thereof, even so shall ye make it... And see that thou make them after their pattern, which hath been showed thee in the mount.*
>
> —Exodus 25:8–9, 40
> (see also Hebrews 8:5)

Having finished the tabernacle and the holy garments of the priesthood, Aaron and his sons, Abihu and Nadab, were brought to the door of the Tabernacle of Meeting where they were purified, invested and anointed for priestly service.

---

24 I. N. Trainin and F. Rosner. Religious Directives in Medical Ethics, in W. T. Reich, ed., Encyclopedia of Bioethics (The Free Press, New York and Collier Macmillan Publishers, London, 1978), Vol. 3, p. 1430a. I have used the quotation by Trainin and Rosner to apply to the Decalogue.

25 The Mosaic Law was repealed under the Gospel, for the incarnate Christ, the Seed of the woman, met all the demands of the law, and now offers salvation only on the condition of faith. It remains, however, binding on all who have not accepted Christ's righteousness by faith, and remains a tutor to sinners to bring them to Christ. However, after faith has come believers are no longer under a tutor (Galations 3:24–25).

And Moses brought Aaron and his sons, and washed them with water. And he put upon him the coat, and girded him with the girdle, and clothed him with the robe, and put the ephod upon him, and he girded him with the skilfully woven band of the ephod, and bound it unto him therewith. And he placed the breastplate upon him: and in the breastplate he put the Urim and the Thummim. And he set the mitre upon his head; and upon the mitre, in front, did he set the golden plate, the holy crown; as Jehovah commanded Moses.

And Moses took the anointing oil, and anointed the tabernacle and all that was therein, and sanctified them. And he sprinkled thereof upon the altar seven times, and anointed the altar and all its vessels, and the laver and its base, to sanctify them. And he poured of the anointing oil upon Aaron's head, and anointed him, to sanctify him. And Moses brought Aaron's sons, and clothed them with coats, and girded them with girdles, and bound head-tires upon them; as Jehovah commanded Moses.

—Leviticus 8:6–13[26]

A cloud then covered the Tabernacle of Meeting, and the glory of the Lord filled the tabernacle. "Here," said the Lord:

...I will meet with thee, and I will commune with thee from above the mercy-seat, from between the two cherubim which are upon the ark of the testimony, of all things which I will give thee in commandment unto the children of Israel.

—Exodus 25:22

The tabernacle and all that pertained to it typified the very presence of God dwelling with His people. Bezaleel, the son of Uri, the son of Hur, of the tribe of Judah, then made the Ark of the Testimony (Ark of the Covenant) of acacia wood, and placed the tablets of stone containing the Ten Commandments written by the finger of God in the ark.[27]

---

26 The holy garments were put on Aaron, and being anointed and sanctified he ministered to God as Israel's first high priest (Exodus 40:12–13). The parents of Aaron were Amran and Jochebed from the tribe of Levi. *"At that time Jehovah set apart the tribe of Levi, to bear the ark of the covenant of Jehovah, to stand before Jehovah to minister unto him, and to bless in his name..."* (Deuteronomy 10:8) Aaron's sons Abihu and Nadab committed sacrilege by offering unauthorized "profane fire" before the Lord, and were devoured by fire (Leviticus 10:1–2).

27 The original two tablets written with the finger of God were broken when Moses on his descend from the mountain found that the people at the command of Aaron had made for themselves a molded calf (Exodus 32:1–5; Deuteronomy 9:10–17).

The five books of Moses were likely dictated between ca. 1450 B.C. and ca. 1410 B.C. All expand on the wilderness wanderings of the Israelites when the Lord went before them by day in a *"pillar of cloud by day, and the pillar of fire by night"* (Exodus 13:22). As the people meandered through the wilderness of Sinai, ever murmuring, rebelling and braking the covenant that God had made with his people, Moses developed for the "stiff-necked people" (2 Chronicles 30:8) who persistently violated God's commandments, the many laws and rituals pertaining to the activities, worship, sacrifices, and commemorative feasts and festivals of the people.[28] The life blood of an unblemished animal (a type of Christ) was offered as a sin offering for the people.

> *For the life of the flesh is in the blood; and I have given it to you upon the altar to make atonement for your souls: for it is the blood that maketh atonement by reason of the life.*
>
> —Leviticus 17:11

Indeed, *"according to the law… all things are cleansed with blood, and apart from shedding of blood there is no remission"* (Hebrews 9:22). The Apostles Matthew, John, Paul, and the author of Hebrews, all write extensively about the cleansing and the forgiveness of sins through the blood of Jesus Christ, the lamb of God:

> *…for this is my blood of the covenant, which is poured out for many unto remission of sins.*
>
> —Matthew 26:28

> *…in [him] we have our redemption through his blood, the forgiveness of our trespasses, according to the riches of his grace…*
>
> —Ephesians 1:7

---

[28] Anonymous. Leviticus: The Mosaic Law, Sacrifices, the Feasts and Festivals; Jesus and the Law. (http://www.byfaith.co.uk/paulb112.htm). The sacrificial offerings mentioned in Leviticus are the Burnt offerings (Leviticus 1:2–17), the Grain offerings (Leviticus 2:1–16), the Peace offerings (Leviticus 3:1–17), the Sin and Guilt offerings (Leviticus 4:1–35) and the Trespass offerings (Leviticus 5:1ff). Also mentioned are the major feasts of the Lord, the Sabbath (Leviticus 23:3), the Feast of First Fruits (Leviticus 23:9–14), the Feast of Weeks or Pentecost (Leviticus 23:15–22), the Feast of Trumpets (Leviticus 23:-23–25), the Day of Atonement or Yom Kippur (Leviticus 23:26–32), and the Feast of Booths or Feast of Tabernacles (Leviticus 23:33–44).

...in [him] we have our redemption [through his blood], the forgiveness of our sins...

—Colossians 1:14

...but if we walk in the light, as he is in the light, we have fellowship one with another, and the blood of Jesus his Son cleanseth us from all sin.

—1 John 1:7

Unto him that loveth us, and loosed us from our sins by his blood.

—Revelation 1:5

And they sing a new song, saying, Worthy art thou to take the book, and to open the seals thereof: for thou wast slain, and didst purchase unto God with thy blood men of every tribe, and tongue, and people, and nation...

—Revelation 5:9

These are they that come out of the great tribulation, and they washed their robes, and made them white in the blood of the Lamb.

—Revelation 7:14

Comparing the Old Testament sacrifices to Christ's atoning blood sacrifice, the author of The Epistle to the Hebrews draws clear contrasts between the earthly tabernacle and the true heavenly tabernacle, between the Levitical priesthood and Christ's high priesthood, between the insufficient animal blood sacrifices of the Old Testament, not efficacious in atoning for sin, and the greatness of Christ's perfecting blood sacrifice, between Moses the intercessor, and Christ the mediator of the new covenant, and between the failing first covenant of works and the new covenant of grace with its better hope, better promise, better sacrifice, and better enduring possession, all better than the old covenant order, or dispensation (Hebrews 7–11).[29]

Just before the death of Moses, the Mosaic Covenant was strengthened by the addition of the Palestinian Covenant between God and Israel. The addition of the Palestinian Covenant reminded the Israelites that: if they would choose to obey the Mosaic law, God would bless the nation abundantly, but that

---

29   There are three dispensations, the Patriarchal (from Abraham to Moses), the Mosaic or Jewish (from Moses to Christ), and the Christian (from Christ's first coming to Christ's second coming).

disobedience would result in His curse upon the nation. Moses the servant of the Lord died soon after on Mount Nebo in the plains of Moab opposite Beth Peor, and the archangel Michael is said to have disputed with the devil about the body of Moses (Jude 9). Be that as it may, the Lord buried him there, and he was not seen again until he reappeared in spirit on the mount of transfiguration, and was seen by Jesus and the Apostles James, Peter and John (Matthew 17:1–3; Mark 9:2–4; Luke 9:28–31).

Now after the death of Moses, the Lord spoke to Joshua (Hoshea) (ca. 1474–1374 B.C.), the son of Nun, saying, *"Moses my servant is dead; now therefore arise, go over this Jordan, thou, and all this people, unto the land which I do give to them, even to the children of Israel"* (Joshua 1:2).

So around ca. 1405 B.C. Joshua ordered the priests and Levites to take up the Ark of the Covenant and cross over the Jordan before the people. When the ark touched the edge of the river the waters miraculously parted and all Israel crossed on dry land. When twelve stones had been placed in the midst of the Jordan for a memorial, the waters returned to their place and overflowed all its banks as before. Joshua then proceeded to Mount Gerizim and Mount Ebal where curses and blessings were read as an awesome and somber warning to those of God's people who would despise His covenant and statutes, abhor His judgments, and choose to disobey His commandments.[30] As explained by Moses:

> *And it shall come to pass, that, as Jehovah rejoiced over you to do you good, and to multiply you, so Jehovah will rejoice over you to cause you to perish, and to destroy you; and ye shall be plucked from off the land whither thou goest in to possess it. And Jehovah will scatter thee among all peoples, from the one end of the earth even unto the other end of the earth; and there thou shalt serve other gods, which thou hast not known, thou nor thy fathers, even wood and stone. And among these nations shalt thou find no ease, and there shall be no rest for the sole of thy foot: but Jehovah will give thee there a trembling heart, and failing of eyes, and pining of soul; and thy life shall hang in doubt before thee; and thou shalt fear night and day, and shalt have no assurance of thy life. In the morning thou shalt say, Would it were even! and at even thou shalt say, Would it were morning! for the fear of thy heart which thou shalt fear, and for the sight of thine eyes which thou shalt see.*
> —Deuteronomy 28:63–67

---

30 Joshua 8:33; Leviticus 26:15; Joshua 8:33.

This dire prophetic warning, that God would bring a sword to execute the vengeance of a broken covenant, foreshadowed the subsequent historical punishment of dispersion and sufferings of the Hebrew people throughout the region during the later Assyrian and Babylonian conquests, and eventually throughout the world. As commented by one noted Bible teacher:

> "These verses of warning were literally fulfilled as so many other promises in relation to the land. The point is made clearly in Scripture that though the ultimate possession of the land at the time of the Second Coming of Christ will certainly be fulfilled, the possession of the land by any one generation of Israel was dependent on the grace of God, and the obedience of Israel to their law."[31]

Having crossed the Jordan it came to pass that:

> *when Joshua was by Jericho, that he lifted up his eyes and looked, and, behold, there stood a man over against him with his sword drawn in his hand: and Joshua went unto him, and said unto him, Art thou for us, or for our adversaries? And he said, Nay; but as prince of the host of Jehovah am I now come. And Joshua fell on his face to the earth, and did worship, and said unto him, What saith my lord unto his servant?*
>
> —Joshua 5:13–14

That this "Commander of the army of the Lord" was no other than the one that had spoken with Moses in Midian, where he saw the bush burning with fire, is apparent for once again the command was issued: "Put off thy shoe from off thy foot; for the place whereon thou standest is holy" (Joshua 5:15).[32] Joshua and Caleb engaged in battle and defeated the occupants of Jericho and Ai, and then proceeded to conquer and possess the promised land of Canaan then occupied by Amorites, Canaanites, Hittites, Hivites, Jebusites, and Perizzites, and still a part of the Egyptian empire.[33] The battle against the Amorite alliance of Adoni-Zedek king of Jerusalem, Hoham king of Hebron, Pira king of Jarmuth, Japia king of

---

31 Walvood, J. F. Major Bible Prophesies: 37 Crucial Prophesies that affect you today (Zondervan Publishing House: Grand Rapids, Michican, 1991), 80.

32 Exodus 3:5; Joshua 5:15.

33 Canaan was possibly part of Egypt under Pharaoh Amenophis III (ca. 1390–1352 B.C.), or Pharaoh Akhnaten (ca. 1353–1349 B.C.).

Lachish and Debir king of Eglon was a battle of epic proportion, for in the Book of Jasher, no longer extant, it is written:

> *Sun, stand thou still upon Gibeon; and thou, Moon, in the valley of Aijalon. And the sun stood still, and the moon stayed, until the nation had avenged themselves of their enemies.*
>
> —Joshua 10:12–13[34]

Having destroyed the nations in the land of Canaan, described as *"flowing with milk and honey"* (Exodus 3:8), Joshua divided the land by lot. The conquest however was incomplete, for the tribes of Manasseh, Ephraim, Zebulun, Asher and Naphtali all failed to drive out the Canaanites, and the children of Dan were forced into the mountains by the Amorites. So by the end of the campaign the Israelites due to their lack of faith were given only a portion of the land that God had sworn to give Abraham their forefather as a possession forever.[35] Joshua died and was buried in the mountains of Ephraim. In his farewell address to the people he encouraged the Israelites to hold fast to the Lord God, and to keep, and do, all that is written in the Book of the Law of Moses. Commenting on the idolatry of the Canaanite tribes Joshua admonished the people:

> *neither make mention of the name of their gods, nor cause to swear by them, neither serve them, nor bow down yourselves unto them; but cleave unto Jehovah your God, as ye have done unto this day.*
>
> —Joshua 23:7–8

Israel served the Lord all the days of Joshua and the days of the elders of Israel who outlived Joshua. Then over the next four hundred and fifty years from the death of Joshua (ca. 1374 B.C.) to the time of the Prophet Samuel (ca. 1100 B.C.), the tribes of Israel were ruled by Judges. It was a period of almost ongoing lawlessness, for *"[i]n those days there was no king in Israel: every man did that which was right in his own eyes"* (Judges 21:25) and *"the word of Jehovah was precious in those days; there was no frequent vision"* (1 Samuel 3:1). When all of Joshua's generation had

---

34 To the saying of Jasper, Joshua adds, *"Is not this written in the book of Jashar? And the sun stayed in the midst of heaven, and hasted not to go down about a whole day"* (Joshua 10:13).
35 Joshua 24:11. For a summary of Joshua's conquests, and the kings conquered by Joshua, and the division of the conquered land see Joshua 11:16–23, 12:7–24, 13:1–19:51.

been gathered to their fathers and another generation arose after them who did not know the Lord, nor the work which the Lord had done for Israel, then:

> *the children of Israel did that which was evil in the sight of Jehovah, and served the Baalim; and they forsook Jehovah, the God of their fathers, who brought them out of the land of Egypt, and followed other gods, of the gods of the peoples that were round about them, and bowed themselves down unto them: and they provoked Jehovah to anger.*
>
> —Judges 2:11–12

To teach the people obedience God delivered them into the hands of plunderers who despoiled them; and He sold them into the hands of their enemies all around so that they could no longer stand before their opponents. However when they cried for deliverance and amended their ways, God mercifully raised up judges who delivered them.[36] The Prophet Samuel (ca. 1094–1014 B.C.) and his sons Joel and Abijah were the last Judges of the period of the Judges.[37] However, Joel and Abijah did not walk in their father's ways; for they turned aside after dishonest gain, took bribes, and perverted justice. Hophi and Phinehas, the two sons of Eli the high priest also turned aside from doing what is right, and the prophet Samuel was sent to announce the destruction of the house of Eli (I Samuel 2:31–35; 3:11–12). Indeed, as had been foretold by Moses and Joshua, the people would not listen to their judges, but turned aside from the way that God had commanded, and played the harlot with other gods, and bowed down to them (Deuteronomy 31:16,20).

> *And when Jehovah raised them up judges, then Jehovah was with the judge, and saved them out of the hand of their enemies all the days of the judge: for it repented Jehovah because of their groaning by reason of them that oppressed them*

---

[36] Twelve Israelite judges are mentioned: Othniel (3:7–11), Ehud (3:12–30), Shamgar (3:31), Deborah (4:1–5:31), Gideon (6:1–8:35), Tola (10:1–2), Jair (10:3–5), Jephthah (10:6–12:7), Ibzan (12:8–10), Elon (12:11–13), Abdon (12:14–15), Samson (13:1–16:31). Abimelech, the son of Gideon, sought to make himself King of Shechem. He ruled for three years and was killed by a woman. He asked his armor-bearer to slay him, lest it be said that he had been killed by a woman (Judges 9:53–54).

[37] K. P. Edgecomb Chronology of the Judges Period (http://www.bombaxo.com/gschron.html) and S. Rudd, Solution to the Chronology of the Book of Judges. (http://www. Bible.ca/archeology/bible-archeology), pp. 1–13, 2012. For comparison see J. H. Walton. Chronological Charts of the Old Testament (Zondervan Publishing House, Michigan, 1979).

and vexed them. But it came to pass, when the judge was dead, that they turned back, and dealt more corruptly than their fathers, in following other gods to serve them, and to bow down unto them; they ceased not from their doings, nor from their stubborn way.

—Judges 2:18–19

Chapter Four

The United Kingdom

Beforetime in Israel, when a man went to inquire of God, thus he said, Come, and let us go to the seer; for he that is now called a Prophet was beforetime called a Seer.
—1 Samuel 9:9
(see also 9:19)

All Israel from Dan to Beersheba knew that Samuel, the son of Elkanah and Hannah, had been established as a prophet of the Lord. He served as circuit judge to the children of Israel, and his duties took him from Ramah to Bethel, Gilgal and Mizpah. At Ramah the elders of Israel, tired of civil conflicts, demanded a king to rule over them (1 Samuel 8:4–5). Pressured by the people Samuel reluctantly gave his consent and anointed Saul (ca. 1052–1010 B.C.) the son of Kish and grandson of Boaz and Ruth, of the tribe of Benjamin, as the first king of a united Israel.[38] Samuel forewarned the people of the consequences of rejecting the Lord God, and of imitating the royal courts of other nations. Carefully, he explained to them the behavior expected of kings who would thereafter reign over them:

> *This will be the manner of the king that shall reign over you: he will take your sons, and appoint them unto him, for his chariots, and to be his horsemen; and they shall run before his chariots; and he will appoint them unto him for captains of thousands, and captains of fifties; and he will set some to plow his ground, and to reap his harvest, and to make his instruments of war, and the instruments of his chariots. And he will take your daughters to be perfumers, and to be cooks, and to be bakers. And he will take your fields, and your vineyards, and your oliveyards, even the best of them, and give them to his servants. And he will take the tenth*

---

[38] 1 Chronicles 8:33.

of your seed, and of your vineyards, and give to his officers, and to his servants. And he will take your men-servants, and your maid-servants, and your goodliest young men, and your asses, and put them to his work. He will take the tenth of your flocks: and ye shall be his servants. And ye shall cry out in that day because of your king whom ye shall have chosen you; and Jehovah will not answer you in that day.

—1 Samuel 8:11–18

Having been anointed king, Saul quickly gathered an army and fought against enemies on every side, against the Philistines in the west, Edomites in the southeast, the Moabites in the east, and the Ammonites in the northeast, but he failed to utterly destroy the Amalekites in the southwest. When contrary to Samuel's instructions Saul offered a burnt offering to appease the Lord, he was rejected by Samuel who said:

[T]hou hast rejected the word of Jehovah, and Jehovah hath rejected thee from being king over Israel… Jehovah hath rent the kingdom of Israel from thee this day, and hath given it to a neighbor of thine, that is better than thou.

—1 Samuel 15:26, 28[39]

The Spirit of the Lord departed from Saul, and Samuel went to Bethlehem. While visiting with Jesse the Bethlehemite he privately anointed with oil Jesse's youngest sheep-tending son David (ca. 1010–970 B.C.), a great-grandson of Boaz and Ruth, to succeed Saul as king over Israel.[40] When the mighty Philistine army shortly after confronted the army of Saul at Socoh in the valley of Elah, young red-haired David volunteered to face in battle the Philistine giant Goliath. With a sling he threw a stone that struck the giant's forehead, and when the giant fell senseless to the ground David cut off his head with the giant's own sword. The Philistines fled in panic and were pursued by the Israelites all the way to Gath and Ekron. For slaying the giant, David gained great popularity and was favored by Saul and Saul's son Jonathan who acknowledged David's right to the throne of Israel, and became David's trusted friend. David initially served as Saul's armor bearer and musician. However, whenever a distressing spirit from God came

---

[39] See also 1 Samuel 13:8–14; 15:22–23, 26, 28; 16:13,14.

[40] David was anointed three times. First informally by Samuel (1 Samuel 16:11–13), then a second time as king of Judah (2 Samuel 2:4), and a third time as king of Israel (2 Samuel 5:3).

upon Saul, he became jealous of David's popularity and tried to kill David with a spear. To escape the vengeance of Saul, David fled into the wilderness regions of Judah where, with a band of followers he temporarily joined himself to Achish the Philistine king of Gath. Due to the misgivings of the Philistine lords he was rejected and compelled to leave. David waged war against the Amalekites and other tribes, and twice he spared the life of King Saul, once in the wilderness of En-gedi, and again in the wilderness of Ziph.

The end of Saul's reign came when the Philistines again invaded Israel and gathered their forces at Shunem. Since the Lord no more answered Saul either by dreams, or by Urim, or by the prophets, he in great fear of the Philistines hired a female medium from the village of En Dor to conduct a seance to bring up the spirit of the prophet Samuel to reveal what he should do (1 Samuel 28:1–23). In reply to Saul's anxious query the spirit of Samuel said:

Wherefore then dost thou ask of me, seeing Jehovah is departed from thee, and is become thine adversary?

—1 Samuel 28:16

Saul and his three sons Jonathan, Abinadab and Malchishua were all killed in battle against the Philistines on Mount Gilboa. Mortally wounded and fearful of being captured by the enemy, Saul fell upon his sword and was killed by an Amalekite (I Samuel 31:1–4; 2 Samuel 1:6–15). When the news of Saul's death reached David at Ziklag, David composed a lamentation over Saul and over Jonathan. Now Jonathan was survived by his five year old son Mephibosheth who was lame in his feet, but for Jonathan's sake David later showed kindness to Mephibosheth (2 Samuel 4:4; 9:1–13; 24:21–22). Concurrently Ishbosheth (ca. 1005–1003 B.C.), the son of Saul, was made king over the northern tribes of Israel in Mahanaim by Saul's cousin Abner who commanded Saul's army. Ishbosheth was forty years old when he began to reign over Israel, but he reigned for only two years, for while there was still war between the house of Saul and the house of David he was stabbed to death while asleep by two guardsmen Rechab and Baanah, the sons of Rimmon the Beerothite.

All the tribes of Israel then came to Hebron and formally anointed David king over a united Israel (2 Samuel 2:1–4; 5:3; 1 Chronicles 11:3).

Behold, we are thy bone and thy flesh. In times past, when Saul was king over us, it was thou that leddest out and broughtest in Israel: and Jehovah said to thee, Thou shalt be shepherd of my people Israel, and thou shalt be prince over Israel.

—2 Samuel 5:1–2
(see also 1 Chronicles 11:2)[41]

To confirm God's binding covenant with the house of David, God sent the prophet Nathan (ca. 1000 B.C.), a contemporary of the prophet Gad (ca. 1000 B.C.), to confirm the promises He had made with the Patriarchs:

When thy days are fulfilled, and thou shalt sleep with thy fathers, I will set up thy seed after thee, that shall proceed out of thy bowels, and I will establish his kingdom. He shall build a house for my name, and I will establish the throne of his kingdom for ever. I will be his father, and he shall be my son: if he commit iniquity, I will chasten him with the rod of men, and with the stripes of the children of men; but my lovingkindness shall not depart from him, as I took it from Saul, whom I put away before thee. And thy house and thy kingdom shall be made sure for ever before thee: thy throne shall be established for ever.

—2 Samuel 7:12–16
(see also 1 Chronicles 17:11–14 and Psalm 89:3–4)

God's covenant with David will never be broken, for He has vowed, "*My covenant will I not break, nor alter the thing that is gone out of my lips*" (Psalm 89:34; see also 105:8–10). The very surety and permanence of God's covenant promises in David are referred to by the later prophet Jeremiah (ca. 650–582 B.C.) who writes:

Thus saith Jehovah: If ye can break my covenant of the day, and my covenant of the night, so that there shall not be day and night in their season; then may also my covenant be broken with David my servant, that he shall not have a son to reign upon his throne; and with the Levites the priests, my ministers. As the host of heaven cannot be numbered, neither the sand of the sea measured; so will I multiply the seed of David my servant, and the Levites that minister unto me... If my covenant of day and night stand not, if I have not appointed the ordinances of heaven and earth; then will I also cast away the seed of Jacob, and of David my

---

41 The Apocrypha: Psalm 151 describes the killing of the giant Goliath, and God's choice of David as king.

servant, so that I will not take of his seed to be rulers over the seed of Abraham, Isaac, and Jacob

—Jeremiah 33:20–22, 25–26

Saul's general Abner, the son of Ner, and commander of the army under Saul and Ishbosheth, then covenanted to bring all Israel to David (2 Samuel 3:12–13,21). However, when Abner sought to promote his own advancement he was treacherously stabbed in the stomach and killed by David's general Joab in revenge for Abner having slain Joab's brother Asahel at Gibeon.

Having reorganized his administration, David (ca. 1000 B.C.) fought against and defeated Hadadezer (Hadarezer) the son of the King of Zobah by the river Euphrates, and as a result Rezon (Hezion) (ca. 940–915 B.C.), the son of Eliadah, abandoned the service of Hadadezer and took Damascus and became king of Syria (1 Kings 11:23–25; 2 Samuel 8:3–8). Rezon (Hezion) thereafter remained an adversary to Israel all the days of David and his son Solomon, and for centuries after the Syrians of Aram-Damascus, first under Rezon, then under Hadadezer (Ben-Hadad) and Hazael, intermittently were at war with Israel. David also subdued the Philistines, Moabites, Edomites and Ammonites and gained major victories and extended his dominion.

It may have been during the war with the Ammonites that David committed adultery with Bathsheba the wife of Uriah the Hittite whose blood he spilled so that he could possess his wife. The judgment of the Lord came quickly, for the prophet Nathan (ca. 1000 B.C.), whose task it was to correct moral and religious abuses, accusingly pointed to David and asked:

Wherefore hast thou despised the word of Jehovah, to do that which is evil in his sight? thou hast smitten Uriah the Hittite with the sword, and hast taken his wife to be thy wife, and hast slain him with the sword of the children of Ammon. Now therefore the sword shall never depart from thy house, because thou hast despised me, and hast taken the wife of Uriah the Hittite to be thy wife. Thus saith Jehovah, Behold, I will raise up evil against thee out of thine own house; and I will take thy wives before thine eyes, and give them unto thy neighbor, and he shall lie with thy wives in the sight of this sun. For thou didst it secretly: but I will do this thing before all Israel, and before the sun.

—2 Samuel 12:9–12[42]

David readily acknowledged the gravity of his evil deed and repented. He understood that by his sin he had given great occasion to the enemies of the Lord to blaspheme, and although he repented and was forgiven he still had to face the consequences, for the child that Uriah's wife bore to David soon after died. For years after, in moments of solitude, David may well have reflected on the words of the ancient Patriarch Job who had said, *"I made a covenant with mine eyes; how then should I look upon a virgin?"* (Job 31:1) Now David reigned in Hebron seven years and six months, and in Jerusalem for thirty-three years. He is perhaps best remembered for making the ancient strong-walled city of the Jebusites on Mount Zion the capital of Israel, and for bringing the Ark of the Covenant up from the house of Abinadab at Kirjath-jearim to the house of Obed-Edom, and from there to Jerusalem where he built an altar to the Lord on the threshing-floor of Araunah the Jebusite (2 Samuel 5:6–9; 6:12; 24:18–24; 1 Chronicles 13:1–14; 15:25–28). Although he had solemnly vowed:

Surely I will not come into the tabernacle of my house, nor go up into my bed; I will not give sleep to mine eyes, or slumber to mine eyelids; until I find out a place for Jehovah, a tabernacle for the Mighty One of Jacob.

—Psalm 132:3–5

Although he had prepared his heart to build a house of rest for the Ark of the Covenant of the Lord, and a footstool of God, and had also made extensive preparations to build it, God said, *"Thou hast shed blood abundantly, and hast made great wars: thou shalt not build a house unto my name, because thou hast shed much blood upon the earth in my sight"* (1 Chronicles 22:8; see also 1 Kings 8:18–19).

David survived two attempts by his sons to dethrone him. His favorite son Absalom by his wife Maacah rebelled and seized power, and was slain by David's

---

[42] The prophesy by the mouth of Nathan that *"I will take thy wives before thine eyes, and give them unto thy neighbor"* and *"he shall lie with thy wives in the sight of this sun"* (2 Samuel 12:11)—was fulfilled when Ahithopel counseled Absalom, *"Go in unto your father's concubines… and Absalom went in unto his father's concubines in the sight of all Israel"* (2 Samuel 16:21–22).

The United Kingdom

general Joab.⁴³ Adonijah, David's son by his wife Haggith, in collusion with Joab the son of Zeruiah, and with Abiathar, seized power and was later put to death by David's son Solomon.⁴⁴ Sheba too, a son of Bichri, deserted David and was killed when pursued by Joab. Sheba's head unceremoniously was thrown to Joab and his brother Abishai by a woman of Beth Maachah.⁴⁵ For directing Joab to conduct an unauthorized census of the whole nation, David was offered as punishment one of three alternatives by the seer Gad: seven years of famine; three months pursued by enemies; or three days of plague. David opted for the latter, for he reasoned that falling into the hand of the Lord and His great mercies, was best.

Having been cared for by Abishag the Shunammite maid in his old age, David died and was buried in Jerusalem the city of David. He reigned for forty years. As commented by the Shilonite prophet Ahijah (ca. 934–909 B.C.), a contemporary of the blind Gershonite prophet Iddo (ca. 935–911 B.C.), and by the prophet Shemaiah (ca. 931–911 B.C.), David, despite his many shortcomings in morals, politics, and his relationship to several of his dysfunctional children, had been a good king, for he faithfully tried to keep the commandments of God, and followed God with all his heart to do what was right in God's eyes (1 Kings 14:8). God even called David *"a man after his own heart"* (1 Samuel 13:14; Acts 13:22). He became the standard to be measured up to, and a spiritual role model for the succeeding kings of Israel and Judah. As suggested by Psalm 119, which deals with David's meditations on the excellencies of the Word of God, his overwhelming desire in life was to be in harmony with God's statutes, testimonies, judgments, precepts, laws and commandments. Despite the faithlessness and wickedness of kings yet to descend from David, God promised David to establish a perpetual kingdom with one of his descendants, the "Seed of the woman," sitting upon the throne of Israel forever (Psalm 2:6–7; Acts 13:33–34; Hebrews 1:5–6; Romans 1:3–4). God's covenant with David thus provided a monarchic lineage through which the incarnate Christ, "the Seed of the woman" will one day govern His people throughout eternity.

Now prior to David's demise, the prophet Nathan and David's wife Bathsheba intervened with David and secured permission to have his son Solomon succeed as king over a theocratic kingdom then stretching from the River Euphrates

---

43 2 Samuel 15:10–13. Absalom when fleeing on his mule from David's servants got his hair caught in the branches of an oak tree and was killed by Joab and his armor-bearers. (2 Samuel 18:9–15).

44 1 Kings 1:5–7; 2:24–25.

45 2 Samuel 20:1–2, 21–22.

to the land of the Philistines, and as far as the river Egypt as prophesied by God in His earlier covenant with Abraham (1 Kings 1:11–31;4:21,24; 2 Chronicles 9:26; Genesis 15:18). Zadok, who had assumed the priestly office of the corrupt priest Eli (ca. 1065–1050 B.C.) then anointed Solomon (co-regent ca. 973–970 B.C./ regent ca. 970–930 B.C.) king of Israel in Gihon (1 Kings 1:34–39). Arrayed in royal garments, perchance less splendid to behold than any lily of the field (Matthew 6:26–29), Solomon began to rule.

In the four hundred and eightieth year after the children of Israel had come out of the land of Egypt, Solomon began to build the house of the Lord in Jerusalem with the assistance of Hiram (ca. 980–947 B.C.), the king of the Sidonians, who made a treaty with Solomon to supply building materials. So Solomon, instead of David, prepared for the works to be done on Mount Moriah. He erected the temple on the threshing floor of Ornan the Jebusite and brought in all the things which his father David had dedicated: the silver and gold and all the furnishings. He laid the foundation of the temple in the forth year of his reign, and it took him seven years to build the temple on Mount Moriah, and in the eleventh year of his reign, having adorned the temple with gold it was finished. The ark of the covenant of the Lord was then brought into the inner sanctuary under the wings of the cherubim overshadowing the place of the ark containing the tablets of stone which Moses had put there in Horeb, and Azariah the Levite ministered as priest. Having completed the work, Solomon in his prayer of dedication thoughtfully mused:

> "But will God in very deed dwell on the earth? behold, heaven and the heaven of heavens cannot contain thee; how much less this house that I have builded!"
> —1 Kings 8:27
> (see also 2 Chronicles, and compare to Acts 7:48–50, 17:24–25)[46]

Following the dedication of the temple, the Lord again appeared to Solomon with the warning that should the people turn away and forsake the Lord's statutes and commandments the temple which He had sanctified would be cast out and laid in ruin - as it subsequently was (2 Chronicles 7:19,21). Solomon also built palaces for himself and for his wife, possibly the daughter of Pharaoh Siamun-meryamun (ca. 978–959 B.C.?) of the 21st Dynasty of Egypt. He built the House of the

---

[46] "Howbeit the Most High dwelleth not in houses made with hands; as saith the prophet, The heaven is my throne, and the earth the footstool of my feet: what manner of house will ye build me? saith the Lord: or what is the place of my rest? Did not my hand make all these things?" (Acts 7:48–50)

Forest in Lebanon, the Hall of Pillars, the Hall of Judgment, and a number of storage cities, fortress cities and military bases for a large number of chariots and cavalry. Despite the warnings of the now deceased prophet Samuel who had foretold the behavior expected from the kings who would rule over them, Solomon brought horses from Egypt and gathered one thousand four hundred chariots and twelve thousand horsemen (2 Chronicles 1:14;9:25,29). He imposed heavy taxes and forced labor on his subjects and drained his kingdom of resources.

Now it happened that a man named Jeroboam, a son of Nebat and Zeredauah, of the Tribe of Ephraim from Zereda, was met by the prophet Ahijah the Shilonite. Jeroboam was a mighty man of valor who assiduously had served as an officer over the labor force of the house of Joseph for a number of years. Quickly approaching, Ahijah tore Jeroboam's new garment in pieces and prophesied the rending of ten tribes from Solomon as punishment for Solomon's sins.

> *And he said to Jeroboam, Take thee ten pieces; for thus saith Jehovah, the God of Israel, Behold, I will rend the kingdom out of the hand of Solomon, and will give ten tribes to thee (but he shall have one tribe, for my servant David's sake and for Jerusalem's sake, the city which I have chosen out of all the tribes of Israel); because that they have forsaken me, and have worshipped Ashtoreth the goddess of the Sidonians, Chemosh the god of Moab, and Milcom the god of the children of Ammon; and they have not walked in my ways, to do that which is right in mine eyes, and to keep my statutes and mine ordinances, as did David his father.*
> —1 Kings 11:31–33[47]

When Ahijah's prophetic announcement came to the attention of King Solomon, Solomon sought to kill Jeroboam, who to preserve his life quickly fled to Pharaoh Shishak I (Shoshenq I) (ca. 945–924 B.C.) of the 22st Dynasty of Egypt who had replaced Pharaoh Psusennes II (ca. 959–945 B.C.) of the 21st Dynasty, and there Jeroboam remained until the death of Solomon (1 Kings 11:40; 2 Chronicles 10:2).[48]

---

[47] At the time of David, the ten tribes of Israel had demanded *"ten parts [shares] in the king, and we have also more right in David than ye"* (2 Samuel 19:43) [that is, "more rights to David than Judah" (2 Samuel 19:43). Jeroboam, the son of Nebat, was given the right to rule over ten shares of the whole kingdom. The prophesy had been made by God to Solomon when he said, *"I will surely rend the kingdom from thee... I will rend it out of the hand of thy son"* (1 Kings 11:11–12).

[48] Sheshonq I (ca. 945–924 B.C.) likely was succeeded by Osorkon I (ca. 890 B.C.) and by Sheshonq I's grandson, Takelot I (ca. 889–874 B.C.) of the Twenty-Second Dynasty.

Solomon administered his kingdom with twelve appointed governors (1 Kings 4:7–19). In addition to his administrative achievements (2 Chronicles 8), he was a prolific writer. He composed and compiled The Book of Proverbs, written perhaps for his firstborn son Rehoboam for many of his proverbs of advice are addressed to "My son" (Proverbs 1:8; 2:1; 3:1; 4:20; 5:1; 6:1; 7:1; etc.). In addition, The Song of Solomon, Ecclesiastes, and a number of Psalms are attributed to him.[49]

Moreover he was an accomplished naturalist. His knowledge of the fauna and flora of Israel was extensive, and he mentions no less than 15 species of animals and 21 varieties of plants. It is also recorded that he knew three thousand proverbs, and that his songs were one thousand and five.

Tragically, despite his great intellect, fabulous wealth and outstanding administrative accomplishments, his heart was not right with God, and the bright day of Solomon's glory ended in clouds and darkness. The theocracy began to crumble, for Solomon entered into numerous diplomatic marriages with foreign wives who brought with them the gods of the surrounding nations. In violation of the law of Moses he had seven hundred wives and three hundred concubines - women of the Moabites, Ammonites, Edomites, Zidonians and Hittites who turned away his heart after the gods Ashtoreth, Milcom, Chemosh, Molech and more. Perhaps the closest to Solomon's heart was a certain Shulamite maiden of whom he writes with such tender affection in The Song of Solomon.[50] Having been blessed by God with wisdom, and with riches and honor, and having tasted the pleasures of life, the lust of the flesh, the lust of the eyes, and the pride of life - Solomon could but sum up his life and experience in few words: *"Fear God, and keep his commandments; for this is the whole duty of man. For God will bring every work into judgment, with every hidden thing, whether it be good, or whether it be evil"* (Ecclesiastes 12:13–14).

Solomon's reign as king in Jerusalem, and over all Israel lasted for forty years. Then impaired by old age he died and was buried in Jerusalem, the city of David. His "dust returned to the earth as it was, and his spirit returned to God who gave it" (Ecclesiastes 12:7). As for the acts of Solomon, all that he did, and his wisdom,

---

49 The Apocrypha adds to Solomon's accomplishments, The Wisdom of Solomon.

50 If the Shulamite virgin (Song of Solomon 1:ff) is the same as the Shunammite virgin Abishag who cared for King David in his old age (1 Kings 1:1–4,15), then the Song of Solomon perhaps could be viewed as a poetic love song between King Solomon and Abishag. Adonijah, David's older brother, unsuccessfully tried to use Abishag as a means to gain control of the kingdom, and was put to death by King Solomon for treason. The Song of Solomon is viewed by Jewish Rabbis as a love song between God and Israel, Christians generally tend to view the Shulamite maiden and her beloved as representing the Church and Christ the Messiah.

they were written in The Book of Nathan the prophet, in The Prophesy of Ahijah the Shilonite, in the The acts of Solomon, and in the Visions of Iddo the seer, books no longer extant (2 Chronicles 9:29; 12:15). He was survived by his son Rehoboam and two daughters Taphath and Basemath (1 Kings 4:11,15).

Rehoboam (ca. 930–913 B.C.) the only son of Solomon and Naamah, the daughter of Hanun the Ammonitess, went to Shechem of Ephraim between Mount Gerizim and Mount Ebal and there he was made king of Israel in Solomon's stead (1 Kings 12:1, 43; 14:31; 2 Chronicles 10:1). He was forty-one years old when he became king, and he reigned seventeen years in Jerusalem, the city which the Lord had chosen out of all the tribes of Israel to put His name (1 Kings 14:21; 2 Chronicles 12:13). Under King Rehoboam the worst features of Solomon's idolatry were perpetuated. He ruled with a hard hand, raised unbearable high taxes to maintain his position and lifestyle, and forced his subjects to do laborious tasks. He oppressed and provoked the people, and when following the death of Solomon the people heard that Jeroboam, the son of Nebat was still in Egypt they sent for him. The whole assembly of Israel then came to plead their case before the throne of Rehoboam. However, Rehoboam "did not listen to the people; for the turn of events was from the Lord that He might fulfill His word which He had spoken by the Levite Ahijah the Shilonite to Jeroboam the son of Nebat" (1 Kings 12:15; 2 Chronicles 10:15). Rehoboam outrightly rejected the counsel of the elders who had stood before his father Solomon, and instead he embraced the advice of the young men who had grown up with him (1 Kings 12:6–8; 2 Chronicles 10:6–8, 13; 13:6–7). After three days Rehoboam, exhibiting no weakness, or willingness to compromise, readdressed the people, and with insolent contempt said:

My little finger is thicker than my father's loins. And now whereas my father did lade you with a heavy yoke, I will add to your yoke: my father chastised you with whips, but I will chastise you with scorpions.

—1 Kings 12:10–11
(see also 2 Chronicles 10:11)

Whereas a soft answer might have turned away wrath, the harsh words of Rehoboam stirred up anger (Proverbs 15:1), and the grievances of the people being unaddressed they rebelled and departed with the words: "*What portion have we in David? neither have we inheritance in the son of Jesse: to your tents, O Israel: now see to thine own house, David. So Israel departed unto their tents"* (1 Kings 12:16; see also 2 Chronicles 10:16).[51]

As foretold by the prophet Ahijah, Jeroboam (ca. 930–909 B.C.) the son of Nebat was then appointed the first king of a politically independent Northern Kingdom of Israel by the rebellious leaders of Shechem.[52] Seceding he tore Israel from the house of David, and drove Israel from following the Lord. None followed the house of David, but the tribes of Judah and Benjamin.

---

51 Samuel 20:1–2. The same words were spoken by the rebel Sheba, the son of Bichri, a Benjamite who had previously rebelled against David for he blew the trumpet, and said, *"We have no portion in David, neither have we inheritance in the son of Jesse: every man to his tents, O Israel. 2 So all the men of Israel went up from following David, and followed Sheba the son of Bichri; but the men of Judah clave unto their king, from the Jordan even to Jerusalem"* (2 Samuel 20:1–2).

52 King Abijah (913–910 B.C.) of Judah, the son of King Rehoboam of Judah subsequently referred to the rebellious leaders of Shechem as "worthless *men*" (2 Chronicles 13:7).

Chapter Five
THE DIVIDED KINGDOM[53]

The Divided Kingdom Period extended from the time of King Rehoboam (ca. 930–913 B.C.), the son of Solomon, to King Zedekiah (ca. 597–586 B.C.) of Judah. Anointed Kings, and their elite followers, with few exceptions, abused and unjustly treated the poor and needy whose only defenders were the prophets. The worship of foreign idols became the national sin especially of the separate northen kingdom of Israel where King Jeroboam (ca. 930–909 B.C.), the son of Nebat, erected and worshiped golden calves at Bethel and at Dan. When the rebels thereafter stoned King Rehoboam's emissary Hadoram (Adoram), who was in charge of the revenue (2 Samuel 20:24; 1 Kings 12:18; 2 Chronicles 10:18), Rehoboam, intending to quash the separatist tribes, quickly departed from Shechem and returned to Jerusalem to assemble an army from the tribes of Judah and Benjamin (1 Kings 12:21;2 Chronicles 10:18; 11:1–4). However due to the word of the Lord that came by the prophet Shemaiah (ca. 931–911 B.C.) "not to fight against their brethren," Rehoboam's planned punitive expedition came to nothing. Jeroboam, the son of Nebat, then rebuilt and fortified Shechem in the mountains of Ephraim and dwelt there as king over the breakaway tribes. To keep the people of Israel from returning to Jerusalem to offer sacrifices

---

53 Chronologies for the kings of Israel (Jeroboam to Hoshea) and of Judah (Rehoboam to Zedekiah) see: (1) Eusebius Preparation for the Gospel (Baker Book House, Grand Rapids, Michigan, 1981), Part 2, Book X, Chapter XIV, p. 539–540; (2) C. Brand, C. Draper and A. England., editors. Holman Illustrated Bible Dictionary: Chronology of the Biblical Period (Holman Bible Publishers, Nashville, Tennessee, 2003), 460–464. See also (3) W. F. Albright, (4) G. Galil, (5) K. Kitchen, (6) J. Jackson, and (7) Steve Rudd in Solved: Divided Kingdom Period Chronology provides the time line from ca. 931–587 B.C. (www.bible.ca). (8) Dates for the kings of Israel and Judah may also be found in the Holy Bible (NIV), Chinese/English version by International Bible Society, Colorado Springs, CO, U.S.A., 1984), Table 2, xii-xiii; and (9) E. R. Thiele, The Mysterious Numbers of the Hebrew Kings (Zondervan Corporation, Grand Rapids, Michigan, U.S.A., 49501, 1983), Maps xii - xv. See also (10) Wikipedia.

in the house of the Lord, Jeroboam ordained a feast. He made two Egyptian Apis Bulls of gold and placed one in Bethel and one in Dan at the extremities of his kingdom, and he offered sacrifices to them as devised in his own heart (1 Kings 12:28,32–33). He dismissed from his mind the commandments of his Maker that:

> *Thou shalt have no other gods before me. Thou shalt not make unto thee a graven image, nor any likeness of any thing that is in heaven above, or that is in the earth beneath, or that is in the water under the earth: thou shalt not bow down thyself unto them...*
> —Exodus 20:3–5

Echoing the very words of Aaron, the brother of Moses, who under pressure had first fashioned a golden calf for the people of Israel, Jeroboam addressed the people: *"[B]ehold thy gods, O Israel, which brought thee up out of the land of Egypt"* (1 Kings 12:28).[54] Then he dismissed the priests of the Lord, the sons of Aaron.

The Levites left their common-lands and their possessions and came to Judah and Jerusalem where they took their stand with Rehoboam. Jeroboam then made priests like the peoples of other lands, and he offered sacrifices on the altar he had made, and burned incense. This was the "sin unto the house of Jeroboam, even to cut it off, and to destroy it from off the face of the earth" (1 Kings 13:34). The priesthood established by Jeroboam was corrupt at its very source. It had no divine sanction, and tragically the sin of Jeroboam thereafter was continued by all subsequent kings of northern Israel for two centuries until Samaria, the capital of Israel, was destroyed by the army of the Assyrians. As Jeroboam stood by the altar he had made a man of God from Judah, perhaps Iddo the seer (ca. 960–911 B.C.), cried out against the altar and prophesied events yet to unfold after a prophetic gap of hundreds of years in the reign of King Josiah (ca. 640–609 B.C.), the son of King Amon (ca. 642–640 B.C.) of Judah.

> *O altar, altar, thus saith Jehovah: Behold, a son shall be born unto the house of David, Josiah by name; and upon thee shall he sacrifice the priests of the high places that burn incense upon thee, and men's bones shall they burn upon thee.*
> —1 Kings 13:2

---

54 *"These are thy gods, O Israel, which brought thee up out of the land of Egypt"* (Exodus 32:8). Luke, in Acts 7:37–43, expands on Israel's rebellion against God in the wilderness.

The Divided Kingdom

Then the man of God added, *"This is the sign which Jehovah hath spoken: Behold, the altar shall be rent, and the ashes that are upon it shall be poured out"* (1 Kings 13:3), and so it happened, the altar was split apart, and the ashes poured out from the altar according to the sign which the man of God had given by the word of the Lord. As Jeroboam reached out to arrest the man of God his arm froze, and unable to regain the use of his arm he had to implore the prophet to restore him as he was before. For the many sins of Jeroboam, the son of Nebat, God then instructed the blind prophet Ahijah to tell Jeroboam:

Thus saith Jehovah, the God of Israel: Forasmuch as I exalted thee from among the people, and made thee prince over my people Israel, and rent the kingdom away from the house of David, and gave it thee; and yet thou hast not been as my servant David, who kept my commandments, and who followed me with all his heart, to do that only which was right in mine eyes, but hast done evil above all that were before thee, and hast gone and made thee other gods, and molten images, to provoke me to anger, and hast cast me behind thy back: therefore, behold, I will bring evil upon the house of Jeroboam, and will cut off from Jeroboam every man-child, him that is shut up and him that is left at large in Israel, and will utterly sweep away the house of Jeroboam, as a man sweepeth away dung, till it be all gone. Him that dieth of Jeroboam in the city shall the dogs eat; and him that dieth in the field shall the birds of the heavens eat: for Jehovah hath spoken it.
—1 Kings 14:7–11

Part of the prophesy of Ahijah against Jeroboam came into effect almost immediately, for as had been foretold to Jeroboam's wife by the prophet Ahijah in Shiloh, Abijah the son of Jeroboam died soon after from an illness. All Israel mourned for the child Abijah, for he was the only one of Jeroboam who would come to the grave, because in him there was found something good towards the Lord God of Israel in the house of Jeroboam.

In the meanwhile King Rehoboam was building cities for defense in Judah and during those early years he walked in the way of David and Solomon, and the tribes of Judah and Benjamin and the priests and Levites remained loyal to him (2 Chronicles 11:5,17). However, as power corrupts and novel ideas often exert a harming influence, the people of Judah gradually forsook the law of the Lord, and did according to all the abominations of the nations which the Lord had cast out before the children of Israel. The apostasy in the south provoked God to anger, and since Rehoboam did not prepare his heart to seek the Lord, God sent the prophet Shemiah (ca. 931–911 B.C.) to Rehoboam with the message: *"Ye have forsaken me, therefore have I also left you in the hand of [Pharaoh Shishak I]"* (2 Chronicles 12:5).[55]

So in the fifth year of Rehoboam [i.e., ca. 925 B.C.], Pharaoh Shishak I (Sheshonq I) (ca. 945–924 B.C.) supported by Lubim, Sukkim and Ethiopian forces invaded Palestine and Judah. He came up against Jerusalem and carried away the treasures of the house of the Lord and the treasures of the kings house including the ceremonial shields of gold that David had taken from the servants of Hadadezer and brought to Jerusalem, and Rehoboam made bronze shields in their place. Shishak I (Sheshonq I) made Judah a vassal state of Egypt, exacted tribute money, and in a show of force he launched a threatening northward drive against his former ally Jeroboam, the son of Nebat. Then he returned to Egypt where soon after he died. The names of the cities captured by Shishak I (Sheshonq I) during his punitive campaign against Judah have been preserved on the temple wall of Amun at Karnak, in Thebes. A battle relief of the 138 cities conquered by Pharaoh Shishak I (Sheshonq I) was likely made by his presumed son Pharaoh Osorkon I (924–889 B.C.).

Then in 913 B.C. King Rehoboam died and was buried in the City of David. The chronicler summarizes his reign saying that *"there was war between Rehoboam and Jeroboam continually"* (1 Kings 14:30; see also 15:6–7) and that *"he did that which was evil, because he set not his heart to seek Jehovah"* (2 Chronicles 12:14). Then in the eighteenth year [i.e., ca. 912 B.C.] of King Jeroboam, the son of Nebat, Rehoboam's favorite son Abijah (Abijam) (ca. 913–910 B.C.), a leader among his brothers, became king over Judah (1 Kings 15:1; 2 Chronicles 13:1–2). His mother's name was Maachar (Michaiah), the daughter of Uriel of Gibeah, and the granddaughter of David's sons Absalom and Abishalom. Following a laudable, but unsuccessful attempt by King Abijah (Abijam) to reunite the tribes under Judah, there was war between Abijah (Abijam) of Judah and Jeroboam of Israel, as there had been continuously between his father Rehoboam and Jeroboam. With an army of four hundred thousand choice men Abijah (Abijam) marched north to fight at Zemaraim southeast of Bethel in the mountains of Ephraim. Facing Jeroboam and his mighty army Abijah (Abijam) called out: *"Hear me, O Jeroboam and all Israel: Ought ye not to know that Jehovah, the God of Israel, gave the kingdom over Israel to David for ever, even to him and to his sons by a covenant of salt?"* (2 Chronicles 13:4–5)

---

55 Shishak (Sheshonq I, ca. 945–924 B.C.), the first ruler of Egypt's Twenty Second Dynasty, succeeded Psusennes II (ca. 959–945 B.C.) of the Twenty-First Dynasty. Shishak was likely followed Osorkon I (ca. 924–889 B.C.).

The Divided Kingdom

Failing to persuade King Jeroboam to return to the house of David, the two sides joined in battle and King Abijah (Abijam) triumphed against Jeroboam's eight hundred thousand men of valor. In that mighty encounter 500,000 of the army of Israel allegedly perished, and the Lord struck Jeroboam the son of Nebat and he died. Jeroboam reigned two and twenty years. His acts, how he reigned, and how he warred were written in the chronicles of the kings of Israel.

Thereafter Israel did not recover strength again in the days of King Abijah (Abijam) of Judah. During the short reign of Abijah (Abijam) he worshiped idols and followed in the ways of his father Rehoboam. The Chronicler writes that he *"walked in all the sins of his father, which he had done before him"* and that *"his heart was not perfect with Jehovah his God, as the heart of David his father"* (1 Kings 15:3). Abijah (Abijam) died in ca. 910 B.C., a year after Jeroboam, and was buried in the city of David (1 Kings 15:9; 2 Chronicles 14:1). The acts of Abijah (Abijam), his ways and sayings, were recorded in the no longer extant commentary of the prophet Iddo (ca. 935–911 B.C.), a Gershomite Levite.

Then in the twentieth year [i.e., ca. 910 B.C.] of King Jeroboam began Asa (ca. 910–869 B.C.), the son of Abijah (Abijam) to rule over Judah and he ruled for 41 years.

In the second year [i.e., ca. 908 B.C.] of Asa king of Judah, Jeroboam was followed in Israel by his son Nadab (ca. 909–908 B.C.) who ruled Israel for only two years (1 Kings 15:25–27). It came to pass when he became king, that he killed all the house of Jeroboam (1 King 15:29–30). He fulfilled the earlier prophesy of Ahijah the Shilonite by killing the remaining members of the Jeroboam dynasty, not leaving to Jeroboam anyone that breathed (1 Kings 14:18–20, 15:25–33). He did evil in the sight of the Lord, and walked in the sin by which his father had made Israel sin. He was the last king of the two generation dynasty of Jeroboam, for while besieging the Philistine town of Gibbethon north of Ekron he was murdered in the third year [i.e., ca. 907 B.C.] of Asa king of Judah by his own captain Baasha (ca. 908–886 B.C.), the son of Ahijah of the house of Issachar. Baasha usurped the throne of Israel and reigned in Tirzah north-east of Shechem for twenty and four years (1 Kings 15:33–34).

Now King Asa, the son of Abijah, initially enjoyed a decade of peace during which time he rebuilt the strength of Judah. He was encouraged by the prophet Azariah (ca. 900–885 B.C.) the son of the prophet Oded (ca. 920 B.C.) who reportedly met Asa and said to him:

Hear ye me, Asa, and all Judah and Benjamin: Jehovah is with you, while ye are with him; and if ye seek him, he will be found of you; but if ye forsake him, he will forsake you. Now for a long season Israel was without the true God, and without a teaching priest, and without law: but when in their distress they turned unto Jehovah, the God of Israel, and sought him, he was found of them. And in those times there was no peace to him that went out, nor to him that came in; but great vexations were upon all the inhabitants of the lands. And they were broken in pieces, nation against nation, and city against city; for God did vex them with all adversity. But be ye strong, and let not your hands be slack; for your work shall be rewarded.

—2 Chronicles 15:1–7

Heeding the prophet, Asa in the fifteenth year of his reign [i.e., ca. 895 B.C.] carried out religious and social reforms. He removed Maachah (Michaiah) as queen mother because she had made an obscene effigy of the sensual Phoenician goddess Asherah (Astarte), and he burned the effigy by the Brook Kidron (1 Kings 15:13; 2 Chronicles 15:10–16). He also banned and removed the idols from all of Judah and Benjamin, and banished the sexually perverted persons from the land.[56] The pagan high places, however, were not removed from Israel. Then in the thirty and fifth year [i.e., ca. 875 B.C.] of the reign of King Asa, Pharaoh Takelot I (ca. 889–874 B.C.), the son of Pharaoh Shoshenq II (ca. 890 B.C.), with Lubim and Cushite support invaded Judah with a huge army of a million men and three hundred chariots, and was decimated in the plain of Zephathah near Mareshah by King Asa who relied on the Lord for victory (2 Chronicles 14:9–13; 16:8; 15:19).[57] Thereafter, in the thirty and sixth year [i.e., ca. 874 B.C.] of Asa king of Judah, King Baasha (ca. 908–886 B.C.) of Israel, the son of Ahijah of the tribe of Issachar, moved south against Judah and began to militarize the city of Ramah on the road to Jerusalem with the intent that he might let none go out or come in to King Asa of Judah. Fearing an imminent attack by Baasha, Asa gathered up all the silver and gold that was left in the treasury of the house of the Lord and in the treasury of the king's house, and sent all to Ben-Hadad I (ca. 900–860 B.C.) of Aram-Damascus with the message: *"There is a league [treaty] between me and thee, as*

---

56 1 Kings 22:46. The sexually perverted persons are referred to in Leviticus 18:22–24; 20:13; Deuteronomy 23:17; Romans 1:26,27. Sexual intimacy outside marriage was considered adultery punishable by death.

57 Asa defeated Zerah the Ethiopian in the Valley of Zephatthah at Mereshah. Zerah allegedly had an army of a million men and three hundred chariots, and Asa an army of three hundred thousand men from Judah and two hundred thousand men from Benjamin.

there was between my father [Abijah] and thy father [Tabrimmon (ca. 915 – 900 B.C.)]" (2 Chronicles 16:3; see also 1 Kings 15:19).[58]

Heeding the plea of King Asa of Judah, Ben-Hadad I ended his treaty with Baasha, and mobilizing his military against Israel he smote several cities in their territory (1 Kings 15:20). Due to this unexpected development Baasha was pressured to withdrew from Ramah and remained in Tirzah his capital. Taking advantage of the situation Asa removed the stones and timbers left behind by Baasha, and built Geba and Mizpah east of Ramah. However, for not inquiring of the Lord regarding his treaty with Ben-Hadad I, Asa was rebuked by the seer Hanani (ca. 920–870 B.C.) who said:

> *Because thou hast relied on the king of Syria, and hast not relied on Jehovah thy God, therefore is the host of the king of Syria escaped out of thy hand. Were not the Ethiopians and the Lubim a huge host, with chariots and horsemen exceeding many? yet, because thou didst rely on Jehovah, he delivered them into thy hand. For the eyes of Jehovah run to and fro throughout the whole earth, to show himself strong in the behalf of them whose heart is perfect toward him. Herein thou hast done foolishly; for from henceforth thou shalt have wars.*
>
> —2 Chronicles 16:7–9

Enraged by the perceived impertinence of the seer, proud King Asa had Hanani incarcerated. Thereafter, the prophet Jehu (ca. 900–848 B.C.), a presumed son of Hanani the seer, brought the word of the Lord to King Baasha of Israel, saying:

> *Forasmuch as I exalted thee out of the dust, and made thee prince over my people Israel, and thou hast walked in the way of Jeroboam, and hast made my people Israel to sin, to provoke me to anger with their sins; behold, I will utterly sweep away Baasha and his house; and I will make thy house like the house of Jeroboam the son of Nebat. Him that dieth of Baasha in the city shall the dogs eat; and him that dieth of his in the field shall the birds of the heavens eat.*
>
> —1 Kings 16:2–4

The prophesy of Jehu the seer to bring an end to the dynasty of Baasha was fulfilled when Elah (ca. 886–885 B.C.), the son of Baasha, in the twenty and sixth year [i.e., ca. 884 B.C.] of Asa the king of Judah, became king of Israel. The followed year while Elah was drinking himself drunk in the house of his steward

---

58 Tabrimmon the son of Rezon I (Hezion) was an adversary of Israel all the days of Solomon.

Arza in Tirzah he was slain by his captain Zimri (ca. 883 B.C.), the commander of half of Elah's chariots, who in the twenty and seventh year [i.e., ca. 883 B.C.] of Asa king of Judah advanced his own agenda, committed high treason, and usurped the throne of Israel (1 Kings 16:9–10, 15). When seated on his throne Zimri had all the members of the household of Baasha massacred - not leaving him one male, neither of his kinsmen nor of his friends (1 Kings 16:12). Having put an end to the two-generation-old dynasty of Baasha, Zimri ruled for only 7 days, for he was rejected by the army while encamped against the Philistines at Gibbethon a few miles north of Ekron, and soon after he died in a fiery palace-blaze plausibly started by himself (1 Kings 16:18).

Then followed a four-year civil war from ca. 885 to 880 B.C., that divided northern Israel between two feuding field commanders Omri (ca. 884–873 B.C.) and Tibni (ca. 885–880 B.C.), the son of Ginath. Half of the people followed Tibni to make him king, and half followed Omri who prevailed over the followers of Tibni, and in the thirty and first year [i.e., ca. 879 B.C.] of King Asa of Judah, Omri became sole king of Israel (1 Kings 16:16, 17, 21–23). He purchased, and built his capital on the Hill of Samaria from Shemer the owner, and then made preparations to relocate his government from the old capital at Tirzah previously established by Jeroboam, the son of Nebat.[59] That Omri and his son Ahab both conducted wars with Moab is confirmed by an inscription by King Mesha carved on a basalt stone discovered at the ancient site of Dibon by the River Jordan. Referred to as the Moabite or Mesha Stone it was set up by King Mesha after Omri's death as a record and memorial. It reads in part: "As for Omri, king of Israel, he humbled Moab many years, for Chemosh was angry at his land. And his son [Ahab] followed him and he also said, 'I will humble Moab.'"[60]

The sheep-breeders of Moab thereafter regularly paid the king of Israel one hundred thousand lambs, and the wool of one hundred thousand rams, until in the days of Ahab's son Joram (Jehoram), Mesha rebelled and attacked Israel (2 Kings 3:4,5). All said, Omri reigned in Tirzah for six years, and altogether twelve years over Israel. He

> *did that which was evil in the sight of Jehovah, and dealt wickedly above all that were before him. 26 For he walked in all the way of Jeroboam the son of Nebat,*

---

[59] The three capitals established by Jeroboam I, son of Nebat were Shechem, Penuel, and Tirzah.

[60] J. B. Pritchard. The Ancient Near East. (Princeton Univ. Press, 1958), Vol. I, p. 209

The Divided Kingdom

and in his sins wherewith he made Israel to sin, to provoke Jehovah, the God of Israel, to anger with their vanities.

—1 Kings 16:25–26

The acts of Omri which he did, and the might that he showed were written in the records of the kings of Israel (1 Kings 16:27). A century and a half after the death of Omri, he was still remembered by the prophet Micah (ca. 738–698 B.C.), a native of Moresheth of Gath, for in Micah's day several statutes of Omri, and the practices of Ahab's house, were still in effect and observed by the Israelites (Micah 6:16).

King Omri was succeeded by his son Ahab (ca. 873/871–852 B.C.) in the thirty and eighth year [i.e., ca. 872 B.C.] of King Asa king of Judah. Ahab reigned over Israel in Samaria for twenty- two years (1 Kings 16:28–30). He was united in marriage to Jezebel a daughter of Ethbaal (ca. 878–847 B.C.) the king of the Sidonians. Due to Jezebel's insidious influence the cults of the Phoenician storm god Baal and of Asherah soon flourished in Israel. Ahab built a temple to Baal in Samaria and abolished the worship of the Lord, and Jezebel continuously hunted down and killed the prophets of the Lord. However, due to the courageous efforts of the Edomite prophet Obadiah (ca. 855–840 B.C. ?) a hundred of the Lord's prophets were hidden from Jezebel, fifty to a cave, and fed with bread and water.

Now it may have been around this time that Ahab's servant Obadiah happened to meet the Tishbite prophet Elijah (ca. 870–845 B.C.) of Giliad who then was the foremost miracle-working prophet in all of Israel. When Ahab learned that Elijah had been found by his servant Obadiah, he went to meet Elijah, whom he tersely addressed, *"Is it thou, thou troubler of Israel?"* (1 Kings 18:17) Answering Elijah used the occasion to challenge Jezebel's four hundred and fifty pagan prophets of Baal and four hundred prophets of Asherah to a competition on Mount Carmel to demonstrate who is God, Baal or the Lord (1 Kings 18:19). The challenge could not have been clearer for Elijah called out to the prophets of Baal and Asherah: *"How long go ye limping between the two sides? if Jehovah be God, follow him; but if Baal, then follow him"* (1 Kings 18:21).

Two bulls were selected, one for the worshipers of Baal and one for Elijah, and it was decided that the God who answers by fire, He is God. Then, after the prophets of Baal and Asherah had performed their miscellaneous Canaanite rites, and failed to have Baal answer by fire, Elijah called upon the Lord who answered by consuming Elijah's sacrifice by fire. God clearly demonstrated to the priests and prophets of Baal and Asherah that the effectual fervent prayer of a righteous prophet avails much, and that the God who answers by fire - He is God. Then, as the sound of an abundance of rain announced the end to a severe drought placed earlier on the land by Elijah, the prophets of Baal were rounded up and executed. When the carnage done by Elijah became known to Queen Jezebel she immediately ordered Elijah killed, and he fearing for his life quickly fled to Beersheba where in great despair he prayed that he might die, but twice was sustained miraculously by an angel. Forty days and forty nights later he arrived at Mount Horeb, the sacred mountain of God where he was instructed to return to Damascus:

> *Go, return on thy way to the wilderness of Damascus: and when thou comest, thou shalt anoint Hazael to be king over Syria; and Jehu the son of Nimshi shalt thou anoint to be king over Israel; and Elisha the son of Shaphat of Abel-meholah shalt thou anoint to be prophet in thy room. And it shall come to pass, that him that escapeth from the sword of Hazael shall Jehu slay; and him that escapeth from the sword of Jehu shall Elisha slay.*
> —1 Kings 19:15–17

Now in king Asa's thirty and ninth year [i.e., ca. 871 B.C.] on the throne of Judah, he was plagued with a severe malady in his feet, and although the pain was severe he did not seek the Lord but the physicians (1 Kings 15:23; 2 Chronicles 16:12). Like the woman, referred to by the Apostle Luke the evangelist, who over a period of twelve years *"had spent all her living upon physicians, and could not be healed of any"* (Luke 8:43), so too Asa had to suffer pain until a few years later in the forty and first year [i.e., ca. 869 B.C.] of his reign, having suffered for two years, he died and was laid in a tomb which he had himself made in Jerusalem the City of David. Asa did what was right in the eyes of the Lord, as did his ancestor King David.

In the fourth year [i.e., ca. 870 B.C.] of King Ahab of Israel, Asa was followed on the throne of Judah by his son Jehoshaphat (co-regent ca. 872–870/ regent ca. 870–848 B.C.) (1 Kings 22:41). Jehoshaphat was thirty-five years old when he became king, and he reigned twenty-five years in Jerusalem. His mother's name was Azubah, the daughter of Shilhi (1 Kings 22:41–42). The Lord was with Jehoshaphat because he walked in the ways of the former King David, and not according to the acts of Israel (2 Chronicles 17:3–4). Anxious to educate the people and to bring about religious reform, he instructed his leaders Ben-Hail, Obadiah, Zechariah, Nethaneel, and Maachah to teach in the cities of Judah from the Book of the Law, and with them went other Levites and priests.

The Divided Kingdom

When the people of Moab and the people of Ammon, and others with them, formed a great and powerful confederacy and came against King Jehoshaphat at Engedi east of the Dead Sea, Jehoshaphat unprepared to fight against the confederacy set himself to seek deliverance from the Lord. While praying for deliverance the Spirit of the Lord came upon the Levite prophet Jahaziel (ca. 870–? B.C.), the son of Zechariah who said:

> *Hearken ye, all Judah, and ye inhabitants of Jerusalem, and thou king Jehoshaphat: Thus saith Jehovah unto you, Fear not ye, neither be dismayed by reason of this great multitude; for the battle is not yours, but God's... Ye shall not need to fight in this battle: set yourselves, stand ye still, and see the salvation of Jehovah with you, O Judah and Jerusalem; fear not, nor be dismayed: to-morrow go out against them; for Jehovah is with you.*
> —2 Chronicles 20:15, 17

As prophesied by Jahaziel, *"the children of Ammon and Moab stood up against the inhabitants of mount Seir, utterly to slay and destroy them: and when they had made an end of the inhabitants of Seir, every one helped to destroy [one] another"* (2 Chronicles 20:23). Indeed, when the people of Judah looked towards the enemy multitude they discovered to their great amazement only dead bodies, for no one had escaped.[61]

Jehoshaphat then bowed before the Lord, and addressing the people he said: *"Hear me, O Judah, and ye inhabitants of Jerusalem: believe in Jehovah your God, so shall ye be established; believe his prophets, so shall ye prosper"* (2 Chronicles 20:20).

Around this time a state of war existed between the militarily-active Hadadezer (Ben-Hadad II) (ca. 860–841 B.C.), the son of Ben-Hadad I (ca. 885–860 B.C.) of Syria, and King Ahab of Israel. In 857 B.C. Hadadezer (Ben-Hadad II) moved against King Ahab of Israel with a coalition of 32 vassal kings and besieged Samaria. Taunting and humiliating Ahab, he demanded everything of value including Ahab's wives and children. Arrogantly he proclaimed for all to hear that he would search Ahab's palace and the houses of his officials. Unintimidated by the Syrian's audacious boasting, Ahab replied, *"Tell him, Let not him that girdeth on his armor boast himself as he that putteth it off"* (1 Kings 20:11).

Then rallying the children of Israel Ahab advanced against Hadadezer (Ben-Hadad II) the son of Ben-Hadad I. Overconfident because of his superior military strength Hadadezer (Ben-Hadad II) relaxed his guard, and while inebriated

---

61 2 Chronicles 20:1–24.

he was defeated and his coalition of thirty-two kings routed by the young leaders of the provinces of Israel. In the confusion Hadadezer (Ben-Hadad II) managed a quick escape by horse. A year later in the spring of 856 B.C., he mounted a second unsuccessful attack against Israel in the plain with his many horses and chariots, and was captured at Aphek on the heights above Chinereth. Coerced by Ahab, Hadadezer (Ben-Hadad II) renounced all prior claims to earlier-seized Israelite towns. Pleading for his life he was then released by a magnanimous Ahab in return for generous trade concessions in Aram-Damascus (1 Kings 20:31–34). However, because Ahab made a covenant with Hadadezer (Ben-Hadad II) and let him go, an unnamed prophet by the roadside met Ahab and said, *"Thus saith Jehovah, Because thou hast let go out of thy hand the man whom I had devoted to destruction, therefore thy life shall go for his life, and thy people for his people"* (1 Kings 20:42).

It might have been after Ahab's two successful campaigns against Hadadezer (Ben-Hadad II) that he found himself coveting a nearby vineyard owned by his Jezreelite neighbor Naboth. It was a fair plot of land that Naboth refused to sell. So Ahab's wicked wife Jezebel hired two scoundrels who bore witness against Naboth and falsely accused him of blasphemy against God and king. On the false evidence presented, Naboth was then stoned to death, and his property confiscated (1 Kings 21:4–21). For murdering Naboth, and for taking possession of his property, the judgment of the Lord came quickly to Ahab by the Tishbite prophet Elijah (ca. 870–845 B.C.) who said:

> *Thus saith Jehovah, Hast thou killed, and also taken possession? And thou shalt speak unto him, saying, Thus saith Jehovah, In the place where dogs licked the blood of Naboth shall dogs lick thy blood, even thine… Behold, I will bring evil upon thee, and will utterly sweep thee away and will cut off from Ahab every man-child, and him that is shut up and him that is left at large in Israel: and I will make thy house like the house of Jeroboam the son of Nebat, and like the house of Baasha the son of Ahijah for the provocation wherewith thou hast provoked me to anger, and hast made Israel to sin.*
> —1 Kings 21:19, 21–22

Hearing this Ahab tore his clothes, put sackcloth upon his flesh and fasted, and because he humbled himself in contrition before God, the calamity on Ahab was delayed to the time of Ahaziah (ca. 853–852 B.C.) the son of Ahab. Then in 853 B.C., during a brief armistice between Israel and Damascus, Ahab out of necessity, and on the urging of his enemy Hadadezer (Ben-Hadad II) joined with other kings of the Levant to face the Assyrian King Shalmaneser III (ca. 859–824 B.C.), the son of Assurnasipal II (ca. 884–859 B.C.), for an Assyrian invasion force was threatening northern Syria as well as Israel. The Bible makes no reference to this threat, but an Assyrian inscription on the Kurkh Monolith of Shalmaneser III propagandizes the event by claiming that Shalmaneser III defeated the anti-Assyrian coalition at Qarqar (Karkar) on the Orontes river, and that King Ahab of Israel allegedly contributed 2000 chariots and 10,000 men - far more than any other in the anti- Assyrian coalition.[62] After the Battle of Qarqar (Karkar), and three more years without war between Syria and Israel, renewed hostilities again resumed between Hadadezer (Ben-Hadad II) and King Ahab. Recognizing Aram-Damascus as a common threat to both Israel and Judah, King Jehoshaphat, the son of Asa, went to visit Ahab who asked:

> *Know ye that Ramoth-gilead is ours, and we are still, and take it not out of the hand of the king of Syria? And he said unto Jehoshaphat, Wilt thou go with me to battle to Ramoth-gilead? And Jehoshaphat said to the king of Israel, I am as thou art, my people as thy people, my horses as thy horses.*
>
> —1 Kings 22:3–4
> (see also 2 Chronicles 18:2–3)

Jehoshaphat's alliance with apostate Israel was then sealed by a diplomatic marriage between Ahab's daughter Athaliah and Jehoshaphat's eldest son Jehoram (Joram) (co-regent ca. 853–848 B.C./regent ca. 848–841 B.C.) (2 Chronicles 18:1).[63] On the mis-guided advice of Ahab's professional court prophets, who spurned the good counsel of the Lord's prophet Michaiah (ca. 870 B.C.), the son of Imlah, and with props of iron mockingly acted out a pretended push against the Syrians, the decision was made to proceed against Hadadezer (Ben-Hadad II) of Aram-Damascus. However, for not casting his vote with Ahab's court prophets, god-fearing Micaiah was struck on the cheek by Zedekiah the son of Chenaanah and escorted to Amon the governor of the city who placed Micaiah in prison (1 Kings 22:24–27; 2 Chronicles 18:10–27). As Michaiah was led away he cried out,

---

62 J. B. Pritchard, editor. The Ancient Near East. An Anthology of Texts and Pictures (Princeton Univ. Pr., 1958), Vol. I, p. 190. "... I fought with them with the support of the mighty forces of Ashur, which Ashur, my lord, has given to me, and the strong weapons which Nergal, my leader, has presented to me (and) I did inflict a defeat upon them between the towns Karkara (Karkar) and Gilzau."

63 The same-named sons of Jehoshaphat and Ahab hereafter are named Jehoram (Joram) of Judah and Joram (Jehoram) of Israel.

"If thou return at all in peace, Jehovah hath not spoken by me. And he said, Hear, ye peoples, all of you" (1 Kings 22:28; see also 2 Chronicles 18:27).

Although forewarned by Micaiah the allied army was scattered like sheep by the Arameans at Ramoth-Giliad. Disguising himself, Ahab was mortally wounded by a bowman when struck by a random arrow between the joints of his armor, and propped up in his chariot he died at the end of the day having bled to death (1 Kings 22:30–34; 2 Chronicles 18:28–34). He was then brought to Samaria and buried. Soon after, when his chariot was washed at the pool in Samaria, the dogs licked up his fresh blood while the harlots bathed, just as foretold by Elijah the prophet (1 Kings 22:29–40; 2 Chronicles 18:28–34). All said, there was *"none like unto Ahab, who did sell himself to do that which was evil in the sight of Jehovah, whom Jezebel his wife stirred up"* (1 Kings 21:25). Thereafter when Jehoshaphat the king of Judah returned unharmed from the battle at Ramoth-giliad to his house in Jerusalem he was met by the prophet Jehu, the son of Hanani, who pointedly asked: *"Shouldest thou help the wicked, and love them that hate Jehovah?"* (2 Chronicles 19:2) The barbed question clearly had a profound impact, for thereafter, due to the added influence of the prophets Jehu, the son of Hanani, of Michaiah, the son of Imlah, and of Eliezer (ca. 870), the son of Dodavah, King Jehoshaphat continued to reform the religious and legal systems of Judah, for he was a good man who had prepared his heart to seek God (2 Chronicles 19:5–11). Among his many accomplishments He nominated a commission of Levites, priests and laymen to teach the people from the Book of the Law, appointed judges, and reportedly set up a final Court of Appeal.

Then in the seventeenth year [i.e., ca. 855 B.C.] of Jehoshaphat king of Judah, Ahaziah (ca. 855–852 B.C.), the son of Ahab and Jezebel, and the brother of Joram (Jehoram), began to reign in Israel in Ahab's place (1 Kings 22:51). Ahaziah was twenty and two years old when he became king, and he reigned for only two years. During this time Jehoshaphat entered into an ill-conceived economic alliance with Ahaziah making ships in Ezion Geber, a port on the shores of the Red Sea originally built by King Solomon. For consenting to this alliance Jehoshaphat was severely rebuked by Eliezer, the son of Dodavah of Mareshah, who prophesied, *"Because thou hast joined thyself with Ahaziah, Jehovah hath destroyed thy works"* (2 Chronicles 20:37). And so it happened, the ships were wrecked by a storm. When Ahaziah therafter again attempted to join Jehoshaphat's merchant ships to Ophir for gold, Jehoshaphat, reminded perhaps of the rebuke of the prophet Eliezer (ca. 853 B.C.), would not allow it (1 Kings 22:48–49). Soon after Ahaziah had the misfortune of falling through the window-lattice of his upper room in the royal palace and was seriously injured (2 Kings 1:2).[64] When he sought healing from Baal-zebub the Philistine god of Ekron the prophet Elijah intercepted the kings messengers escorting the prophet of Baal-zebub, and pointedly asked, *"Is it because there is no God in Israel, that ye go to inquire of Baal-zebub, the god of Ekron?"* (2 Kings 1:3)

The prophet of Baal-zebub was then sent by Elijah to King Ahaziah with the message that he would soon die. Displeased with the message, Ahaziah immediately dispatched a captain with fifty soldiers to bring Elijah in for questioning. However, on the command of Elijah fire fell from heaven and consumed the captain and his soldiers. A second band likewise was dispatched and fared no better. Finally when a third band was sent, Elijah agreed to accompany the captain to the king where he repeated the judgment of the Lord God. So, in the eighteenth year [i.e., ca. 854 B.C.] of King Jehoshaphat of Judah, Ahaziah the son of Ahab having ruled for two years died according to the word of the Lord which Elijah had spoken (2 Kings 1:17; 3:1). All said, Ahaziah had acted very deviously, he committed evil in the sight of the Lord, and the historian comments that he served Baal and worshiped him, and provoked the Lord of Israel to anger according to all that his father Ahab had done (1 Kings 22:51–53). Since Ahaziah had no sons of his own, he was succeeded in Israel in the second year [i.e., ca. 851 B.C.] of King Jehoram (Joram), the son of Jehoshaphat of Judah, by his brother Joram (Jehoram) (ca. 852–841 B.C.) who ruled Israel for twelve years to ca. 841 B.C.

In the meanwhile the prophets Elijah (ca. 870–845 B.C.) and Elisha (ca. 845–800 B.C.) were observed by the river Jordan by fifty men of the sons of the prophets in Jericho. Having crossed the river, Elijah was caught up into heaven in a whirlwind by the "Chariot of Israel and its horsemen" (2 Kings 2:1–15).[65] On seeing the miraculous transport of the prophet Elijah, Elisha cried out: "My father, my father, the *chariots* of Israel and *the* horsemen *thereof*!" (2 Kings 2:12)

When Elisha thereafter arrived in Damascus, accompanied by his attendant Gehazi, a son of the local prophets was dispatched to anoint Jehu (ca. 841–814 B.C.), the son of Nimshi, as king over Israel, charging him to strike down the whole house of Ahab in accordance with what Elijah had prophesied regarding the calamity that the Lord would bring on Ahab's posterity (1 Kings 21:21; 2

---

64 King Ahaziah, perhaps like Eutychus of Troas in the New Testament (Acts 20:9), may have fallen into a deep sleep and fallen from a window.

65 As for Elijah he was not seen again until he and Moses were seen by the Apostles Peter, James and John at the transfiguration of Jesus (Matthew 17:1–3; Mark 9:2–4; Luke 9:28–31).

Kings 9:1–13). Elated by the good news the associates of Jehu blew their trumpets, and excitedly proclaimed *"Jehu is king"* (2 Kings 9:13). From that time Jehu, an important military commander under King Joram (Jehoram) of Israel, conspired against the King (2 Kings 9:14).

Now when Mesha the king of the Moabites learned that King Ahab had been killed in battle at Ramoth Giliad he immediately ceased paying the tribute to Israel that he had been paying since the days of King Omri. He announced his independence and formed a powerful confederacy with the surrounding nations to fight against Israel. King Joram (Jehoram) (ca. 852–841 B.C.) of Israel quickly responded to the threat by raising an army, and then invited the much older King Jehoshaphat of Judah to join him against King Mesha, and the Moabite confederacy. By a roundabout route the two kings marched for seven days by the wilderness of Edom where they were joined by the king of Edom. Recalling the earlier deliverance from Ammon and Moab by the prophet Jahaziel at Engedi, Jehoshaphat asked for a prophet who could assure them of victory. When told that the prophet Elisha, the son of Shaphat, unknown to all had accompanied them on the expedition, the three kings went to see Elisha. Ignoring Joram (Jehoram) the king of Israel with undisguised disdain, Elisha informed Jehoshaphat that the Lord God would deliver the Moabites into their hands. As the coalition arrived in Moabite territory, the valley in the meanwhile had been filled with runoff water from Edom, and as the morning sun cast its rays on the reddish-colored muddy waters collected in ditches round about, it appeared from a distance as human blood to the Moabites. Imagining that the Israelites had killed one another, the Moabites went for the delusory spoil only to be attacked and driven back. The further advance of the coalition towards Kir Haraseth, the stronghold of the Moabites, was strategic and purposive. Every choice city was attacked by the Israelites. From a Moabite perspective the damage inflicted by the advancing enemy was devastating, for every good tree was cut down, every spring of water was stopped up, and every good piece of land ruined (2 Kings 3:19, 25).[66] Hard pressed King Mesha was driven back to Kir Haraseth, and following a failed counterattack from his stronghold, and the horrible sacrifice of Mesha's eldest son to the Moabite god Chemosh, Joram (Jehoram) and Jehoshaphat withdrew from the tragic scene.

---

66 *"Only the trees of which thou knowest that they are not trees for food, thou shalt destroy and cut them down; and thou shalt build bulwarks against the city [Kir Haraseth] that maketh war with thee, until it fall"* (Deuteronomy 20:20).

The Divided Kingdom

After Mesha's Moabite rebellion had been defeated by the combined forces of Joram (Jehoham) of Israel and Jehoshaphat of Judah, war again broke out between Syria and Israel. When the Syrian king Hadadezer (Ben-Hadad II) (ca. 860–841 B.C.) was told that every word spoken by him in his own bedroom was known to Elisha, he sent raiders to the city of Dothan to apprehend the spy and the prophet. When the raiders surrounded the city with horses and chariots, and Elisha prayed for deliverance, the invaders miraculously were struck with blindness and led captive to King Joram (Jehoram) in Samaria where their eyes were opened. So the invasion by the Syrian raiders at this time was prevented by Elisha (2 Kings 6:8–23). Thereafter around 850 B.C., King Joram (Jehoram) was again besieged in Samaria by Hadadezer (Ben-Hadad II) the king of Syria, who is referred to by Elisha as the *"son of a murderer"* (2 Kings 6:32). During the siege there was a great famine, and the people of Samaria were forced by extreme hunger to cannibalize their children (2 Kings 6:24–30).[67] However when all seemed lost, the Lord caused the army of the Syrians to hear in the rustling leaves of the surrounding mulberry trees, the sound of marching soldiers and the noise of chariots and horses. Imagining that the Hittites, or perhaps the Egyptians headed perhaps by Pharaoh Osorkon II (ca. 872–837 B.C.), were coming to assist King Joram (Jehoram), they raised the siege on Samaria and fled in panic.

Then in ca. 848 B.C. King Jehoshaphad of Judah died. He had sought the Lord with all his heart, and his kingdom was prosperous when in the fifth year [i.e., ca. 847 B.C.] of Joram (Jehoram), the son of Ahab and Jezebell, he was succeeded in Judah by his eldest son Jehoram (Joram) (co-regent ca. 853–848 B.C./regent ca. 848–841 B.C.). When the Edomites learned that Jehoshaphad had died they rebelled against Judah's authority, ceased paying tribute to Jehoram (Joram) (2 Chronicles 21:16–17), declared their independence, and attacked the Judeans south of the Dead Sea in Idumea. Responding Jehoram (Joram) sent all his chariots, but found himself outnumbered by the Edomites (2 Kings 8:20–22). Soon after the Levitical city of Libnar revolted, and near the end of the reign of Jehoram (Joram) (2 Chronicles 21:10), raiding Philistines and Arabians invaded and plundered the royal palace in Jerusalem and killed the older brothers of Jehoram (Joram) (2 Chronicles 20:31; 21:1–3,13). They carried off the rest of his family except his youngest son Ahaziah by his wife Athaliah, the daughter of King Ahab and Jezebel (2 Chronicles 21:16–17).[68] Now Jehorem (Joram) did evil in the sight

---

67 Cannibalization of children is referred to twice as chastisement for disobedience (Leviticus 26:28–29; Deuteronomy 28:53).
68 Azariah is also referred to by the name Jehoahaz (2 Chronicles 21:17).

of the Lord. He led Judah astray by causing the inhabitants of Jerusalem to commit harlotry (2 Kings 8:18; 2 Chronicles 21:6–12). Yet despite his many sins the Lord would not destroy Judah for the sake of King David, as He had promised David to give a lamp to him and his sons forever (2 Kings 8:19). In ca. 841 B.C., Jehoram (Joram) having reigned for eight years in Jerusalem died. As had been prophesied by Elijah, the Lord struck him in the intestines with an incurable bowel disease, and at the end of two years, at the age of 40, his intestines came out because of his sickness (2 Chronicles 21:12–20; 2 Kings 8:7). To no one's sorrow he died and was buried in the city of David, but not in the tombs of the kings of Israel just as the house of Ahab had, for Athaliah the daughter of Ahab was his wife (2 Kings 8:18; 2 Chronicles 21:6).

Now Ahaziah, the son of King Jehoram (Joram), and grandson of King Jehoshaphat (co-regency ca. 872–871/regency 871–848 B.C.), was twenty and five years old when in 841 B.C. he became king of Judah. But he only reigned for one year in Jerusalem. His mother was Athaliah the daughter of Ahab and the granddaughter of Omri.[69] During his brief reign Ahaziah walked in all the ways of the house of Ahab, for his mother and the whole house of Ahab counseled him (2 Chronicles 22:4).

In the meanwhile, when King Hadadezer (Ben-Hadad II) of Aram-Damascus became ill he dispatched his servant Hazael to the prophet Elisha to learn if he was to live, or to die. Elisha foreknew all the evil that Hazael would do to the children of Israel, how he would set the strongholds of Israel on fire, kill their young men with the sword, and dash their children, and rip open their women with child. Even so, the prophet sent Hazael the servant back to Hadadezer (Ben-Hadad II) with the laconic, but paradoxical message: *"Thou shalt surely recover; howbeit Jehovah hath showed me that he shall surely die"* (2 Kings 8:10).

Having delivered Elisha's laconic message, Hazael (ca. 841–800 B.C.) on seeing an opportune occasion to promote his own agenda suffocated Hadadezer (Ben-Hadad II) on his sick-bed with a wet blanket, and in the same year Jehu was anointed king over Israel, Hazael became king over Aram- Damascus (2 Kings 8:7–15). Also in the same year, Syria was invaded, and Damascus besieged by the Assyrian King Shalmaneser III (ca. 859–824 B.C.), the son of Ashur-nasipal II (ca. 884–858 B.C.), but Hazael survived this attack as well as two subsequent attacks by the Assyrians in ca. 837 B.C ? and 836 B.C ?

---

69 Merril F. Unger. The New Unger's Bible Dictionary (Moody Press, Chicago, 1988), 38b2 and 121b.

The Divided Kingdom

Now in the eleventh year [i.e., ca. 841 B.C.] of King Joram (Jehoram), the son of Ahab, his namesake King Jehoram (Joram) of Judah was succeeded by his twenty-two-year-old son Ahaziah (Azariah) (841 B.C.), the namesake of Ahab's predeceased son Ahaziah (ca. 853–852 B.C.). Ahaziah (Azariah) was twenty-two years old when he became king in Judah and he reigned one year in Jerusalem (2 Kings 8:26). During this time he was counseled by the house of Ahab to join King Joram (Jehoram) of Israel on a military expedition against Hazael the king of Aram-Syria at Ramoth Giliad. In the battle that followed, which was won by Hazael, King Joram (Jehoram) was wounded and taken to Jezreel to recover.[70] While there he was visited by Ahaziah (Azariah) the king of Judah who had also fought at Ramoth Giliad. Visiting the injured Joram (Jehoram) at Jezreel was God's occasion for the downfall of Ahaziah (Azariah) the king of Judah, for Jehu (ca. 841–814 B.C.), the son of Nimshi, whom the prophet Elisha had anointed king of Israel, instead of King Joram (Jehoram), now fulfilled the prophesy against the house of Ahab. Leaving Ramoth Giliad with Bidcar his captain, Jehu in great haste rode to Jezreel where twice he was met on the road by guardsmen dispatched by the convalescent King Joram (Jehoram) of Israel and King Ahaziah (Azariah) of Judah. Since the mounted guardsmen did not return to Jezreel with news as expected, Joram (Jehoram) and Ahaziah (Azariah) themselves rode to meet Jehu in the portion of Naboth the Jezreelite. When Joram (Jehoram) saw Jehu he called out, *"Is it peace, Jehu?"* Jehu angrily responded, *"What peace, so long as the whoredoms of thy mother Jezebel and her witchcrafts are so many?"* (2 Kings 9:22)

Joram (Jehoram) quickly turned his horse around to escape, and as he attempted to flee he cried out a warning to Ahaziah: *"There is treachery, O Ahaziah!"* Jehu quickly drew his bow, and with murder in his heart he killed King Joram (Jehoram) the last king of the House of Omri and ordered Bidcar his captain to throw the corpse into the nearby tract of the field of Naboth the Jezreelite. Jehu then pursued Ahaziah (Azariah) the young king of Judah by the road to Berth Haggan and ordered him shot in his chariot at the ascent of Gur. Seriously wounded young king Ahaziah (Azariah) of Judah managed to flee to Megiddo west of Jerusalem where in the year 841 B.C. he died (2 Kings 9:27–28).[71] Commenting on the life of Ahaziah (Azariah), the historian reports that he "walked in the way

---

[70] Following Hazael's victory in 841 B.C. over Joram (Jehoram) of Israel and Ahaziah of Judah, he erected a victory stele at Tel Dan to commemorate the event.

[71] The chronicler in 2 Chronicles 22:9 writes that Ahaziah was caught hiding in Samaria, and then brought to Jehu and killed. He was buried because he was *"the son of Jehoshaphat, who sought Jehovah with all his heart"* (2 Chronicles 22:9).

of the house of Ahab, and did evil in the sight of the Lord as the house of Ahab had, for he was the son-in-law of the house of Ahab" (2 Kings 8:27). Moreover, the mother of Ahaziah *"was his counsellor to do wickedly. And he did that which was evil in the sight of Jehovah, as did the house of Ahab; for they were his counsellors after the death of his father, to his destruction"* (2 Chronicles 22:3–4). Entering the gate at Jezreel Jehu quickly made his way to the palace where Queen Jezebel was residing. Having seen from her palace-tower the murder of King Joram (Jehoram), she mockingly likened Jehu to the ill-famed murderer Zimri (ca. 885 B.C.) of Israel who half a century before had murdered all the members of the household of King Baasha. Paraphrasing the last words spoken by King Joram (Jehoram) of Israel before he died, Jezebel sarcastically called out, *"Is it peace, thou Zimri, thy master's murderer?"* (2 Kings 9:31)[72]. Those were her last words, for when Jehu demanded to know, "Who is on the Lord's side," Queen Jezebel was thrown by several willing eunuchs from the height of the palace wall, and when her blood spattered on the wall below, the frightened horses panicked and trampled her body underfoot as had indeed been prophesied by Elijah the Tishbite:

> *In the [plot of ground] of Jezreel shall the dogs eat the flesh of Jezebel; and the body of Jezebel shall be as dung upon the face of the field in the portion of Jezreel, so that they shall not say, This is Jezebel.*
>
> —2 Kings 9:36–37

Jehu made the house of Ahab like the house of Jeroboam, the son of Nebat, and like the house of Baasha, the son of Ahijah. For his service as God's obedient, but merciless executioner, he was praised by God:

> *Because thou hast done well in executing that which is right in mine eyes, and hast done unto the house of Ahab according to all that was in my heart, thy sons of the fourth generation shall sit on the throne of Israel.*
>
> —2 Kings 10:30

When Jehonadab, a son of Rechab, thereafter met Jehu on his way to Samaria, Jehu asked, *"Is thy heart right, as my heart is with thy heart?"* Jehonadad answered, *"It is."* Jehu then said, *"If it be, give me thy hand."* So Jehu took Jehonadab up to him into the chariot and said, *"Come with me, and see my zeal for Jehovah"* (2 Kings 10:15–16).

---

[72] Zimri had become a symbol for the slave who turns against his master.

When they came to Samaria, Jehu proceeded to murder King Ahaziah's forty-two brothers as well as the sons of Ahaziah's brothers, and Ahab's seventy sons. By a cunning stratagem he also cut off a large number of Baal-worshiping priests and princes and many others affiliated with the four- generation-old Omride dynasty (2 Kings 9:27–29; 10:1–13, 17–28; 2 Chronicles 22:8).[73] Nothing of what the Lord had said to His servant Elijah concerning the house of Ahab fell to the earth, for Jehu killed all who remained of the house of Ahab in Jezreel, all his great men and close acquaintances and his priests. His savage slaughter of the enemies of God was subsequently criticized by the prophet Hosea (ca. 758–725 B.C.), the son of Beeri, who on the joyful occasion of the birth of his own son Jezreel wrote, *"Call his name Jezreel; for yet a little while, and I will avenge the blood of Jezreel upon the house of Jehu, and will cause the kingdom of the house of Israel to cease"* (Hosea 1:4).

Jezebel, too, it may seem, was subsequently remembered, for in the New Testament Apocalyse letter to the corrupt church in Thyatira, the Apostle John writes: *"And I gave her time that she should repent; and she willeth not to repent of her fornication"* (Revelation. 2:21).

When Athaliah (ca. 841–835 B.C.), the daughter of King Ahab and granddaughter of King Omri of Israel learned that Ahaziah (Azariah) her son had been killed by orders of King Jehu, she immediately destroyed her grandchildren and remaining heirs to the house of Judah and usurped the right to govern Judah (2 Kings 11:1,2; 2 Chronicles 22:10–12). By her ruthless action she almost managed to destroy the Davidic monarchy. However, the child Joash (Jehoash), the son of Ahaziah (Azariah), miraculously escaped the slaughter.[74] To protect the endangered child from his murderous grandmother he was hidden away by his aunt Jehosheba (Jehoshabeath), daughter of King Joram (Jehoram) and sister of Ahaziah, and raised by the priest Jehoiada his uncle who secretly conspired to have Queen Athaliah killed possibly by Carian Cherethite or Pelethite mercenaries assigned by Jehoiada to protect the legitimate boy king.[75] At the age of seven Joash (Jehoash) (ca. 835–796 B.C.) was finally presented as the rightful Davidic king of Judah and crowned by the priest Jehoiada. Acting as interim regent, Jehoiada

---

73 The four generation dynasty of Omri consisted of Omri, Ahab, Ahaziah and Joram (Jehoram). The Assyrian kings referred to Omri's successors as the "House of Omri."

74 To distinguish between the sons of Ahaziah of Judah and Jehoahaz of Israel, the former is referred to as Joash (Jehoash) and the latter as Jehoash (Joash).

75 The Cherethites and Pelethites may have been ethnic groups of Carian mercenaries from Asia Minor.

addressed those assembled and said, *"Behold, the king's son shall reign, as Jehovah hath spoken concerning the sons of David"* (2 Chronicles 23:3). When much too late Queen Athaliah discovered that she had been deceived by Jehoiada the priest serving as interim regent, she angrily tore her clothes and cried out, *"Treason! treason!"* (2 Kings 11:14; 2 Chronicles 23:13).

Having arrested and executed Queen Athaliah, the last survivor of the house of Omri, the coronation ceremony of the boy king was followed by a joyous festival such as had not been observed since the earlier days of King Asa (ca. 910–869 B.C.) of Judah (2 Chronicles 15:9–15; 29:10; 34:31–32).[76] The young child began to reign in the seventh year [i.e., ca. 834 B.C.] of King Jehu of Israel, and he reigned in Jerusalem for nearly forty years. His mother's name was Zibiah of Beersheba. Joash (Jehoash) initially did what was right in the sight of the Lord all the days in which his righteous mentor Jehoiada the priest instructed him. He collected census and assessment money for the repair of the temple, broke the Phoenician idols in pieces, demolished the sanctuary of Baal, ordered the execution of Mattan the high priest of Baal in Jerusalem (2 Kings 11:18), and also hired masons and carpenters to restore the house of the Lord with monies collected in a wooden alms chest with a bored hole in its lid placed by the altar. However, "after the death of Jehoiada the priest, when the leaders of Judah came and bowed down to the King, he listened to them (2 Chronicles 24:17–18). Therefore they left the house of the Lord God of their fathers, and served wooden images and idols. The high places were not taken away; and the people continued to sacrifice and burn incense to their pagan gods on the high places. Then the Spirit of God came upon Zechariah, the son of Jehoiada the priest who in the meanwhile had succeeded his father as high priest. With righteous indignation he condemned the growing apostasy in Judah and prophesied, *"Thus saith God, Why transgress ye the commandments of Jehovah, so that ye cannot prosper? because ye have forsaken Jehovah, he hath also forsaken you"* (2 Chronicles 24:20). Willfully blind to the kindness which Jehoiada his mentor had shown him, King Joash (Jehoash) ordered Zechariah the priest to be stoned to death in the court of the house of the Lord, and as Zechariah breathed out his last breath he cried, *"Jehovah look upon it, and [repay it]"* (2 Chronicles 24:22). During the remaining spiritual decline of Joash (Jehoash), the prophet Joel (ca. 835–796 B.C.), the son of Pethuel, preached on the end-of-time coming Day

---

76 Like joyous festivals were also observed in the days of the Kings Hezekiah (727–697 B.C.) and Josiah (640–609 B.C.) of Judah.

of the Lord with its judgments and eventual restoration, the outpouring of God's spirit, and the re-gathering of the captives of Judah and Jerusalem.[77]

Within a year of the execution of Zechariah the priest, Hazael the Syrian went up and fought against Gath of the Philistines, and then set his face to go to Jerusalem where he defeated King Joash (Jehoash). To buy off Hazael, Joash (Jehoash) took all the sacred things and the gold found in the treasuries of the kings house, the sacred things that his fathers Jehoshaphat and Jehoram (Joram) and Ahaziah had dedicated, as well as his own sacred things, and gave all to Hazael who then went away from Jerusalem to confront the Assyrian King Adad-nirari III (ca. 810–782 B.C.), the son of Shamshi-Adad V (ca. 824–810 B.C.) then laying siege to Damascus (2 Kings 12:17–18).

In 814 B.C., towards the end of the reign of the Assyrian King Shamsi-Adad V, King Jehu of Israel died and was buried in Samaria.[78] Although he had struck down the whole house of Ahab as prophesied by Elijah and Elisha, and had rooted out Baal from Israel, he did not himself turn away *"from the sins of Jeroboam the son of Nebat, wherewith he made Israel to sin, Jehu departed not from after them, to wit, the golden calves that were in Beth-el, and that were in Dan"* (2 Kings 10:29). He *"took no heed to walk in the law of Jehovah, the God of Israel, with all his heart: he departed not from the sins of Jeroboam, wherewith he made Israel to sin"* (2 Kings 10:29–31). He reigned over Israel in Samaria twenty and eight years, and according to one perceptive commentator, he was:

> One of those decisive, terrible, and ambitious, yet prudent, calculating, and passionless men whom God from time to time raises up to change the fate of empires and execute His judgment on the earth.[79]

Indeed, the Most High determines the rise and fall of nations. He rules in the kingdom of men, and gives it to whomever He chooses (Daniel 2:21; 4:25).

---

[77] Joel's messianic prophesy concerning the outpouring of God's Holy Spirit is quoted by the Apostle Peter (Acts 2:1–4, 16–21) when at Pentecost the Holy Spirit like a rushing mighty wind fell like tongues of fire upon the assembled disciples.

[78] 2 Kings 10:34–36. When the Assyrian King Shalmaneser III (ca. 858–824 B.C), the father of Shamsi-Adad V (ca. 824–810 B.C.) campaigned against and put pressure on the kingdoms of Hamath and Aram Damascus, Jehu was compelled to pay tribute to the Assyrian king.

[79] The Ultimate Bible Dictionary (Jazzybee Verlag Jurgen Beck 86450 Altenmunster, Germany, 2012), and in Matthew George Eaton. Illustrated Bible Dictionary. Vol. 2: G–N, 3rd ed. (Thomas Nelson, 1897).

He removes kings and raises up kings (Job. 12:23); He puts down one, and exalts another (Psalm 75:7).

Then in the twenty and third year [i.e., ca. 812 B.C.] of Joash (Jehoash) the king of Judah, Jehu was followed on the throne of Israel by his son Jehoahaz (Joahaz) (ca. 814–798 B.C.) who reigned seventeen years and inherited the troubles his father Jehu had with Aram-Damascus (2 Kings 10:35;13:1–5). Since he did not depart from the sins of Jeroboam, the son of Nebat, the Lord was aroused against Israel, and He delivered Israel into the hands of the tyrannicide Hazael and his son Ben-Hadad III (ca. 806–770 B.C.), all their days (2 Kings 13:22). The Syrians left Jehoahaz (Joahaz) with only *"fifty horsemen, and ten chariots, and ten thousand footmen"* (2 Kings 13:7), hardly enough to pay the required tribute to Hazael, and hardly enough to put up a symbolic parade guard for visiting dignitaries.[80] Therefore Jehoahaz (Joahaz) pleaded with the Lord, and the Lord listened to him; for He saw the oppression of Israel by the king of Syria (2 Kings 13:4). Jehoahaz (Joahaz) like his father "did evil in the sight of the Lord; and did not depart from all the sins of Jeroboam, the son of Nebat, who had made Israel sin" (2 Kings 13:2,6). Then Jehoahaz (Joahaz) died and was buried in Samaria, and in the thirty and seventh year [i.e., ca. 798 B.C.] of king Joash (Jehoash) of Judah, he was followed on the throne of Israel by his son Jehoash (Joash) (798–782 B.C.) (2 Kings 13:10).

Around this time the prophet Elisha became sick and was visited by King Jehoash (Joash) of Israel. Facing Jehoash (Joash), Elisha ordered the king to strike the ground with his arrows, one representing "the Lord's deliverance" and the other "deliverance from Syria." Complying Jehoash (Joash) struck the ground three times and then stopped. Angrily Elisha cried out, *"Thou shouldest have smitten five or six times: then hadst thou smitten Syria till thou hadst consumed it; whereas now thou shalt smite Syria but thrice"* (2 Kings 13:19). Then around ca. 800 B.C. Elisha, having performed a great variety of miraculous acts, died from his illness.[81] On seeing the dead prophet on his death-bed, Jehoash (Joash) wept, and repeating the words that Elisha had spoken when Elijah was taken to heaven in a whirlwind he cried out, *"My father, my father, the chariots of Israel and the horsemen thereof!"* (2 Kings 13:14)

Responding to the earlier plea of Jehoahaz, the father of Jehoash (Joash), the Lord then gave Israel and Judah a deliverer, for the Assyrian King Adad-nirari III

---

80   Michael D. Coogan, ed., The Oxford History of the Biblical World (Oxford University Press, UK: 1998), 305.

81   For the miraculous acts of Elisha see (2 Kings 2:21, 23; 3:9–20; 4:1–7, 18–37, 42–44; 5:1–27; 6:1–7). Hearsay has it that when the corpse of another man subsequently was placed in Elisha's tomb and touched the bones of the dead prophet, the man's corpse revived and stood on its feet (2 Kings 13:21).

(ca. 810–783 B.C.), who had succeeded King Shamsi-Adad V (ca. 824–810 B.C.), invaded and crushed Aram-Damascus and killed Hazael. The house of Hazael was set on fire and the flames rapidly spread and devoured the palaces of Ben- Hadad. Then following the succession of Hazael's son Ben-hadad III (ca. 800–770 B.C.), the stage was set for Jehoash (Joash) (ca. 798–782 B.C.), the son of Jehoahaz, and grandson of Jehu, to reassert Israel's independence (2 Kings 13:10). In the second year [i.e., ca. 796 B.C.] of his reign he recaptured from the hand of Ben-Hadad III the cities which had been taken out of the hand of Jehoahaz his father (2 Kings 13:25). In three wars, the number of times he had struck the ground at the command of the dying prophet Elisha, Jehoash (Joash) took back territories captured by the Damascenes, and drove Ben-Hadad III out of Israel.

Also in 796 B.C. Joash (Jehoash), the king of Judah, was conspired against and murdered in Jerusalem by two of his officials Zabad, an Ammonite, and Jehozabad, a son of Shomer a Moabite (2 Kings 12:20–21). He was killed on his bed in the house of the Millo in Jerusalem as revenge for the earlier bloody execution of Zechariah the son of Jehoiada the priest (2 Kings 12:19–21; 2 Chronicles 24:26). Ironically they buried him in the sepulchers of the kings in Jerusalem, the city of David, next to Jehoiada his faithful childhood mentor (2 Chronicles 24:15–16). He was followed on the throne of Judah by Amaziah (ca. 796–767 B.C.) his son (2 Kings 14:1–4). Amaziah was twenty and five years old when he began to reign, and he reigned twenty and nine years in Jerusalem. His mother's name was Jehoaddan of Jerusalem. He executed the servants who had murdered his father Joash (Jehoash), but did not kill their children as it is written in the Law of the Book of Moses: *"The fathers shall not be put to death for the children, neither shall the children be put to death for the fathers: every man shall be put to death for his own sin"* (Deuteronomy 24:16; see also 2 Chronicles 25:4).

Amaziah gathered together Judah and set over them captains of thousands and captains of hundreds according to their father's houses throughout Judah and Benjamin, and he numbered them from twenty years old and above, and found them to be three hundred thousand choice men of war who could handle spear and shield. Supplemented by a mercenary force of 100,000 Israelite soldiers hired for a hundred talents he made plans to subdue the Edomites. To his annoyance, however, and perhaps to the greater annoyance of the hired mercenaries, he was ordered by a man of God to discharge them (2 Chronicles 25:5–10). Then leading his people he marched to the Valley of Salt between Judah and Edom south of the Dead Sea where he killed ten thousand of the people of Seir and took captive another ten thousand alive - only to have them thrown from the top of a rock and killed. When he returned from the slaughter of the Edomites he carried with him the images and idols of the gods of the people of Seir, and set them up to be his own gods. A prophet was then sent by the Lord who asked Amaziah: *"Why hast thou sought after the gods of the people, which have not delivered their own people out of thy hand?"* (2 Chronicles 25:15) Angered by the rebuke Amaziah replied, *"Have we made thee of the king's counsel?"* The prophet replied no, adding, "I know that God *hath* determined to destroy *thee*, because *thou hast* done this, and *hast* not hearkened unto my counsel" (2 Chronicles 25:16). Having soundly defeated the Edomites, proud Amaziah unwisely proceeded to provoke and challenge King Jehoash (Joash) (ca. 798–782 B.C.) of Israel, the son of Jehoahaz (ca. 814–798 B.C.) and grandson of Jehu (ca. 841–814 B.C.), to face him in battle (2 Kings 14:8; 2 Chronicles 25:17). With words heavily loaded with sarcasm King Jehoash (Joash) of Israel replied:

> *The thistle that was in Lebanon sent to the cedar that was in Lebanon, saying, Give thy daughter to my son to wife: and there passed by a wild beast that was in Lebanon, and trod down the thistle. Thou hast indeed smitten Edom, and thy heart hath lifted thee up: glory thereof, and abide at home; for why shouldest thou meddle to thy hurt, that thou shouldest fall, even thou, and Judah with thee?*
> —2 Kings 14:9–10
> (see also 2 Chronicles 25:18–19)

Amaziah's challenge was accepted, and in 793 B.C. the two kings looked one another in the face at Beth Shemesh. The army of Judah was routed and King Amaziah taken prisoner (2 Kings 14:11–13; 2 Chronicles 25:21–23). Jehoash (Joash) then advanced on Jerusalem and broke down the wall from the gate of Ephraim to the corner gate, about four hundred cubits. He took all the gold and silver found in the house of the Lord and the treasuries of the king's house, and returned to Samaria with hostages - that included the disgraced King Amaziah of Judah (2 Kings 14:13–14; 2 Chronicles 25:23–24). The following year the people of Judah took Uzziah (Azariah) (co-regent ca. 792–767/regent 767–740 B.C.), the son of Amaziah, who at the time was sixteen years old, and appointed him to replace his father Uzziah (Azariah) as co-regent (2 Kings 14:19–20; 2 Chronicles 25:27).[82]

---

[82] The dating of Uzziah (Azariah) is based on the conjecture that he was made co-regent in 792 B.C. following the capture of his father Amaziah by Joash the king of Israel, and made sole regent immediately following the death of Amaziah in 767 B.C.

The Divided Kingdom

Uzziah (Azariah) was sixteen years old when he began to reign, and he reigned fifty and two years in Jerusalem. His mother's name was Jecoliah (2 Chronicles 26:3).

In 782 B.C. Jehoash (Joash) died peacefully in Samaria and was succeeded, in the fifteenth year [i.e., ca. 782/781 B.C.] of Amaziah of Judah by his son Jeroboam II (co-regent ca. 793–782/regent ca. 782–753 B.C.) (2 Kings 14:23). As a goodwill gesture Jeroboam II released Amaziah, the son of Joash (Jehoash) king of Judah, who then went on to reign for another fifteen years in Judah as regent with his son Uzziah (Azariah) as co-regent (2 Kings 14:17; 2 Chronicles 25:25). In 767 B.C. at the age of fifty-four, the humiliated Amaziah was conspired against and killed at Lachish where he had sought refuge from his people. His body was brought upon horses to Jerusalem where he was buried in the royal sepulcher. He did what was right in the sight of the Lord, yet not like King David.

He lived fifteen years after the death of King Jehoash, the son of Jehoahaz, the king of Israel.

The year following, which was the twenty and seventh year [i.e., ca. 766 B.C.] of Jeroboam II of Israel, Uzziah (Azariah) (co-regent ca. 792–766/regent ca. 766–740 B.C.) the son of King Amaziah finally became sole regent in Judah (2 Kings 14:21; 15:1; 2 Chronicles 26:1; Amos 1:1).[83] He reigned fifty and two years in Jerusalem, and in the days of the prophet Zechariah, the son of Berechiah who had understanding in the wisdom of God, he "was much indebted to him for his wise counsel, and God made him prosper (2 Chronicles 26:4–5).[84] He built towers and fortified them with military engines, and equipped a large army that made war against the Philistines of Gath and Ashdod. Moreover he had an army of well equipped fighting men that went out to war by bands. In alliance with King Jeroboam II of Israel he retook Aram-Damascus and Hamath on the river Orontes from Ben-hadad III, and extended Israel to its former limits:

---

[83] Around 760 B.C., during the long reign of Uzziah (Azariah), a major earthquake may have affected the entire region (Zechariah 14:5).

[84] Jesus stated that Zechariah's father Berechiah was murdered between the temple and the altar (Matthew 23:31–35). Like Zechariah, the son of Jehoiada, he was likely stoned "in the court of the house of the Lord" (2 Chronicles 24:20–21). Zechariah referred to here is not the same as his later name sake the Prophet Zechariah (ca. 520–509 B.C.).

> *He restored the border of Israel from the entrance of Hamath unto the sea of the Arabah, according to the word of Jehovah, the God of Israel, which he spake by his servant Jonah the son of Amittai, the prophet, who was of Gath-hepher.*
> —2 Kings 14:25
> (see also 2 Chronicles 26:6–15, Zephaniah 1:16)[85]

The successes of Jeroboam II in the north-east and north may be attributed in part to the progressive weakening of the Aramean kingdom caused by the earlier campaigns by the Assyrian Kings Adad- Nirari III (ca. 810–783 B.C.), by Shalmaneser IV (ca. 782–773 B.C.) and by Ashur-dan III (ca. 773–754 B.C). Turning south-east Jeroboam II also subdued the Ammonites and Moabites. During his long reign the people began to enjoy the fruits of their dominance, and the kingdom of Israel prospered with a wealthy class of landowners. The upper classes enjoyed a material prosperity, and a softness of living that over time progressively sapped the physical and moral vigor of the nation (Amos 3:11–15; 5:11; 6:4–5,8). The prophets Amos (ca. 765–754 B.C.) of Tekoa and Hosea (ca. 758–725 B.C.), the son of Beeri, both strongly condemned the Samaritans for their extravagant lifestyle and lack of social justice, for the elites trampled upon the poor and afflicted the just (Amos 2:6–8; 5:10–12; Hosea 4:1–2; 7:1–7). Speaking for the Lord, Amos strongly denounced the prescribed irreligious sacrifices of the priests, and the immorality and pagan worship of the Samarian people:

> *I hate, I despise your feasts, and I will take no delight in your solemn assemblies. Yea, though ye offer me your burnt-offerings and meal-offerings, I will not accept them; neither will I regard the peace-offerings of your fat beasts. Take thou away from me the noise of thy songs; for I will not hear the melody of thy viols. But let justice roll down as waters, and righteousness as a mighty stream.*
> —Amos 5:21–24

The high-priest Amaziah of Bethel responded to what he rightly perceived to be Amos's attack on the priesthood of the Israelites, and even accused Amos of conspiring against King Jeroboam II. Derisively he told Amos, "O thou seer, go,

---

[85] Jonah (ca. 781–753 B.C. ?) was twice commissioned to go to Nineveh. The ancient cities of Babel and Nineveh were built by Nimrod the son of Cush and subsequently re- founded by the Assyrian King Shalmaneser I (ca. 1263–1234 B.C.), the son of Adad-Nirari (ca. 1295–1264 B.C.). Jonah disobeyed the first commission and was punished (Jonah 1:3; 2:10), and then obeyed the second commission which resulted in the repentance of the Ninevites (Jonah 3:1–10). Nineveh was spared after Jonah's mission for more than a century.

The Divided Kingdom

flee thou away into the land of Judah, and there eat bread, and prophesy there: but prophesy not again any more at Beth-el" (Amos 7:12–13). Denouncing the affluent and hedonistic elites of Samaria, and saddened by Israel's unpreparedness for the coming onslaught of the Assyrian host, Amos prophesied that Israel would go captive as the first of the captives, that *"Jeroboam [II] shall die by the sword, and Israel shall surely be led away captive out of his land"* (Amos 7:11). Then departing he said:

> *[Woe to you] that put far away the evil day, and cause the seat of violence to come near; that lie upon beds of ivory, and stretch themselves upon their couches, and eat the lambs out of the flock, and the calves out of the midst of the stall; that sing idle songs to the sound of the viol; that invent for themselves instruments of music, like David; that drink wine in bowls, and anoint themselves with the chief oils; but they are not grieved for the affliction of Joseph.*
>
> *Therefore shall they now go captive with the first that go captive; and the revelry of them that stretched themselves shall pass away.*
>
> —Amos 6:3–7

However, the people of Samaria did not believe that evil would overtake them, as evil subsequently did, for *"judgment springeth up as hemlock in the furrows of the field"* (Hosea 10:4).[86] Then in the thirty and eighth year [i.e., ca. 754 B.C.] of King Uzziah (Azariah) of Judah, Jeroboam II, now an old man in his seventies, died and was buried with his ancestors. He reigned forty-one years, and did not depart from the sins of his earlier namesake Jeroboam (ca. 930–909 B.C.), the son of Nebat, who had introduced the calf-worship at Dan and Bethel a century and a half before (2 Kings 14:23–24).

Jeroboam II was succeeded by his son Zechariah (ca. 753–752 B.C.) who ruled over Israel in Samaria for only six months, for he was conspired against and killed by Shallum (ca. 753 B.C.), the son of Jabesh, who usurped the throne of Israel and ruled in Zechariah's stead. The death of Zechariah ended the five-generation-old dynasty of King Jehu, and fulfilled the word of the Lord which He had spoken years earlier saying to Jehu: *"Thy sons to the fourth generation shall sit upon the throne of Israel"* (2 Kings 15:12). The rule of Shallum, the son of Jabesh, was characterized by lawlessness and revolution, and the chronicler writes, *"And he did that which was evil in the sight of Jehovah, as his fathers had done: he departed not from the sins of Jeroboam the son of Nebat, wherewith he made Israel to sin"* (2 Kings 15:9).

---

[86] Hemlock (L. Conium maculatum) a highly poisonous perennial herbaceous flowering plant here likened to a noxious weed.

Having killed Zechariah, Shallum only reigned for one month in Samaria, for in the thirty and ninth year [i.e., ca. 753 B.C.] of Uzziah (Azariah) of Judah, while inebriated he was dethroned and assassinated by Menahem (ca. 753–738 B.C.), the son of Gadi, who for ten years prior, while serving as commander in Tirzah, had conspired to make himself king of Israel. Menahem's rule over Israel was distinguished by great wickedness, war and excessive taxation. He brutally smote the inhabitants of Tiphsah (Tappuah) along the coast because they opened not their gates to him, and he ripped up all the women that were with child (2 Kings 15:16, 29; Isaiah 9:1). When the Assyrian King Tiglath-pileser III (Pul) (ca. 744–727 B.C.), the son of Asshur-nirari V (ca. 754–745 B.C.) in 739 B.C. moved against an anti-Assyrian coalition organized by Uzziah (Azariah) of Judah and entered Israel, Menahem quickly exacted of each man fifty shekels of silver as a burdensome tax, and bought-off the Assyrian king with a thousand talents (2 Kings 15:19–20; 1 Chronicles 5:26).[87] Having collected tributes from Menahem as well as from Rezin (ca. 750–732 B.C.) of Damascus and Hiram of Tyre, Tiglath-pileser III departed and returned to Assyria.

When King Uzziah (Azariah) of Judah was strong and his fame had spread as far as the entrance of Egypt his heart was lifted up to his destruction, for he transgressed against the Lord his God by entering the temple of the Lord to burn incense on the altar of incense (2 Chronicles 26:16–23). For presumptuously sinning in this manner he was ordered by Azariah the high priest to leave the sanctuary. When he responded in great anger the Lord struck him, and while he was angry with the priests, leprosy broke out on his forehead (2 Chronicles 26:19).[88] Like Miriam, the sister of Moses, who had sinned by considering herself not unequal to Moses, her brother, and was made "as white as snow for her assumption" (Numbers 12:1–10), so too Uzziah (Azariah) was struck by the Lord, and until

---

[87] A fragmentary annalistic text reads: "As for Menahem, I (Tiglath-pileser) ov]erwhelmed him [like a snowstorm] and he ... fled like a bird, alone, [and bowed to my feet(?)], I returned him to his place [and imposed tribute upon him, to wit:] gold, silver, linen garments with multicolored trimmings... great... [I re]ceived from him Israel (lit.: "Omri-Land"... all its inhabitants (and) their possessions I led to Assyria." See: J. B. Pritchard The Ancient Near East. An Anthology of Texts and Pictures. 1973. Vol. I, p. 193–194. Another building inscription on clay reads: "I (Tiglath-pileser) received tribute from Rezon of Damascus and Menahem of Samaria."

[88] As noted by G. Rawlinson, The kings of Israel and Judah (London), Uzziah's act was a flagrant assumption, not only of the priestly, but of the high priestly office (Exodus 30:7,8). If tamely submitted to, it would have practically subordinated the entire priesthood to the monarch, and have gone far to destroy the whole Mosaic system." George Rawlinson. The Kings of Israel and Judah (James Nisbet and Co., UK, 1889), 154.

the day of his death he remained a leper and lived separately in his private house excluded from public life and cut off from the house of the Lord (2 Chronicles 26:18–21).[89]

During his time of self-imposed quarantine, his son Jotham (co-regent ca. 750–740) was ruler over his father house judging the people of Judah (2 Kings 15:5,7; 2 Chronicles 26:21,23). Apart from the transgression which earned Uzziah (Azariah) the rebuke of the temple priests and the anger of God, he did what was right in the sight of the Lord, according to all that his father Amaziah had done (2 Chronicles 26:4; 2 Kings 15:3). However, since the corpse of a leper would have polluted the burial field of the kings of Judah, the corpse of Uzziah (Azariah), like the polluted corpse of Jehoram (Joram), the son of King Jehoshaphat of Judah, was denied burial there, and instead was interred somewhere near it.

In the fiftieth year [i.e., ca. 742 B.C.] of Uzziah (Azariah) of Judah, King Menahem having ruled for ten years in Israel died. The Prophets Hosea and Amos both draw depressingly dismal pictures of the ungodliness of Menahem's reign, for he did evil in the sight of the Lord, and did not depart all his days from the sins of Jeroboam, the son of Nebat, who had made Israel sin. Also in the fiftieth year of Uzziah (Azariah), Pekahiah (ca. 742–740 B.C.), the son of Menahem, became king in his father's stead and ruled Israel for two years. Then following the death in the fiftieth and second year [i.e., ca. 740 B.C.] of Uzziah (Azariah) king of Judah, Pekahiah was conspired against and murdered in the royal palace of Samaria by Pekar, the son of Remaliah, who prior to this time (ca. 752–740 B.C.) had served Pekahiah as a captain in Giliad. With the death of King Pekahiah the two generation-old dynasty of Menahem came to an end, and with Menahem and Pekahiah out of the way Pekah (ca. 740–732 B.C.) dared to usurp the throne of Israel with the aid of a band of Gileadites.

Now Jotham the son of King Uzziah was twenty and five years old when he began to rule, and he ruled for a total of sixteen years in Jerusalem first as co-regent with his father Uzziah (Azariah), and then as sole regent (ca. 740–735 B.C.) (2 Chronicles 27:1). He became sole regent in Judah in the second year [i.e., ca. 740 B.C.] of King Pekah of Israel (2 Kings 15:7, 30, 32; 16:1; 2 Chronicles 26:21–23). The name of Jotham's mother was Jerusha, the daughter of Zadok. Jotham fought successfully against the king of the Ammonites and defeated them and forced them to pay tribute. He became mighty "because in all his ways he made the Lord his guide (2 Chron. 27:6). He died in 735 B.C. having done what was right in the sight of the Lord according to all that his father Uzziah (Azariah) had

---

[89] The laws concerning leprosy are referred to in Leviticus 13:1–14:57.

done, and he was buried in the city of David. However the people still sacrificed to their idols, burned incense on the high places, and acted corruptly. Then in the seventeenth year [i.e., ca. 743 B.C.] of Pekah, the son of Remaliah, King Jotham was succeeded on the throne of Judah by his son Ahaz (Jehoahaz) (co-regent ca. 743–732 B.C./regent ca. 732–719 B.C.) (2 Kings 16:1; 2 Chronicles 27:9). He was twenty years old when he began to reign, and he reigned as regent over Judah for 16 years (2 Kings15:32–38; 16:1–2; 2 Chronicles 27:9; 28:1). Around this time Pekah, the King of Israel, and King Rezin II (ca. 770–732 B.C.) of Aram, mockingly referred to by the Prophet Isaiah (ca. 760–673 B.C.), the son of Amoz, as "smoking firebrands," secretly allied themselves in an anti-Assyrian coalition against King Tiglath-pileser III (ca. 744–727 B.C.) of Assyria, and took evil council against Ahaz the king of Judah (2 Kings 15:29; Isaiah 7:4). They expected by strength of force to coerce King Ahaz the son of Jotham to strengthen their anti-Assyrian alliance, or failing that, to unseat Ahaz and install in his stead on the throne of Judah a certain "son of Tabeel," perhaps an Ephraimite in the army of Pekar, the son of Remaliah, or a Syrian in the army of Rezin II (Isaiah 7:6). Coming to Jerusalem they besieged Ahaz, but could not prevail against him. Ahaz firmly declined to join them, and because he refused to cooperate, King Rezin II of Syria and Pekah of Israel attacked Judah. In one day they killed one hundred and twenty thousand including Maaseiah the king's son and Elkanah who was second to the king, and they carried a large number captive to Samaria for they proposed to force the children of Judah and Jerusalem into slavery (2 Kings 16:5; 2 Chronicles 28:5–15).[90] To make matters worse for Ahaz, the Edomites and the Palestinians invaded the land from the south and from the west. Deeply distressed by the affairs of state King Ahaz sent messengers with large quantities of silver and gold taken from the house of the Lord and the houses of the princes to Tiglath-pileser III, the son of Ashur-nirari V (ca. 754–745 B.C.), saying, *"I am thy servant and thy son: come up, and save me out of the hand of the king of Syria, and out of the hand of the king of Israel, who rise up against me"* (2 Kings 16:7).

The plea being heard, the stage was set for the fall of Israel, for the Assyrian King Tiglath-Pileser III in 732 B.C. went against Aram-Damascus, previously weakened beyond recovery by Jeroboam II, and easily took it by force. Rezin II (ca. 750–732 B.C.) the last king of Aram-Damascus was assassinated and his hometown totally destroyed (2 Kings 16:9). Tiglath-pileser III also took several Israelite cities and carried away captive 13,500 Israelites to Assyria. To save

---

[90] Due to the intervention of the prophet Oded, the prisoners were well treated by their captors and repatriated.

The Divided Kingdom

Jerusalem King Ahaz of Judah went to Damascus to render homage to the Assyrian king. While there he eyed a magnificently-carved pagan altar, and drawn by desire to possess one like it he forwarded the pattern of it to Urijah (Uriah), a priest of the house of Ahaz in Jerusalem, who then proceeded to construct an altar after the pattern seen in Damascus. From then on while the Assyrian king advanced westward against the Philistines, King Ahaz became increasingly unfaithful to the Lord. He encouraged moral decline in Judah, introduced idolatrous customs, and continually was unfaithful to the Lord. He sacrificed to the gods of Damascus on the Syrian altar that Urijah (Uriah) the priest had artfully carved for him, for he said, *"Because the gods of the kings of Syria helped them, therefore will I sacrifice to them, that they may help me"* (2 Chronicles 28:23).

> *[Ahaz] did not that which was right in the eyes of Jehovah, like David his father; but he walked in the ways of the kings of Israel, and made also molten images for the Baalim. Moreover he burnt incense in the valley of the son of Hinnom, and burnt his children in the fire, according to the abominations of the nations whom Jehovah cast out before the children of Israel. And he sacrificed and burnt incense in the high places, and on the hills, and under every green tree.*
> —2 Chronicles 28:1–4

He even cut in pieces the articles of the house of the Lord and made for himself pagan altars in every corner of Jerusalem and throughout Judah, and shut up the doors of the house of the Lord (2 Chronicles 28:24–25). As commented by the chronicler, this *"brought Judah low because of Ahaz king of Israel"* (2 Chronicles 28:19). Having thoroughly provoked to anger the Lord God of his fathers, Ahaz died. Having reigned for sixteen years he died at the age of thirty-five and was buried in the City of David - but not in the sepulchers of the kings of Israel. He did not do what was right in the sight of the Lord his God, as David had. The moral and spiritual wickedness of Judah, particularly under the rule of Ahaz, is described in vivid anatomical details by the prophet Isaiah, the son of Amoz:

> *Ah sinful nation, a people laden with iniquity, a seed of evil-doers, children that deal corruptly! they have forsaken Jehovah, they have despised the Holy One of Israel, they are estranged and gone backward. Why will ye be still stricken, that ye revolt more and more? the whole head is sick, and the whole heart faint. From the sole of the foot even unto the head there is no soundness in it; but wounds, and*

bruises, and fresh stripes: they have not been closed, neither bound up, neither mollified with oil.

—Isaiah 1:4–6

Then in the twelfth year [i.e., ca. 730 B.C.] of Ahaz king of Judah, began Hoshea, the son of Elah, to reign in Samaria. He led a conspiracy against Pekah and killed him, for Pekah like Remaliah his father *"did that which was evil in the sight of Jehovah: he departed not from all the sins of Jeroboam the son of Nebat, wherewith he made Israel to sin"* (2 Kings 15:24). In Pekar's stead the Assyrian King Tiglath-Pileser III, in the twentieth year [i.e., ca. 730 B.C.] of Jotham the king of Judah, placed Hoshea (ca. 731–722 B.C.) on the throne of Israel in Samaria, and he reigned eight years (2 Kings 15:30; 17:1).[91] In 727 B.C. when Tiglath-Pileser III died and Shalmaneser V (ca. 726–722 B.C.) became king of Assyria, Hoshea rebelled against the Assyrians and brought no tribute payments to the king of Assyria as he had done year after year. Instead he aligned himself with Pharaoh So (Tefnakht ?) (ca. 724–717 B.C.) of the 24th dynasty of Egypt (2 Kings 17:4). Around the same time, in the third year [i.e., ca. 727 B.C.] of Hoshea, Hezekiah (ca. 727–697 B.C.) the son of Ahaz at the age of twenty-five became king of Judah and reigned in his fathers place thirty years in Jerusalem (2 Kings 16:19–20; 17:1; 18:1–2; 2 Chronicles 29:1). His mother's name was Abi (Abijah) the daughter of Zechariah. Also in the third year [i.e., ca. 727 B.C.] of Hoshea, which was the first year [i.e., ca. 726 B.C.] of Hezekiah's reign, Hezekiah reopened the doors of the house of the Lord that his father Ahaz had closed. Moreover all the holy utensils which King Ahaz in his reign had cast aside in his transgression Hezekiah repaired, sanctified and replaced before the altar of the Lord. With the encouragement of the Prophet Isaiah (ca. 760–673 B.C.), whose activity began around 740 B.C., the year that King Uzziah (Azariah) died, he set in order the service of the house of the Lord and celebrated the Passover, for the people had not kept the Passover in the prescribed manner since the time of Solomon the son of David (2 Chronicles 29:3–31:21). Moreover he tore down the pagan high places and destroyed the bronze snake that Moses centuries before had set up in the wilderness to save the people from snake bites (Numbers 21:4; 2 Kings 18:3–7; 2 Chronicles 29:2–19). He also made his scribes copy the memorable proverbs of King Solomon (Proverbs 25:1). In the

---

91 "They overthrew King Pekar and I placed Hoshea as king over them. I received from them 10 talents of gold, 1,000 talents of silver as their [tri]bute and brought them to Assyria" (James B. Pritchard, ed., *The Ancient Near East: An Anthology of Texts and Pictures* [Princeton, NJ: Princeton University Press, 1958], 194).

The Divided Kingdom

seventh year [i.e., ca. 723 B.C.] of King Hoshea of Israel, which was the third year [ca. 724 B.C.] of Hezekiah king of Judah, the Assyrian King Shalmaneser V (ca. 726–722 B.C.), having succeeded his father Tiglath-Pileser III, dispatched a messenger to King Hezekiah with a threatening letter which Hezekiah read before the Lord and was replied to with the assistance of the Prophet Isaiah who exhorted the people to place their dependence on God (Isaiah 37:6, 9–20, 21–29). Then in the seventh year [i.e., ca. 723 B.C.] of Hoshea which was the fourth year [i.e., ca. 723 B.C.] of King Hezekiah of Judah, the Assyrian King Shalmaneser V (ca. 727–722 B.C.) having uncovered a conspiracy by Hoshea, invaded Israel and came up against the rebellious house of Hoshea. Israel had given itself wholly to idolatry and suffered the consequences - the vengeance of a broken covenant. Because of continual and consistent sinning, and the rejection of spiritual light, the northern kingdom with its capital of Samaria was besieged. In the ninth year [i.e., ca. 721 B.C.] of Hoshea, which was the sixth year [i.e., ca. 721 B.C.] of Hezekiah of Judah, the Assyrians took Samaria, bound Hoshea in prison, and carried a major portion of the ten tribes of Israel away to Assyria, and placed them in the cities of Halah and Habor by the river Gozan, and in other cities of the Medes (2 Kings 17:1–11; 18:9–11).[92] As had been foretold by the Prophet Amos, Samaria was overtaken by evil *"like hemlock in the furrows of the field"* (Hosea 10:4).[93] Three times God had disciplined the people, but they had not accepted correction (Amos 4:6,8–9), so God's patience with Israel's ongoing rebellion had finally come to an end. Then Shalmaneser V mysteriously died, or was deposed by the usurper Sargon II (ca. 721–705 B.C.) who took credit for the conquest of Samaria and continued to advance through Gaza and Israel to the border of Egypt ruled by Pharaoh Piye (ca. 743–712 B.C. ?), a Cushite Ethiopian of the 25th Dynasty of Egypt. By ca. 705 B.C. Sargon II had moved on to Asia Minor where, while fighting the encroaching Cimmerians, he was *"thrust through with [a] sword"* (Isaiah 14:19) and died. Sargon's successor on the throne of Assyria was his son Sennacherib II (ca. 705–681 B.C.) who when faced with rebellions in client states proceeded to drive the usurper Merodach-baladan II (ca. 722–710, 703–702 B.C.) out of Babylon.

---

92 For King Hoshea's prior futile reliance on Pharaoh So (Tefnakht) (ca. 724-717 B.C) of Egypt, and for withholding tribute payments to the king of Assyria, he was imprisoned and likely died in captivity (2 Kings 17:4). Settlers from Syria and Mesopotamia were transplanted to Samaria. J. B. Pritchard. An Anthology of Texts and Pictures. Sargon II (721–705): The Fall of Samaria. 1.195–196.

93 Hemlock (L. *Conium maculatum*) a highly poisonous perennial herbaceous flowering plant here likened to a noxious weed.

Having existed as a separate kingdom for about two hundred and fifty years, Samaria was crushed by the rod and staff of God's anger and indignation - and was no more. As prophesied centuries before by the blind prophet Ahijah when he passed judgment on the House of Jeroboam the son of Nebat, the rebellious nation of Israel was never again inhabited entirely by Israelites, but was resettled by transplanted settlers. As for the title "Israel" it was thereafter generally applied to Judah.

> "Of the nine distinct dynasties that successively ruled the dissevered tribes, three ended with the total extirpation of the reigning family. The kingdom continued for a period of about two hundred and fifty years, and the inspired records of those eventful two-and-a-half centuries of Israel's kings and people furnish us with little more than repeated and fearful exhibitions of lawlessness and evil. Out of the nineteen kings that reigned from the great schism to the deportation to the land of Assyria, only seven died natural deaths (Baasha, Omri, Jehu, Jehoahaz, Jehoash, Jeroboam II, and Menahem); seven were assassinated (Nadab, Elah, Joram, Zachariah, Jehoahaz, Pekaiah, and Pekar); one committed suicide (Zimri); one died of injuries received in battle (Ahab); one was 'struck' by the judgment of God (Jeroboam); one died of injuries received from a fall (Ahaziah); and the other, and last (Hoshea), apparently was 'cut off as foam upon the water.'"[94]

Then in the fourteenth year [i.e., ca. 713 B.C.] of Hezekiah king of Judah, Sennacherib II came up against all the fortified cities of Judah and took them. As for Hezekiah he immediately sent to the king of Assyria in Lachish saying: *"I have offended; return from me: that which thou puttest on me will I bear"* (2 Kings 18:14).

The king of Assyria charged King Hezekiah of Judah three hundred talents of silver and thirty talents of gold " (2 Kings 18:9–10, 13–14), and Hezekiah gave him all the silver that was found in the house of the Lord and in the treasures of the kings house. He even cut off the gold from the doors of the temple of the Lord, and from the pillars which he had overlaid, and gave it all to the king of Assyria. Not satisfied with the payoff the king of Assyria sent Tartan and his generals Rabsaris and Rabshakeh from Lachish with a great army against Jerusalem where they taunted and reproached the Israelites in the Hebrew language, urging them

---

[94] Knapp, C. The Kings of Judah and Israel. (Loizeaux Brothers, Inc., Publishers. 1972), 292. As in the case of the kings of Israel and Judah the deeds of lawlessness and evil by the people of the Lord give *"great occasion to the enemies of Jehovah to blaspheme"* (2 Samuel 12:14).

The Divided Kingdom

not to trust Hezekiah their king (2 Kings 18:17–32). Insulted the servants of the Lord came to the prophet Isaiah who said,

> *Be not afraid of the words that thou hast heard, wherewith the servants of the king of Assyria have blasphemed me. Behold, I will put a spirit in him, and he shall hear tidings, and shall return to his own land; and I will cause him to fall by the sword in his own land.*
>
> —2 Kings 19:6–7

The Assyrians then surrounded Jerusalem with earthwork and enclosed Hezekiah like "a bird in a cage."[95] However, by divine intervention the city was miraculously spared, for:

> *…it came to pass that night, that the angel of Jehovah went forth, and smote in the camp of the Assyrians a hundred fourscore and five thousand: and when men arose early in the morning, behold, these were all dead bodies. So Sennacherib [II] king of Assyria departed, and went and returned, and dwelt at Nineveh.*
>
> —2 Kings 19:35–37
> (see also 2 Chronicles 32:21–22)

Now it came to pass that King Hezekiah, the son of King Asa of Judah, became ill and was told by the Prophet Isaiah, "*Set thy house in order; for thou shalt die, and not live*" (2 Kings 20:1; see also 2 Chronicles 32:24). Saddened by the news Hezekiah prayed earnestly for healing, and desiring a sign that the Lord would indeed cure him he asked the Prophet Isaiah for a sign. Replying the prophet said:

> *And this shall be the sign unto thee from Jehovah, that Jehovah will do this thing that he hath spoken: behold, I will cause the shadow on the steps, which is gone down on the dial of Ahaz with the sun, to return backward ten steps.*
>
> —Isaiah 38:7–8

Astonishingly the sun returned ten degrees on the sundial by which it hade gone down, and for a bonus God graciously added fifteen more years to Hezekiah's life with promises of deliverance from the hand of the king of Assyria (2 Kings 20:1–11; 2 Chronicles 32:31; Isaiah 38:5–8). When the news of the sundial

---

[95] Michael D. Coogan. The Oxford History of the Biblical World (Oxford University Press, 1998), 334.

miracle reached Babylon, King Merodach-Baladan (ca. 721–710 B.C.), the son of Baladan, dispatched envoys to Jerusalem to enquire about the sundial. Arriving in Jerusalem they were shown the treasures of Hezekiah. Indeed there was nothing in his dominion that the naive but hospitable Hezekiah did not show them, and when the prophet Isaiah learned of this freely- volunteered expose to a potential enemy he prophesied that the day would soon come when all the treasures of Hezekiah, and his family would be carried off to Babylon as prisoners (2 Kings 20:12–19; Isaiah 39:1–8).

In Sennacherib's campaign against Lebanon, Palestine and Judea several Palestinian cities subject to King Hezekiah were subdued and plundered, and several rulers of cities deported to Assyria. The citizens of the Philistine city of Ekron refused to submit to Sennacherib II, and for their rebellion they were severely punished. The details of what took place in Ekron are preserved in Assyrian script on the six-sided Prism of Sennacherib, as follows:

> "The officials, the patricians and the common people of Ekron - who had thrown Padi, their king, into fetters (because he was) loyal to (his) solemn oath (sworn) by the god Ashur, and had handed him over to Hezekiah, the Jew - (and) he (Hezekiah) held him in prison, unlawfully, as if he (Padi) be an enemy... I assaulted Ekron and killed the officials and patricians who had committed the crime and hung their bodies on poles surrounding the city. The (common) citizens who were guilty of minor crimes, I considered prisoners of war. The rest of them, those who were not accused of crimes and misbehavior, I released."[96]

In the fourteenth year of Hezekiah [i.e., ca. 713 B.C.] Sennacherib II again came up against all the fortified cities of Judah and ordered his commander Rabshakeh to lay siege to Jerusalem (2 Kings 18:13; Isaiah 36:1).[97] The siege likely was interrupted temporarily by Pharaoh Shabaka (ca. 712–698 B.C.), the father of Pharaoh Shebitku (ca. 698–690 B.C.), both of whom are referred to with scorn by the Rabshakeh as *"broken reeds"* (2 Kings 18:19–21, NKJV). King Hezekiah only survived the siege by paying a heavy tribute to the Assyrians. As for Padi, the king of

---

[96] J. B. Pritchart. The Ancient Near East. An Anthology of Texts and Pictures. Sennacherib: The siege of Jerusalem (Princeton Univ. Pr., 1973). Sixth paperback printing, I. 199–201; M. F. Unger and R. K. Harrison and H. F. Vos, editors. The New Unger's Bible Dictionary. (Moody Press, Chicago, 1988), p. 1157b. Revised and updated edition.

[97] J. B. Pritchard. The Ancient Near East. An Anthology of Texts and Pictures. Sennacherib: The siege of Jerusalem. (Princeton Univ. Pr., 1973), Sixth paperback printing, I.199–201.

Ekron, he was made to come from Jerusalem and reinstalled as lord on the throne of Ekron, imposing upon him the tribute due to Sennacherib II his overlord.

When King Hezekiah of Judah again rebelled against his Assyrian masters and withheld tribute, Sennacherib II returned, and once more laid siege to Jerusalem. In anticipation of the renewed onslaught by the Assyrians, Hezekiah in the meanwhile had strengthened his garrisons throughout Judah and fortified the defensive wall around Jerusalem. Moreover, to deprive Sennacherib II's army of water, and to ensure a liberal supply to Jerusalem for a prolonged siege, he had dug a 1,780 foot long Siloam tunnel through solid rock, and brought the waters of the Gihon spring within the walls of the city (2 Chronicles 32:3–4).[98] In this way an abundant supply of fresh water to the city was assured.

Then in 697 B.C. Hezekiah the son of King Ahaz died. He was greatly honored by the people of Jerusalem, and was buried in the upper tombs of the sons of David. With the encouragement of the Prophet Isaiah he had done

> *that which was good and right and faithful before Jehovah his God. And in every work that he began in the service of the house of God, and in the law, and in the commandments, to seek his God, he did it with all his heart, and prospered.*
> —2 Chronicles 31:20–21

Following the death of Hezekiah, his only son Manasseh (co-regency ca. 697–687 B.C./regent ca. 687–642 B.C.) set the stage for Judah's final destruction by reversing the good reforms made by his father. Manasseh was twelve years old when he began to reign, and he reigned 55 years. His mother's name was Hephzibah. Despite the reproof and warnings of the Prophets Isaiah and Micah, Manasseh did evil in the sight of the Lord, according to the detestable abominations of the Amorites whom the Lord had cast out before the children of Israel.

> *For he built again the high places which Hezekiah his father had destroyed; and he reared up altars for Baal, and made an Asherah, as did Ahab king of Israel, and worshipped all the host of heaven, and served them. And he built altars in the house of Jehovah, whereof Jehovah said, In Jerusalem will I put my name. And he built altars for all the host of heaven in the two courts of the house of Jehovah. And he made his son to pass through the fire, and practised augury, and used enchantments, and dealt with them that had familiar spirits, and with wizards: he wrought much evil in the sight of Jehovah, to provoke him to anger. And he set the*

---

[98] The Siloam Inscription (700 B.C.) celebrates the creation of the tunnel by Hezekiah.

graven image of Asherah, that he had made, in the house of which Jehovah said to David and to Solomon his son, In this house, and in Jerusalem, which I have chosen out of all the tribes of Israel, will I put my name for ever.

—2 Kings 21:3–7
(see also 2 Chronicles 33:1–9)

Provoked by the idolatry of Manasseh the Lord said:

Behold, I bring such evil upon Jerusalem and Judah, that whosoever heareth of it, both his ears shall tingle. And I will stretch over Jerusalem the line of Samaria, and the plummet of the house of Ahab; and I will wipe Jerusalem as a man wipeth a dish, wiping it and turning it upside down. And I will cast off the remnant of mine inheritance, and deliver them into the hand of their enemies; and they shall become a prey and a spoil to all their enemies; because they have done that which is evil in my sight, and have provoked me to anger, since the day their fathers came forth out of Egypt, even unto this day.

—2 Kings 21:12–15[99]

Although Manasseh later repented of his idolatry, the Lord did not turn from the fierceness of His great wrath with which His anger was aroused against Judah because of the provocations with which Manasseh had provoked Him.[100]

And I will cause them to be tossed to and fro among all the kingdoms of the earth, because of Manasseh, the son of Hezekiah, king of Judah, for that which he did in Jerusalem.

—Jeremiah 15:4

As had been prophesied by Isaiah, the Assyrian King Sennacherib II was assassinated in 681 B.C. He was slain in Nineveh in the temple of Nisroch by his sons Adrammelech and Sharezer who for safety fled to the mountains of Armenia (2 Kings 19:36–37; 2 Chronicles 32:21; Isaiah 37:37–38). Sennacherib II was succeeded first by his son Esarhaddon (ca. 680–669 B.C.) and then by Ashurbanipal

---

99 God always makes justice the plumb line, the measuring line, and the level to test the religious and political leadership of His people. They will be measured against a standard, the Law of God, and will be found either in alignment with, of out of alignment with the standard.

100 The Apocrypha includes The Prayer of Manasseh when carried off to Babylon.

(ca. 669–633 B.C.) both of whom, in separate campaigns against Pharaoh Tirhakah (Taharqa) (ca. 690–664 B.C.) and his cousin Pharaoh Tanutamun (Tantamani) (ca. 664–653 B.C.) of the 25th Dynasty of Egypt, captured the ancient city of Memphis. Esarhaddon describes the Assyrian invasion of Egypt as follows:

"I fought daily, without interruptions, very bloody battles against Tarqu (Taharqa), king of Egypt and Kush, the one accursed by the great gods. Five times I hit him with the point of my arrows, inflicting wounds from which he should not recover... I destroyed it [Memphis], tore down its walls and burnt it down. His 'queen', the woman of his palace, Ushanahuru his heir apparent, his other children, his possessions, horses, large and small cattle beyond counting, I carried as booty to Assyria. All Kushites I deported from Egypt - leaving not even one to do homage to me."[101]

Also deported at this time was King Manasseh of Judah. The captains of the army of the king of Assyria took Manasseh with hooks, bound him with bronze fetters, and carried him off to Babylon (2 Chronicles 33:11–20). In his dire affliction he implored the Lord his God, and humbled himself and prayed, and the Lord his God received his entreaty, heard his supplication, and brought him back to Jerusalem as vassal king of a tribute-paying Assyrian province. Then in 642 B.C., following a reign of 55 years, Manasseh died and was buried in Jerusalem in the garden of Uzza near the king's palace (2 Kings 21:17–18; 2 Chronicles 33:20). As for the acts of Manasseh, his prayer and how God received his entreaty, and all his sin and trespass, and the sites where he built high places and set up wooden images and carved images before he was humbled, they are written among the sayings of the seers.

Amon (ca. 643/642–641/640 B.C.), the son of Manasseh, was twenty-two years old when he followed his father on the throne of Judah, and he reigned two years in Jerusalem (2 Chronicles 33:18–21). His mother's name was Meshullemeth the daughter of Haruz of Jotbah, and he married Jedidah, the daughter of Adaiah of Bozkath. During his brief reign he continued as his father Manasseh had to dismantle the faith of the Jews in Judah (2 Chronicles 33:21–25). The prophet Zephaniah refers to the moral depravity during Amon's reign. The prophets in the land were insolent, treacherous people, the priests polluted the sanctuary and did violence to the law, and the proud and haughty people were unashamed of their evil deeds (Zephaniah 1:4; 3:4, 11). All said, Amon did evil in the sight of the Lord,

---

[101] ANET, pp. 293, 295, modified by H. T. Aubin. The Rescue of Jerusalem (Doubleday Canada, 2002), pp. 281–282 and p. 399 ftn. 37 and 38.

as his father Manasseh had, for he walked in all the ways that his father walked; and he served the carved images which his father had made and worshiped them. He did not humble himself before the Lord as his father Manasseh had humbled himself, but forsook the Lord God of his fathers, and trespassed more and more. Perhaps because of his close association with the Assyrians, he was himself conspired against by his servants and killed in his own house. Like his father he was buried in the garden in Uzza (2 Kings 21:18, 26).

The people of the land slew all the conspirators against King Amon; and they made Josiah (ca. 640–609 B.C.) his son king of Judah (2 Kings 21:24; 2 Chronicles 33:25). Josiah's mother's name was Jedidah, the daughter of Adaiah of Boscath. He was eight years old when he was anointed king and he reigned thirty-one years in Jerusalem. In the eighth year of his reign [i.e., ca. 632 B.C.], while he was still a youth, he began to seek the god of King David, and in the thirteenth year [i.e., ca. 627 B.C.] of his reign, with the help of the prophet Jeremiah, the son of Hilkiah of the priests who were in Anathoth, he took away all the abominations out of all the countries that pertained to the children of Israel. He also broke down the pagan altars, beat into powder the wooden images, burned the bones of the priests on their altars, and made all that were present in Israel to serve the Lord their God (2 Kings 23:2–16, 19–20; 2 Chronicles 34:3–8, 33; Jeremiah 1:2–3). In the eighteenth year [i.e., ca. 622 B.C.] of his reign, when he had purged the land and the temple, he sent Shaphan the scribe to see Hilkiah the high priest with instructions to repair the damages done to the house of the Lord (2 Kings 22:3). Within the neglected house of the Lord was found the long lost Book of the Law of Moses. Having read from it he tore his clothes and wept. Then he asked the high-priest Hilkiah (ca. 639–609 B.C.) to have the prophetess Huldah (ca. 609 B.C.), the wife of Shallum, son of Tikvah, to inquire of the Lord concerning what was written in the Book of the Law. Having examined it carefully the prophetess reported:

> *Thus saith Jehovah, Behold, I will bring evil upon this place, and upon the inhabitants thereof, even all the words of the book which the king of Judah hath read. Because they have forsaken me, and have burned incense unto other gods, that they might provoke me to anger with all the work of their hands, therefore my wrath shall be kindled against this place, and it shall not be quenched. But unto the king of Judah, who sent you to inquire of Jehovah, thus shall ye say to him, Thus saith Jehovah, the God of Israel: As touching the words which thou hast heard, because thy heart was tender, and thou didst humble thyself before Jehovah, when thou heardest what I spake against this place, and against the inhabitants*

thereof, that they should become a desolation and a curse, and hast rent thy clothes, and wept before me; I also have heard thee, saith Jehovah. Therefore, behold, I will gather thee to thy fathers, and thou shalt be gathered to thy grave in peace, neither shall thine eyes see all the evil which I will bring upon this place. And they brought the king word again.

—2 Kings 22:16–20
(see also 2 Chronicles 34:22–28)

Fearing the wrath of the Lord, Josiah heeded the instructions of the prophetess. He assembled the inhabitants of Jerusalem and read to them the words of The Book of the Covenant which had been found in the house of the Lord, and he made all present take a stand. Then he earnestly proceeded with the religious reform he had already started.[102] He exterpated idolatry, and restored and purified Solomon's Temple. He brought to completion the prophesy of the unnamed man of God who centuries before had cried out against the altar made by Jeroboam the son of Nebat (1 Kings 13:1–3). Then he and the people of Judah sanctified themselves and celebrated the long neglected ceremony of the Passover in the restored temple of Solomon in Jerusalem. [103] Such a Passover had never been held since the days of the Judges who judged Israel, or since the days of Samuel the seer, nor in all the days of the kings of Israel and the kings of Judah.

Following the death of King Ashurbanipal of Assyria in 627 B.C. and the rise to power of Nabopolassar (Nabu-apla-usur) (ca. 625–605 B.C.) in Babylon, the Assyrian cities of Ashur (ca. 614 B.C.) and then Nineveh (ca. 612 B.C.) fell to a Medo-Scythian-Babylonian alliance as had been prophesied by Nahum (ca. 658–615 B.C.) the Elkoshite, and by Zephaniah (ca. 640–626 B.C.) the son of Cushi. Nahum had foretold the complete destruction of Nineveh, then the capital of the Assyrian empire (Nahum 3:1). The Assyrian king Sin-shur-ishkun (ca. 621–612 B.C.) was killed in the assault on Nineveh, and Ashur-uballit II (ca. 612–609 B.C.) managed to escape to Haran where he was proclaimed the new

---

[102] For Josiah's cultural revolution see 2 Kings 23:1–24.

[103] Based on artifacts from the period, it appears that the high priest Hilkiah may have had silver amulets made for Josiah's sons inscribed with blessings. One of these amulets discovered in 1979 in a burial cave at Ketef Hinnom west of Jerusalem, and translated in 1986 by student archaeologists from the University of Tel Aviv, was inscribed with the priestly benediction: *"Jehovah bless thee, and keep thee: Jehovah make his face to shine upon thee, and be gracious unto thee: Jehovah lift up his countenance upon thee, and give thee peace"* (Numbers 6:24–26).

Assyrian emperor.[104] To strengthen Egypt against the oncoming and threatening Babylonian alliance, Pharaoh Necho II (Nekau II) (ca. 610–595 B.C.), the son of Psamtik I (Psammetichus I) (ca. 664–610 B.C.), and father of Psamtik II (Psammetichus II) (ca. 595–589 B.C.) of the 26th dynasty of Egypt, decided to ally himself with his former Assyrian enemies against Babylon, and in 610 B.C. he advanced northward to assist the Assyrians at Haran and Carshemish by the River Euphrates. En route the Egyptian relief force was attacked near Megiddo by King Josiah of Judah who in his thirty and first year as king [i.e., ca. 609 B.C.], despite the words of Necho II (Nekau II) to desist, nonetheless attacked the Egyptian relief force and was mortally wounded by a random arrow (2 Kings 22:1; 23:29; 2 Chronicles 35:20–23). His servants carried him dead in a chariot from the plain of Esdraelon to Megiddo, and from there south by way of Hadad Rimmon where he died, and onward to Jerusalem where he was buried in one of the tombs of his fathers. The prophet Jeremiah lamented for Josiah, for Josiah *"did that which was right in the eyes of Jehovah, and walked in all the way of David his father, and turned not aside to the right hand or to the left"* (2 Kings 22:2). It was well with him for he *"judged the cause of the poor and needy; then it was well. Was not this to know me? saith Jehovah"* (Jeremiah 22:10).

Following the death in 609 B.C. of King Josiah at Megiddo, his son Jehoahaz (609 B.C.) by his mother Hamutal, the daughter of Jeremiah of Libnah, was anointed king by the people of Judah (2 Kings 23:30–36; 2 Chronicles 36:1–5).[105] Jehoahaz was twenty and three years old when he began to reign, and he reigned for only three months in Jerusalem. During his brief reign he built his house by unrighteousness and his chambers by injustice, and he used the services of his people unjustly and unfairly without wages. His eyes and heart was for nothing but covetousness, for shedding innocent blood, and for practicing oppression and violence (Jeremiah 22:13–14, 17). Indeed, seeing his people in need, and shutting up his heart from them, how could the love of God abide in him. He may have gloried in his spacious chambers paneled with cedar and painted with vermillion, and enjoyed sin for a season, but writes Jeremiah:

Thus saith Jehovah, Let not the wise man glory in his wisdom, neither let the mighty man glory in his might, let not the rich man glory in his riches; but let him

---

104 J. B. Pritchard, ed. The Ancient Near East. An Anthology of Texts and Pictures. The Fall of Nineveh. Princeton Univ. Pr., Sixth paperback printing, 1973, pp. 202–203.

105 The sons of Josiah were, the firstborn Johanan, the second Jehoiakim, the third Zedekiah, the fourth Jehoahaz (Shallum) (1 Chronicles 3:15–16).

that glorieth glory in this, that he hath understanding, and knoweth me, that I am Jehovah who exerciseth lovingkindness, justice, and righteousness, in the earth: for in these things I delight, saith Jehovah.

—Jeremiah 9:23–24

Pharaoh Necho II (Nekau II) on his return from Haran which fell in 610/609 B.C., deposed King Jehoahaz and led him captive to Egypt where he died (2 Kings 23:31–34; 2 Chronicles 36:3; Jeremiah 22:10–12). Yet, the death of Jehoahaz like that of his father was lamented by the prophet Jeremiah who writes:

For thus saith Jehovah touching Shallum the son of Josiah, king of Judah, who reigned instead of Josiah his father, and who went forth out of this place: He shall not return thither any more; but in the place whither they have led him captive, there shall he die, and he shall see this land no more.

—Jeremiah 22:11–12

Pharaoh Necho II (Nekau II) then took Eliakim, the brother of Jehoahaz and Josiah's eldest son, and placed him on the throne of Judah and gave him the throne name Jehoiakim (ca. 609–598 B.C.) (2 Kings 23:33–36; 24:6; 2 Chronicles 36:4–9). Jehoiakim was twenty and five years old when he began to reign and he reigned eleven years in Jerusalem. His mother was Zebudah, the daughter of Pedaiah of Rumah. In 605 B.C., which was the fourth year of Jehoiakim (Eliakim), the remnant of the army of Pharaoh Necho II (Nekau II) was annihilated at Carchemish on the River Euphrates by the Babylonian commander Nebuchadnezzar II (ca. 605–562 B.C.), the son of Nabopolassar. The victory of the Babylonians at Carchemish, which ended the rule of Egypt, was not unexpected, for under the Assyrian Kings Sin-shur-ishkun (ca. 621–612) and Ashur-uballit II (ca. 612–608 B.C.) the Assyrians, fighting to hold off nomadic Cimmerian hordes encroaching in Asia Minor from the north, had gradually ceased to be a significant military force. Nebuchadnezzar II then marched south by way of Hamath and Ashkelon and invaded Judah and came against Jerusalem. Having made Jehoiakim (Eliakim) a tribute-paying vassal to Babylon he departed, and in the year that followed he took Gaza (2 Kings 24:1; 2 Chronicles 36:6; Daniel 1:1–2; Jer. 25). Then when in 601 B.C. Jehoiakim (Eliakim) rebelled against Nebuchadnezzar his overlord, and turned to Pharaoh Necho II (Nekau II) of Egypt for help, Nebuchadnezzar returned to Jerusalem (2 Kings 23:35) . The prophet Habakkuk (608–598 B.C.) was shocked for he could not believe that a righteous God would allow an unrighteous nation to capture Jerusalem. Watching from the rampart of the city he raised his voice to God and asked, *"O Jehovah, how long shall I cry, and thou wilt not hear? I cry out unto thee of violence, and thou wilt not save"* (Habakkuk 1:2). But God replied,

> *For, lo, I raise up the Chaldeans, that bitter and hasty nation, that march through the breadth of the earth, to possess dwelling-places that are not theirs. They are terrible and dreadful; their judgment and their dignity proceed from themselves. Their horses also are swifter than leopards, and are more fierce than the evening wolves; and their horsemen press proudly on: yea, their horsemen come from far; they fly as an eagle that hasteth to devour. They come all of them for violence; the set of their faces is forwards; and they gather captives as the sand. Yea, he scoffeth at kings, and princes are a derision unto him; he derideth every stronghold; for he heapeth up dust, and taketh it. Then shall he sweep by as a wind, and shall pass over, and be guilty, even he whose might is his god.*
>
> —Habakkuk 1:6–11

Jehoiakim (Eliakim) surrendered to Nebuchadnezzar II, and bound in bronze fetters he was carried off to Babylon with other hostages together with the sacred vessels of the temple. Also deported to Babylon were Jehozadak the son of Seraiah, and the Judean youths Hananiah (Shadrach), Mishael (Meshach), Azariah (Abed-Nego), and Daniel (Belteshazzar) (ca. 620–559 B.C.) the dream-interpreter yet to be of Nebuchadnezzar's apocalyptic visions regarding a colossal statue prophetically symbolizing four successive world powers, Babylon, Medo-Persia, Greece and Rome, and his famous but complex "Seventy-Weeks Prophesy" from the close of the Babylonian captivity to the coming and demise of the Messiah, the promised Seed of the woman.[106]

All said, Jehoiakim (Eliakim), like his brother Jehoahaz, "did evil in the sight of the Lord, according to all that his father had done" (2 Kings 22:19; 23:35–37; 24:4; Jeremiah 26:20–24). He reigned for eleven years and during his reign the prophets Urijah (Uriah) (ca. 630 B.C.), the son of Shemaiah, and Jeremiah, the son of Hilkiah, suffered bitter persecution for their pro-Babylonian positions. Urijah (Uriah) who did not want to bring his neck under the yoke of the king of Babylon

---

[106] Daniel 9:24–27. The prophesy of Daniel consists of an initial 49 years (i.e., seven sevens of weeks) commencing with Artaxerxes's decree to Ezra to rebuild the temple and walls of Jerusalem, then another 434 years (i.e., sixty-two sevens) ending with the crucifixion of Jesus Christ, for a total of 483 years. Finally at the end of the Church Age yet another 7 years (i.e., one week of seven). In all the entire prophesy covers a time frame of ca. 490 prophetic years (70 weeks of sevens).

tried to escape to Egypt, but was brought back and killed with the sword (Jeremiah 26:20–25; 27:20).

When the prophesies of Jeremiah regarding the invasion of the Babylonians, and the captivity were brought to the attention of King Jehoiakim (Eliakim) by Jeremiah's secretary Baruch (ca. 630 B.C.), the son of Neriah (ca. 660 B.C.), the king in great anger cut the written scrolls with a knife, threw them into the fire, and placed Jeremiah under severe restraint in the court of the prison in the kings house (Jeremiah 36:1–32).[107] Jeremiah was let down with robes into the dungeon of Malchiah the king's son. However, because of the earnest intercession of the Ethiopian eunuch Ebed-melech with the king, Jeremiah was saved from imminent death (Jeremiah 38:7–13; 39:15–18). When Jehoiakim (Eliakim) died he was not lamented by the prophet Jeremiah, as was his brother, but he was *"buried with the burial of an ass, drawn and cast forth beyond the gates of Jerusalem"* (Jeremiah 22:19; see also 36:30).

King Jehoiakim (Eliakim) was then succeeded by his eight year old son Jeconiah (Coniah) who assumed the throne name Jehoiachin (1 Chronicles 3:16; 2 Chronicles 36:8).[108] Jehoiachin (Jeconiah, Coniah) (ca. 597 B.C.), whose mother was Nehushta the daughter of Einathan of Jerusalem, reigned only three months and ten days in Jerusalem, for when Nebuchadnezzar in the eighth year of his reign [i.e., ca. 587 B.C.] came against Jerusalem for the second time and built a siege wall against it all around, Jehoiachin (Jeconiah, Coniah), his mother, his servants, his princes, his eunuchs, and his officers all went out to the king of Babylon and surrendered (2 Kings 24:12). Nebuchadnezzar demanded a heavy tribute and then returned to Babylon with 10,000 captives, and with Jehoiachin (Jeconiah, Coniah) caged and bound in chains (2 Kings 24:14–16). That Jehoiachin greatly provoked the Lord to anger is evident, for the prophet Jeremiah delivering God's message to Jehoiachin (Jeconiah, Coniah) writes:

> *As I live, saith Jehovah, though Coniah the son of Jehoiakim king of Judah were the signet upon my right hand, yet would I pluck thee thence; and I will give thee into the hand of them that seek thy life, and into the hand of them of whom thou art afraid, even into the hand of Nebuchadrezzar king of Babylon, and into the hand of the Chaldeans. And I will cast thee out, and thy mother that bare thee, into another country, where ye were not born; and there shall ye die. But to the land whereunto their soul longeth to return, thither shall they not return. Is this man Coniah a despised broken vessel? is he a vessel wherein none delighteth? wherefore*

---

[107] The Apocrypha in Baruch deals with Israel's sins as the cause of the Babylonian exile.
[108] The sons of Jehoiakim (Eliakim) were Jeconiah (Coniah) and Zedekiah.

are they cast out, he and his seed, and are cast into the land which they know not? O earth, earth, earth, hear the word of Jehovah. Thus saith Jehovah, Write ye this man childless, a man that shall not prosper in his days; for no more shall a man of his seed prosper, sitting upon the throne of David, and ruling in Judah.

—Jeremiah 22:24–30[109]

Although, beginning with King David's coronation in ca. 1010 B.C., an uninterrupted succession of kings ruled over the house of David, that succession ceased when the southern Kingdom under King Jehoiachin (Jeconiah, Coniah) surrendered to Nebuchadnezzar II of Babylon and was deported. He was the last in succession who sat on the throne of David, for he was exiled together with the princes of Judah, with the carpenters and smiths, and imprisoned (Jeremiah 24:1). A false prophet at the time named Hananiah, the son of Azur, prophesied that within two years God would break the yoke that Babylon had put on the neck of all conquered nations, and bring back Jehoiachin (Jeconiah, Coniah), the son of Jehoiakim (Eliakim) as well as the treasures and captives of Judah that Nebuchadnezzar II had taken and carried off to Babylon (Jeremiah 28:1–4). The words of this self-serving and self- promoting false prophet were quickly dismantled by the prophet Jeremiah who angrily called Hannaniah a liar to his face:

Hear now, Hananiah: Jehovah hath not sent thee; but thou makest this people to trust in a lie. Therefore thus saith Jehovah, Behold, I will send thee away from off the face of the earth: this year thou shalt die, because thou hast spoken rebellion against Jehovah.

—Jeremiah 28:15–16

In all thirteen thousand of the general population of Jerusalem were deported, but the city was spared (2 Kings 24:12–16; Jeremiah 52:28–29). Among the captives exiled and taken to Babylon were Ezekiel (ca. 620–570 B.C.), the son of Buzi, whose prophetic activity extended for about 23 years to ca. 571 B.C., and Kish the great grandfather of Mordecai (ca. 500 B.C.) the Jew mentioned in the Book of Esther. Also carried away by Nebuchadnezzar II were the false prophets

---

[109] Jehoiachin (Jeconiah, Coniah) is mentioned by name by Matthew in his genealogy of Jesus Christ: "Josiah begot Jeconiah and his brothers about the time they were carried away to Babylon" (Matthew 1:11). Because of God's curse on Jeconiah the Joseph mentioned in Matthew could not be the biological father of Jesus but rather the adoptive father, for Jesus was conceived by the Holy Spirit and born of the Virgin Mary.

Ahab, the son of Kolaiah, and Zedekiah, the son of Maaseiah, who both prophesied falsely in the name of the Lord, and were roasted in the fire by the king of Babylon (Jeremiah 29:21–22). These false prophets did not have, as had Shadrach, Meshach and Abed-Nego, a protector "like the Son of God" to deliver them in the midst of fire (Daniel 3:16–24).[110]

Recalling the trials endured by the exiles in Babylon one unnamed patriot poet writes:

> *"By the rivers of Babylon there we sat down, yea, we wept when we remembered Zion. We hung our harps upon the willows in the midst of it. For there those who carried us away captive required of us a song, and those who plundered us required of us mirth, saying: 'Sing us one of the songs of Zion!' How shall we sing the Lord's song in a foreign land? If I forget you, O Jerusalem, let my right hand forget her skill! If I do not remember you, let my tongue cling to the roof of my mouth – if I do not exalt Jerusalem above my chief joy. Remember, O Lord, against the sons of Edom the day of Jerusalem, who said: 'Raze it, raze it, to its very foundation!' O daughter of Babylon, who are to be destroyed, happy shall he be who repays you as you have served us! Happy shall he be who takes and dashes your little ones against the rock!"*
>
> —Psalm 137:1–9[111]

Yet, the exiles had not been left without hope, for in their despair they remembered God's covenant with the Patriarchs Jacob and Isaac: *"that, when they are in the land of their enemies, I will not reject them, neither will I abhor them, to destroy them utterly, and to break my covenant with them"* (Leviticus 26:44–45)

From the time of Jehoiachin (Jeconiah, Coniah), no one of Jehoiachin's seed afterward reigned over Judah (Jeremiah 22:30).

The theocratic viceroyalty ceased; the temporal kingdom of the house of David was dissolved, Jehovah, being rejected by His covenant people and idolatry substituted for His worship, forsook His temple, discontinued

---

110 The Apocrypha introduce several additions to the Book of Daniel. They are The Prayer of Azariah and The Song of the Three Jews (their prayers and deliverance), Susanna (in which Daniel cross-examines the accusers of an adulteress), and Bel and the Dragon (in which Daniel mocks the idol Bel and an unnamed dragon god, and is miraculously delivered by the prophet Habakkuk.

111 C. H. Spurgeon. Psalm CXXXVII in The Treasury of David (Zondervan Publishing House, Grand Rapids, Michigan, 1969), Volume 3, pp. 226–229.

His former theocratic relation, ceased to manifest Himself in the Shekina, and turned to execute His wrath upon Judah and Israel for their idolatrous abominations, and upon the surrounding nations whose idols they worshiped, and by whom they had been seduced and oppressed.[112]

In 597 B.C., Mattaniah the brother of Jehoiakim (Eliakim) was installed in the place of Jehoiachin (Jeconiah, Coniah) by Nebuchadnezar II and given the throne name Zedekiah (ca. 597–586 B.C.) (2 Kings 24:17–18; 2 Chronicles 36:10; Jeremiah 37:1). Zedekiah (Mattaniah) was the third son of Josiah, and his mother's name was Hamutal, the daughter of Jeremiah of Libnah. He was twenty and one years old when he began to reign and he reigned eleven years in Jerusalem. He was the last king to rule over Judah. Then in the fourth year [i.e., ca. 593 B.C.] of Zedekiah (Mattaniah) the false prophet Hananiah died according to the word of the Lord by Jeremiah.

In the ninth year [i.e., ca. 588 B.C.] of Zedekiah (Mattaniah), Nebuchadnezzar II again returned and encamped against Jerusalem, and built a siege wall against it all around. Zedekiah (Mattaniah) in collusion with Edom, Moab, Ammon, Tyre and Sidon briefly considered opposing the Babylonians, but the plan was condemned by Jeremiah and came to naught (Jeremiah 27:3; 37:11–16; 2 Chronicles 36:13). In the meanwhile Pharaoh Necho II (Nekau II) of Egypt had died and was succeeded first by Pharaoh Psamtik II (Psammetichus II) (ca. 595–589 B.C.), and then by Pharaoh Hophra (Apries) (ca. 589–570 B.C.), the son of Psamtik II (Psammetichus II). When Pharaoh Hophra (Apries) rebelled and declared his independence from Babylon, King Zedekiah (Mattaniah) of Judah also rebelled, ceased paying tribute to Nebuchadnezzar II and joined the rebellion of Pharaoh Hophra (Apries). To deal with this development Nebuchadnezzar II partially lifted the siege on Jerusalem and advanced against Pharaoh Hophra (Apries) who, hard-pressed by the Babylonians, retreated to Egypt. As Nebuchadnezzar again drew near to the gates of Jerusalem and besieged the city, King Zedekiah (Mattaniah) deprived of much needed Egyptian military assistance, sent Pashhur, the son of Maaseiah the priest, to inquire of the prophet Jeremiah what the Lord would do to make the king of Babylon go away. Jeremiah's response effectively crushed the hopes and expectations of King Zedekiah (Mattaniah):

---

[112] E. Lord. *The Messiah in Moses and the Prophets* (Jazzybee Verlag, Loschberg, Germany. 2013), p. 95–96 [EPUB]. "Jehovah had withdrawn not to reappear until he would come, the Messenger of the Covenant, in fulfilment of Malachi's prediction." (p. 107, Malachi 3:1–3). For the gradual withdrawal of the Shekina see Ezekiel 8:4–6; 9:3; 10:4,18; 11:23.

The Divided Kingdom

Thus shall ye say to Zedekiah: Thus saith Jehovah, the God of Israel, Behold, I will turn back the weapons of war that are in your hands, wherewith ye fight against the king of Babylon, and against the Chaldeans that besiege you, without the walls; and I will gather them into the midst of this city. And I myself will fight against you with an outstretched hand and with a strong arm, even in anger, and in wrath, and in great indignation. And I will smite the inhabitants of this city, both man and beast: they shall die of a great pestilence. And afterward, saith Jehovah, I will deliver Zedekiah king of Judah, and his servants, and the people, even such as are left in this city from the pestilence, from the sword, and from the famine, into the hand of Nebuchadrezzar king of Babylon, and into the hand of their enemies, and into the hand of those that seek their life: and he shall smite them with the edge of the sword; he shall not spare them, neither have pity, nor have mercy.

—Jeremiah 21:3–7

The city was besieged unto the eleventh year [i.e., ca. 586 B.C.] of King Zedekiah (Mattaniah) (2 Kings 25:2; Jer. 39:2; 52:5). Although Zedekiah (Mattaniah) tried to escape by way of the king's garden, he was captured with his entourage in the plains of Jericho and brought to Riblah in Syria where his sons were killed while he watched in horror (2 Kings 25:7; Jeremiah 39:4–7; 52:8–11). Then Zedekiah was himself blinded, and bound with bronze fetters he was carried off to Babylon where he eventually died (2 Kings 25:4–7; Jeremiah 52:8–11).

And Jehovah, the God of their fathers, [had] sent to them by his messengers, rising up early and sending, because he had compassion on his people, and on his dwelling-place: but they mocked the messengers of God, and despised his words, and scoffed at his prophets, until the wrath of Jehovah arose against his people, till there was no remedy.

—2 Chronicles 36:15–16

Justice was made the measuring line, and righteousness the plummet (Isaiah 28:17). God brought against Jerusalem the overflowing scourge of the Chaldeans, and they trampled the people down, killing their young men with the sword in the house of their sanctuary, having no compassion on neither young man or virgin, nor on the aged or the weak. He gave them all into the hand of Nebuchadnezzar, for God's patience with Judah had run out (Isaiah 28:14–18; 2 Chronicles 36:15–17). As commented by the Apostle Paul, it is well to remind ourselves of what happened to Israel and to Judah throughout their respective histories, for *"these things were our examples, to the intent we should not lust after evil things, as they also lusted"* (1 Corinthians 10:6, 11. See also NKJV). Indeed, the Apostle Peter reminds us that the cities of Sodom and Gomorrah were destroyed, *"having made them an example unto those that should live ungodly"* (2 Peter 2:6). With few exceptions none of the kings of Israel and none of the kings of Judah could have faced their subjects and said as the ancient seer Samuel (ca. 1100 B.C.) in good conscience had once said:

> *Here I am: witness against me before Jehovah, and before his anointed: whose ox have I taken? or whose ass have I taken? or whom have I defrauded? whom have I oppressed? or of whose hand have I taken a ransom to blind mine eyes therewith? and I will restore it you.*
> —1 Samuel 12:3

Not many could have faced their kings and replied, *"Thou hast not defrauded us, nor oppressed us, neither hast thou taken aught of any man's hand"* (1 Samuel 12:4).

The prophet Jeremiah, who was an eyewitness to the famine and disease that spread throughout Jerusalem during the long siege, writes in great detail of the unendurable sufferings of the inhabitants of the City of David that God now in His awful fury had cast out from his presence. Distressed in spirit "the weeping prophet" poured out his deep lament:

> *The tongue of the sucking child cleaveth to the roof of his mouth for thirst: the young children ask bread, and no man breaketh it unto them. They that did feed delicately are desolate in the streets: they that were brought up in scarlet embrace dunghills. For the iniquity of the daughter of my people is greater than the sin of Sodom, that was overthrown as in a moment, and no hands were laid upon her. Her nobles were purer than snow, they were whiter than milk; they were more ruddy in body than rubies, their polishing was as of sapphire. Their visage is blacker than a coal; they are not known in the streets: their skin cleaveth to their bones; it is withered, it is become like a stick. They that are slain with the sword are better than they that are slain with hunger; for these pine away, stricken through, for want of the fruits of the field. The hands of the pitiful women have boiled their own children; they were their food in the destruction of the daughter of my people. Jehovah hath accomplished his wrath, he hath poured out his fierce anger… because of the sins of her prophets, and the iniquities of her priests, that have shed the blood of the just in the midst of her.*
> —Lamentations 4:4–11, 13

Nebuzaradan the servant of the king of Babylon had the city burned with fire - not only the house of the Lord, but also the king's house and all the houses of the great men of Jerusalem. The articles and treasures from the house of God, great and small, and the treasures of the king and of his leaders, all these were taken. What happened to the Ark of the Covenant is not known. Perhaps it was destroyed when the city was taken by the Babylonians and the captives deported. Only a very small number of vine-dressers and husbandmen were permitted to remain in the land, and of these, who could now confidently be persuaded that the promise of the land made to their fathers would be their abiding place forever, and that howsoever they behaved themselves towards God they could not again be removed from it?[113] To raise morale Jeremiah had purchased the property of his cousin Hanameel, and by reference to God's promises he indicated that Jerusalem would yet be rebuilt and be an habitable place to return to (Jeremiah 32:6–9,12).

Following the capture of Jerusalem and the senseless destruction of life, property, and the deportation of yet another group of captives to Babylon by Nebuzaradan, Nebuchadnezzar II appointed a pro-Babylonian puppet governor named Gedaliah (ca. 597–586 B.C.), a son of Ahikam. Gedaliah made Mizpah northwest of Jerusalem his headquarters. He ordered Nebuzaradan to show kindness towards the prophet Jeremiah, to look after him, and to do him no harm. So Jeremiah was taken from the court of the prison and committed to Gedaliah who brought him to Mizpah (Jeremiah 39:11–14). Gedaliah was forewarned by Johanan, a son of Kareah, that Ishmael the son of Nethaniah of the royal family with ten co-conspirators backed by Baalis the Ammonite king had been sent to murder him. Johanan offered to kill Ishmael and thus prevent the evil plot, but Gedaliah ignored the warning and was murdered a couple of months later when Ishmael was attending a dinner at the governor's house (2 Kings 25:25, 26; Jer. 40:13–16; 41:1–10). Others were murdered as well, and many more were thrown by Ishmael into the midst of an old reservoir or cistern constructed centuries earlier in the days of King Asa (ca. 910–869 B.C.) of Judah and King Baasha (ca. 908–886 B.C.) of Israel. Fearing instant reprisals by the Babylonians for the daring assassination of Gadaliah by Ishmael and his co-conspirators, Johanan escaped to Egypt with a remnant including the prophet Jeremiah and his faithful amanuensis Baruch (Jeremiah 43:6). The escape was made just in time, for in 581 B.C. Jerusalem experienced yet another deportation of its citizens by the Babylonian

---

[113] "In fact, the promise of the land in its ultimate fulfillment fails to find completion in the entire Old Testament." John F. Walvoord. Major Bible Prophesies (Zondervan Publishing House, Michigan, 1991), 82.

captain Nebuzaradan. As for Jeremiah he allegedly died in Egypt in the reign of Evil-Merodach (Amel-Marduk) (ca. 561–560 B.C.), the son of King Nebuchadnezzar II.

In the meanwhile Pharaoh Hophra (Apries) (ca. 589–570 B.C.) had been unseated in a rebellion by Pharaoh Amasis II (Ahmose II) (ca. 570–526 B.C.), the father of Pharaoh Psamtik III (Psammeticus III) (ca. 526–525 B.C.). To regain his position the dethroned Hophra (Aphries) joined up with King Nebuchadnezzar II, and in 567 B.C. he invaded Egypt only to be driven back by Pharaoh Amasis II (Ahmose II).

Then following the death of Nebuchadnezzar II in 562 B.C., his son Evil-Merodach (Amel-Marduk) (ca. 562–560 B.C.) became king of Babylon. In the first year of the reign of Evil-Merodach (Amel-Marduk), which was the thirty and seventh year of the captivity of King Jehoiachin (Jeconiah, Coniah) of Judah, Jehoiachin due perhaps to the influence of the exiled prophet Daniel was finally released from prison in Balylon and provided for all the days of his life at the king's table until Evil-Merodach (Amel-Marduk) was murdered by Nergal-sharezer (Neriglissar) (ca. 560–556 B.C.) his brother-in-law who succeeded him as king of Babylon (2 Kings 25:27–30; Jeremiah 52:31–34). Then in succession followed Labashi-Marduk (ca. 556 B.C.), Nabonidus (Nabu-na'id) (ca. 556–539 B.C.) and his son Belshazzar (Bel-shar-usur) who was made regent in Babylon. In 539 B.C., Cyrus II the Great (ca. 559–530 B.C.), the founder of the Achaemenid dynasty of Persia absorbed Mesopotamia and Babylon, and ended the rule of Nabonidus the last king of the Neo-Babylonian Empire.

In the first year [i.e., ca. 558 B.C.] of Cyrus II king of Persia, that the word of the Lord spoken by the mouth of Jeremiah might be fulfilled, the Lord stirred up the spirit of Cyrus the Great so that he made a proclamation throughout all his kingdom, and also put it in writing, saying:

> *Thus saith Cyrus king of Persia, All the kingdoms of the earth hath Jehovah, the God of heaven, given me; and he hath charged me to build him a house in Jerusalem, which is in Judah. Whosoever there is among you of all his people, Jehovah his God be with him, and let him go up.*
>
> —2 Chronicles 36:23
> (see also Ezra 1:1–4)[114]

---

114 According to Ezra the scribe, Cyrus decreed, "[L]et the house be builded, the place where they offer sacrifices, and let the foundations thereof be strongly laid; the height thereof threescore cubits, and the breadth thereof threescore cubits" (Ezra 6:3).

The Divided Kingdom

Cyrus then repatriated those Judeans held captive in Babylon since the earlier deportations of King Nebuchadnezzar II and his general Nebuzaradan. He appointed a descendant of the Davidic dynasty named Sheshbazzar (Shenazar), a presumed son of King Jehoiachin (Jeconiah, Coniah), as governor of the restored Persian "Province of Judah," and allowed the returning Judeans to build a new temple in Jerusalem. We are told by the prophet Daniel (ca. 620–540 B.C.) that when Belshazzar (Bel-shar- usur) (ca. 553–539 B.C.), the son of Nabonidus (ca. 556–539 B.C.), was feasting and praising the gods of gold and silver, bronze and iron, wood and stone, the fingers of a man's hand wrote on the wall of the king's palace the mysterious words: *"Mene, Mene, Tekel, Upharsin"* (Daniel 5:1–29).[115] As translated the message read:

> *mene; God hath numbered thy kingdom, and brought it to an end. tekel; thou art weighed in the balances, and art found wanting. peres; thy kingdom is divided, and given to the Medes and Persians.*
>
> —Daniel 5:26–28

That very night Cyrus II's general Gobryas attacked Babylon and killed Belshazzar (Bel-shar-usur), the son of Nabonidus.[116] Thereafter, the oppression by Babylon ceased, and her dominant role in Near Eastern politics came to a gradual end.[117] The prophesy against Babylon, as viewed from a eschatological point of view however remains an event yet to be fulfilled at some future time in the "Day of the Lord," for as prophesied earlier by the prophet Isaiah:

> *And Babylon, the glory of kingdoms, the beauty of the Chaldeans' pride, shall be as when God overthrew Sodom and Gomorrah. It shall never be inhabited, neither shall it be dwelt in from generation to generation… And it shall come to pass in the day that Jehovah shall give thee rest from thy sorrow, and from thy trouble, and from the hard service wherein thou wast made to serve, that thou shalt take up this parable against the king of Babylon, and say, How hath the oppressor ceased! the golden city ceased! Jehovah hath broken the staff of the wicked, the sceptre of the rulers; that smote the peoples in wrath with a continual stroke, that ruled the nations in anger, with a persecution that none restrained. The whole earth is at rest,*

---

115 Daniel 5:1–29.
116 Miller, W. tr., Xenophon. Cyropaedia VII.24–32. (LCL. pp.271–275).
117 The city continued as an important economic center during the remainder of Persian rule and subsequently into the early second century A.D. when it was finally abandoned.

and is quiet: they break forth into singing... Sheol from beneath is moved for thee to meet thee at thy coming; it stirreth up the dead for thee, even all the chief ones of the earth; it hath raised up from their thrones all the kings of the nations. All they shall answer and say unto thee, Art thou also become weak as we? art thou become like unto us? Thy pomp is brought down to Sheol, and the noise of thy viols: the worm is spread under thee, and worms cover thee.
—Isaiah 13:19; 14:3–7, 9–11

In ca. 535 B.C., which according to the prophesy of Jeremiah ended the 70 years of captivity begun in 605 B.C., a first group of about 50,000 returning exiles led by Zerubbabel the son of Shealtiel, governor of Judah and a direct descendant of King David, assisted by a priest named Joshua, began building upon the foundation of the second Jerusalem temple begun by Sheshbazzar (Shenazzar) (Ezra 5:14,16).

But many of the priests and Levites and heads of fathers' houses, the old men that had seen the first house, when the foundation of this house was laid before their eyes, wept with a loud voice; and many shouted aloud for joy...
—Ezra 3:12

Then in 530 B.C. Cyrus II (the Great) died. He was succeeded by his son Cambyses II (ca. 525–522 B.C.) who defeated Pharaoh Psamtik III (Psameticus III) (ca. 526–525 B.C.) the last king of the 26th Dynasty of Egypt. To retain control in Persia, Cambyses II had his brother Bardiya (Smerdis) (ca. 522–521 B.C.) assassinated. When a pretender named Gaumata then impersonated Bardiya his brother, Cambyses II returned to Persia, but died before he could deal with the revolt. Gaumata was himself overthrown by Darius I (Hystaspes) (ca. 521–486 B.C.), the successor to King Cyrus (the Great). In the meanwhile preparatory work on the temple in Jerusalem was delayed due to the determined efforts of a Persian official named Tattenai (ca. 520–502 B.C.) who complained to Darius I (Hystaspes) asserting that the Jews were insubordinate and defiant. When Darius I (Hystaspes) looked into the matter and discovered that the Jews already had the necessary royal permission from King Cyrus II (the Great) he decreed that the work should proceed at Tattenai's expense. Then in the second year [i.e., ca. 519 B.C.] of King Darius I (Hystaspes) the word of the Lord came by the prophet Haggai (ca. 520–505 B.C.) to Zerubbabel, the son of Shealtiel and grandson of Jehoiachin, the penultimate king of Judah, then serving as governor of Judah, and to Joshua, the son of Jehozadak, the high priest saying:

Thus speaketh Jehovah of hosts, saying, This people say, It is not the time for us to come, the time for Jehovah's house to be built... Is it a time for you yourselves to dwell in your ceiled houses, while this house lieth waste? Now therefore thus saith Jehovah of hosts: Consider your ways... Thus saith Jehovah of hosts: Consider your ways. Go up to the mountain, and bring wood, and build the house; and I will take pleasure in it, and I will be glorified, saith Jehovah.

—Haggai 1:2, 4–5, 7–8
(see also 2 Chronicles 36:22–23 and Ezra 1:1–3)

So the Lord stirred up the spirit of all the remnant of the people, and the work on the house of the Lord was restarted in the second year [i.e., ca. 518 B.C.] of the reign of Darius I (Hystaspes) the king of Persia (Ezra 4:24; Haggai 1:14).

And the elders of the Jews builded and prospered, through the prophesying of Haggai the prophet [ca. 520 B.C.] and Zechariah the son of Iddo [ca. 522–509 B.C.]. And they builded and finished it, according to the commandment of the God of Israel, and according to the decree of Cyrus, and Darius, and Artaxerxes king of Persia.

—Ezra 6:14

Zechariah, who had witnessed the laying of the foundation of the temple by the hands of Zerubbabel, ministered to the returned exiles, encouraging them with his many visions, dreams, ethical exhortations and Messianic prophesies. By the sixth year [ca. 515 B.C.] of the reign of King Darius I (Hystaspes) the second temple was finally finished and dedicated (Ezra 6:15). However, local opposition to the repairing and rebuilding of the walls of Jerusalem continued well into the reign of King Xerxes I (Ahasuerus) (ca. 486–465 B.C.), the son of Darius I (Hystaspes), and following his assassination into the reign of Artaxerxes I (Longimanus) (ca. 465–424 B.C.), the son of Xerxes I (Ahasuerus).[118]

---

118 The Book of Esther outlines events during the first decade [i.e., ca. 483–474 B.C.] of the Persian King Xerxes I (Ahasuerus) (ca. 486–466 B.C.). Vashti the queen of Persia was dethroned during a festival and the Jewish maiden Esther was made queen. Haman, the vizier, then schemed to kill all the Jews in the Empire, but his plot was discovered by a Jew named Mordecai who by Esther informs King Ahasuerus. Haman is then hanged on the gallows he built for Mordecai, and Mordecai is appointed vizier in his place. The events gave rise to the Jewish feast of Purim (Adar 14–15), a festival of deliverance from oppression. The Septuagint (Apography) introduces several additional passages to the Book of Esther.

History, Part One: Old Testament

In the seventh year [i.e., ca. 458 B.C.] of King Artaxerxes I (Longimanus) of Persia, following the Davidic governorship of Zerubbabel, a presumed grandson of King Jehoiachin (Jeconiah, Coniah) of Judah, the priestly scribe Ezra (ca. 480–440 B.C.), the grandson of Seraiah, arrived in Jerusalem with a second group of returning exiles. Having been raised in captivity, many of the returnees had remarried pagan wives and raised children, and many had replaced their own native tongue with Aramaic. Their customs and traditions had changed in captivity, and they needed to be reconnected to their Jewish roots. Ezra therefore began to conduct public readings from the Mosaic Law explaining and interpreting the Scriptures to the people (Nehemiah 8:1–12). He was an excellent teacher, and it was said of him that "the hand of the Lord his God was upon him… for the Law of his God was in his hand" (Ezra 7:6, 14). He was the first non-Davidic Governor of Judah, and likely came to Jerusalem in the seventh year [i.e., ca. 458 B.C.] of Artaxerxes I (Longimanus) (ca. 465–424 B.C.) and some time ahead of Nehemiah, the son of Hecaliah, who was appointed governor of Judah in the twentieth year [i.e., ca. 445/444 B.C.] of Artaxerxes I (Longimanus), and remained governor of Judah until the thirty and second year [i.e., ca. 432 B.C.] at which time he was temporarily recalled to Persia to serve his royal master at Shushan, or perhaps Ecbatana (Ezra 7:7–8; Nehemiah 2:1; 5:14; 13:6). Thereafter, having arrived with another group of exiles in Jerusalem, the scribes Ezra and Nehemiah set the stage for ongoing religious reform, and the rebuilding of the walls of the city of Jerusalem that had been restored and fortified on several prior occasions in the days of the Judean Kings Uzziah (Azariah) (ca. 792–740 B.C.) and Jotham (ca. 750–732 B.C.), and subsequently extended in the days of King Manasseh (ca. 697–642 B.C.) to include the temple. The remaining opponents to the rebuilding project were Sanballat, the hereditary governor of the province of Samaria and grandson of Sanballat the Horonite (?), as well as Geshem the Arabian, Tobiah the Ammonite, and the high priest Eliashib. Despite their efforts to obstruct the work, the walls of Jerusalem were completed and dedicated by 437 B.C. ?

Chapter Six
THE INTERTESTAMENTAL PERIOD[119]

The Intertestamental Period extended from the time of the prophet Malachi (ca. 465–430 B.C.) to the time of King Herod the Great (ca. 40/37–4 B.C.). The Book of Malachi the prophet, contemporary with Ezra (ca. 465–430 B.C.) and Nehemiah (ca. 445–425 B.C.), was probably written during the post-exile period after the rebuilding of the Zerubbabel Temple (second temple) in Jerusalem. The importance of the Book of Malachi is not in what men may get from God, but what God should be given by men such as honor, reverence, and fear of His holy name - like the fear and reverence of ancient Levi (Malachi 2:4–6). With the death of Malachi in ca. 430 B.C. the spiritual gift of prophesy went silent and Israel entered upon a period of prolonged silence devoid of prophetic revelations. The concept of a coming earthly messianic kingdon gradually developed within the apocalyptic literature of Judaism. The concept of a coming kingdom was incorrectly perceived by the Jews as a kingdom to be ruled over by the anticipated coming of King Messiah, a conquer-king who would inaugurate a nationalistic Golden Epoch in which the hopes of the prophets, as understood by the learned Rabbis, would become a political reality for the nation.

In 423 B.C. the Persian King Artaxerxes I (Longimanus) died and was quickly succeeded by his son Xerxes II (ca. 424–423 B.C.), then by Sogdianus (ca. 424–423 B.C.) and by Darius II (Nothus) (ca. 423–404 B.C.). Throughout these years, and subsequently under the rule of Artaxerxes II (Mnemon) (ca. 404–359 B.C.), then of Artaxerxes III (Ochus) (ca. 359–338 B.C.) and of Artaxerxes IV (Arses) (ca. 338–335 B.C.) the people of Jerusalem enjoyed a measure of autonomy until the defeat of Darius III (Codomanus) (ca. 335–331 B.C.) at Gaugamela on the River Tigris near Arbela by the Greek-Macedonian ruler Alexander III (the Great) (ca. 336–323 B.C.), the son of Philip II of Macedonia (ca. 359–336 B.C.), and the murder soon after of Darius III (Codomanus) by Artaxerxes V (Bessus) (d.

---

[119] The Intertestamental period lasted from ca. 450 B.C. to ca. 70 A.D.

329 B.C.), the Satrap of Bactria. Alexander the III (the Great) inherited possession of Judea in 332 B.C. He was welcomed in peace by the Jews, and as a result Jerusalem was spared. Then in 323 B.C. Alexander died in Babylon. His empire was quickly partitioned by his generals, as had been prophesied by the dream-interpreter Daniel in his apocalyptic overview of history (Daniel 2:31–45).[120] Palestine then came under the rule of Alexander's general Ptolemy I (Soter) (ca. 323–285 B.C.). Under his successor Ptolemy II Philadelphus (ca. 285–246 B.C.) the Hebrew Scriptures were translated by Egyptian Jews into Greek.[121] Known as the Septuagint (LXX), it included the Apocrypha containing a variety of wisdom literature, historical fiction, fictitious romantic tales, and additions to the Books of Daniel and Esther. The Athenian orator Demetrius Phalerus (ca. 350–280 B.C.), a pupil of Theophrastus, was appointed over the king's library in Alexandria, and he, in communication with the High Priest Eleazar (?) of Jerusalem arranged for six elderly experienced men from each tribe, learned in all matters of Jewish Law, to translate the Hebrew Law of the Jews into Greek.[122] After the Egyptian Ptolemies, the semi-autonomous Jewish theocracy in Jerusalem came under Syrian-based Seleucid rulers (ca. 198–164 B.C.).[123] When the Syrian King Seleucus IV (Philopater) (ca. 187–175 B.C.), the son of Antiochus III (Megas) (ca. 223–187 B.C.) was assassinated, and his brother Antiochus IV (Epiphanes) (ca. 175–163 B.C.) became king, his oppressive actions against the Jews of Jerusalem in 167 B.C. struck at the very heart of Judaism and almost destroyed the monistic faith of the Jews. To promote Greek values Antiochus IV (Epiphanes), nicknamed "the madman" (Epimanes), attempted to eradicate Jewish religion and culture. Jewish customs and ceremonies were forbidden, Torah scrolls were seized and burned, and the second temple, the Temple of Zerubbabel in Jerusalem, was plundered and turned into a place of worship for the Greek god Zeus Olympius. Epiphanes' intolerance of the Jews only served to ignite the Maccabean War of Independence

---

120 The image's head was of fine gold, its chest and arms of silver, its belly and thighs of bronze, its legs of iron, its feet partly of iron and partly of clay. The colossal statue symbolized the Babylonians, Medo-Persians, Greeco-Roman empires, and a still future revival of the Roman Empire.

121 After Ptolemy II (Philadelphus) (ca. 285–246 B.C.) came Ptolemy III (Euergeter) (ca. 246–222/221 B.C.), Ptolemy IV (Philopater) (ca. 221–203 B.C.) and Ptolemy V (Epiphanes) (ca. 203–180 B.C.).

122 Eusebius. Preparation for the Gospel (Baker Book House, Grand Rapids, Michigan, 1981), Part 1, Book VIII, Chapters I to V, Pages 377–385 (348b-355b).

123 Antiochus III (Megas) (ca. 223–187 B.C.), Seleucus IV(Philopater) (ca. 187–175 B.C.), Antiochus IV (Epiphanes) (ca. 175–164 B.C.).

The Intertestamental Period

(ca. 167–163 B.C.) led by the Maccabean-Hasmorian priestly family of Mattathias Harmonean (ca. 168–166 B.C.)[124] The Maccabees founded the Hasmonian dynasty which ruled from 168 B.C. to 37 B.C. The Hasmonians were traditionalists and leaders of the conservative party. They reacted against the process of Hellenization in Jerusalem promoted by the liberal section of the Jewish aristocracy. The ultimate provocation to the Maccabeans was the installation of a Syrian garrison in the city of Jerusalem, and a pagan cult in the temple. After the death of Mattathias in 166 B.C., the dynasty was ruled by a succession of high priests. Mattathias's son Judah (Judas) Maccabaeus (ca. 166–160 B.C.) and Judah's son Jonathan Maccabaeus (ca. 160–143 B.C.) assumed leadership. Judah (Judas) and his brothers Jonathan, Simon (ca. 143–135 B.C.), and Johanan all fought valiantly against the Seleucid commander Apollonius, then Governor of Samaria, and against Apollonius's subordinate Seron to the west of Jerusalem near Emmaus. Concurrently Lysias, the viceroy of the Seleucid Empire, previously appointed by Antiochus IV (Epiphanes), was dispatched to relieve the isolated Seleucid garrison of Aca facing the "Temple Mount" in Jerusalem and to destroy the city with infantry, cavalry and units of war elephants commanded by the Seleucid generals Nicanor, Ptolemy and Gorgias. Advancing by way of Beth-Zur and Beth-Zechariah in the foothills of Judea south of Jerusalem Lysias arrived and prepared to take Jerusalem. He was forced however to withdrew his troops to Syria when Philip, the escort of Antiochus IV (Epiphanes) and regent for Epiphanes' son Antiochus V (Eupator) (ca. 163–162 B.C.) took control of the Seleucid empire. For failing to take Jerusalem Lysias and Antiochus V (Eupater) were both put to death by Demetrius I (Soter) (ca. 162–150 B.C.), the cousin of Antiochus V (Eupater) and father of Demetrius II (Nicator) (ca. 145–138 B.C.). Again in 160 B.C. Demetrius I (Soter) dispatched his general Bacchides against Judah (Judas) Maccabaeus (ca. 166–160 B.C.) in Jerusalem, and in the ensuing encounter Judah (Judas) was killed. The leadership of the Hasmonians then went to his brother Jonathan Maccabaeus (ca. 160–143 B.C.) who ingeniously entered into a military alliance with Rome against Syria, and thereby relieved the military pressure from Syria. When Jonathan Maccabaeus was then killed by a supporter of Antiochus VI (Epiphanes Dionysius) (ca. 145–142/138 B.C.), the leadership went to Simon Maccabeus (ca. 143–135 B.C.) the last remaining son of Mattathias. Simon Maccabaeus was supported by Demetrius II (Nicator) (ca. 145–139 B.C.) and by Antiochus VII (Eu-

---

[124] The Jewish uprising against the Syrians (ca. 165 B.C), and the rededication of the temple of Jerusalm that followed the war was subsequently commemorated as the Festival of Lights (Hanukkah).

ergetes Eusebes Soter Sidetes) (ca. 139–129 B.C.), both of whom exempted the Jews from taxes associated with Jewish bondage to the Syrian empire. Following the death of Simon Maccabaeus in 135 B.C. the leadership went to his son John Hyrcanus I (ca. 135–104 B.C.) and to John's eldest son Judah Aristobolus I (ca. 104–103 B.C.).[125]

Following the Maccabean War of independence the Jewish people were granted a measure of autonomy, and the Seleucid kingdom thereafter entered upon a period of gradual disintegration as the Parthians, from the time of King Mithradates I (ca. 171–138 B.C.) to King Mithradates II (ca. 123–88 B.C.) enlarged their territory in the east, defeated the Bactrians, conquered Media, and had their first contact with Rome. By 129 B.C. the Seleucid Empire had been reduced to Cilicia, Syria, Palestine and Mesopotamia. Thereafter Judea continued as an independent monarchy under Hasmonian priest-kings who assumed authority in almost all political, legal and religious matters. John Hyrcanus I was followed by Judah Aristobolus I (ca. 104–103 B.C.), and after him by Alexander Jannai (Jannaeus) (ca. 103–76 B.C.) and Queen Alexandra Salome (ca. 76–67 B.C.). During this time the divisions between Sadducees, Pharisees, and Essenes, reflecting the diversity of the Jewish community, emerged and took root in the religious life of the Jews.[126] When in 67 B.C. Alexandra Salome died, civil war quickly broke out between her two sons John Hyrcanus II (ca. 76–66 B.C.) and Judah Aristobolus II (ca. 67–63 B.C.). Aristobolus II, the more dominant of the two brothers won, and Hyrcanus II on the advice of Antipater II (ca. 100–43 B.C.) the governor of Idumaea, and father of Herod I (ca. 73–4 B.C.), fled to Petra to regroup.

Thereafter in ca. 65 B.C. Hyrcanus II assisted by Antipater II laid siege to Jerusalem. The siege, however, was lifted in ca. 64 B.C. by the intervention of Marcus Aemilius Scaurus (96–53 B.C.), the namesake son of the Roman General Marcus Aemilius Scaurus (ca. 163–89 B.C.), who had moved his forces from Damascus to Jerusalem to sort out the dynastic problems in Judea. The dispute between the two brothers Aristobulus II and Hyrcanus II continued until the arrival in Jerusalem of the Roman General Gnaeus Pompeius Magnus (ca. 106–48 B.C.) and the fall of Jerusalem to the Romans soon after in 63 B.C. Pompeius made Judea a Roman province, and Gabinius (ca. 57–55 B.C.) his legate soon

---

125 The Jewish festival of Chanukah (Lights/ or Dedication) celebrates the victory of the Jews over the Syrians during the Maccabean revolt and the rededication of the temple desecrated by Antiochus Epiphanes IV.

126 P. Richardson. Herod. King of the Jews and Friend of the Romans (Univ. South Carolina Press, 1996), 74.

after divided Judea into 5 administrative districts. Judah Aristobulus II was taken prisoner and sent to Rome where he was put to death, and John Hyrcanus II (ca. 63–40 B.C.) was reinstalled and made Ethnarch with the title High Priest of the Jews. Pompeius did not deny the Jews the customs of their forefathers in assembling for sacred and religious purposes, and of doing all things according to their own traditional laws.

A decade later, but before the assassination in 44 B.C. of the Roman Emperor Gaius Julius Caesar (ca. 100–44 B.C.), Antipater the Idumaean (ca. 60–43 B.C.) was appointed by Caesar as procurator of Judea in recognition of his assistance during the Roman Civil War. Antipater's two sons were made governors, Phasael I (ca. 43–40 B.C.) in Jerusalem, and Herod the Idumaean in Galilee. When Antipater I soon after was murdered, Herod the Idumaean was elevated by the Roman General Mark Antony (ca. 83–30 B.C.) and the Roman Senate to the rank of Tetrach of Jerusalem and Galilee, and subsequently he was made vassal king of Judea by the Roman Emperor Octavian (Augustus) (ca. 27 B.C.-A.D. 14), the posthumously adopted nephew and heir of Gaius Iulius Caesar. The Hasmonean period finally came to an end under King Herod I, the Great (ca. 40/37–4 B.C.).

As noted by one eminent Jewish writer:

"If one looks closely at historical events… the spread of Jewish people… throughout the known world, and the rise of Messianic expectations, it is clear that the hand of God was preparing the way for the coming Redeemer… the events of the Inter-testamental Period set the stage for the coming of the Mashiach, Yeshua of Nazareth. The opening words of Matthew say it quite simply and naturally from a Jewish perspective: 'The book of the genealogy of Yeshua ha-Mashiarc, Ben David, Ben-Avraham' (Matthew 1:1). A first century rabbi by the name of Shaul/Paul said it this way: 'But when the fullness of time came, God sent out His Son' (Galatians 4:4). The Intertestamental Period prepared God's people for the world-transforming event"[127] (Slightly edited).

---

[127] Rabbi Barney Kasdan, The Intertestamental Period (400 BCE-4BCE), in The Messianic Jewish Family Bible (Destiny Image Publishers, Inc., Shippensburg, PA, 2012), 1064.

History
Part II
New Testament

Chapter Seven

THE CHURCH AGE

The Church Age marks the end of the Intertestamental Period, and the onset of the Age of Grace, for "the law was given through Moses, but grace and truth came through Jesus Christ" (John 1:17). As explained by the Apostle Paul:

> *For if, by the trespass of the one [Adam], death reigned through the one; much more shall they that receive the abundance of grace and of the gift of righteousness reign in life through the one, even Jesus Christ. So then as through one trespass the judgment came unto all men to condemnation; even so through one act of righteousness the free gift came unto all men to justification of life. For as through the one man's disobedience the many were made sinners, even so through the obedience of the one shall the many be made righteous. And the law came in besides, that the trespass might abound; but where sin abounded, grace did abound more exceedingly: that, as sin reigned in death, even so might grace reign through righteousness unto eternal life through Jesus Christ our Lord.*
>
> —Romans 5:17–21

The age of the church intervenes within the program of God for Israel, and must be completed before God can resume His millennial program with Israel and bring it to completion. As customary, the Scriptures were read by the Rabbis every Sabbath to remind the people that the adoption, the glory, the covenants, the giving of the law, the service of God, and the promises made by God to the Patriarchs, as proclaimed from Moses to Malachi, all pertained to them (Acts 13:27; Romans 9:4). The rulers and those who dwelt in Jerusalem did not know that the prophet Daniel (ca. 620–540 B.C.) in his "Seventy-Weeks Prophesy," had foretold that the Messiah would come in the flesh and be "cut off:"

Know therefore and discern, that from the going forth of the commandment to restore and to build Jerusalem unto the anointed one, the prince, shall be seven weeks, and threescore and two weeks: it shall be built again, with street and moat, even in troublous times. And after the threescore and two weeks shall the anointed one be cut off, and shall have nothing: and the people of the prince that shall come shall destroy the city and the sanctuary.

—Daniel 9:25–26

Perhaps the people and their rulers did not really care to know about their Prophets. After all, which of the Prophets had their fathers not persecuted, and which of the Prophets, who had foretold the coming of the Just One, had their fathers not killed? (Luke 11:49–51; Acts 7:52; 13:27). Like their fathers they pretended to honor God with their lips. In vain they worshiped Him laying aside the commandments of God, and they taught as doctrines the commandments and traditions of men" (Isaiah 29:13; Mark. 7:6–9).

Now when Emperor Caesar Augustus (63 B.C.-A.D. 14) decreed that all the world should be registered, and Publius Sulpicius Quirinus (10 B.C.-A.D. 6.) was governor of Syria, it happened that not far from Jerusalem in a little town named Bethlehem, a woman by the name of Mary unknown to all but to her husband Joseph, the son of Jacob, and a few shepherds keeping watch over their flock, brought forth her firstborn who is Christ the Lord, the Incarnate Son of God (Luke 2:1–2).[128] The fullness of the time had come, when God sent forth His Son, the "Seed of the woman" conceived by the Holy Spirit, born under the law to redeem those who were under the law (Galatians 4:4–5).

And the Word became flesh, and dwelt among us (and we beheld his glory, glory as of the only begotten from the Father), full of grace and truth.

—John 1:14

---

128 As to the divine nature of Jesus Christ He is the Son of God. As to His human nature He is the Son of Man. The Roman poet Claudius Claudianus (ca. A.D. 394) in his De salvatore XXXII (XCV) writes that: "... the unwed mother, destined to give birth to her own Creator, was astonished at the unborn child that grew within her body. A mortal womb hid the artificer of the heavens: the Creator of the world became a part of human nature. In one body was conceived the God who embraces the whole wide world, and He whom nor earth nor sea nor sky can contain was enclosed by the limbs of a little child... " M. Platnauer, tr. Claudian (Cambridge Massachusetts: Loeb Classical Library, 1972), 2, 261–263.

The Church Age

The apostle Luke tells us,

And suddenly there was with the angel a multitude of the heavenly host praising God, and saying, Glory to God in the highest, and on earth peace among men in whom he is well pleased.
—Luke 2:13–14

Then wise Magi from the east, possibly Chaldean astrologers or stargazers familiar no doubt with Daniel's "Seventy-Weeks Prophesy," arrived from afar bringing gifts to Him who was born "King of the Jews." When eight days were completed for the circumcision of the newborn child, He was brought to Jerusalem and dedicated in the temple according to Jewish custom, and given the name Jesus. Two righteous temple octogenarians Simeon and Anna on seeing the holy child confessed Him to be the long-awaited-for Savior and light of revelation to the Jews and Gentiles. When King Herod was told about the prophesy of Micah, that out of Bethlehem of Judea a ruler should come to shepherd the people of Israel (Micah 5:2), Herod supposing his kingdom to be in danger, in imitation of the ancient Pharaoh who killed the Hebrew children when Moses was born, proceeded to slay all the children that were in Bethlehem, and in all the coasts thereof from two years old and under. Being warned in a dream Joseph and Mary managed to escape with the child to Egypt where they remained until around 4 B.C. when Herod died a violent death. An angel of the Lord struck him because he did not give glory to God, and as recorded by the apostle Luke: "Herod was eaten by worms and died" (Acts 12:20–23). His kingdom was divided by the Roman Emperor Octavian (Augustus) between Herod's three sons. Herod Archelaus (ca. 23 B.C.-A.D. 18), who had replaced his father, was dethroned in A.D. 6 and replaced by the first Roman Prefect of Judea named Coponius (ca. A.D. 6–9). Coponius removed the legal authority, or scepter of the Sanhedrin, and thus fulfilled the prophesy of the Patriarch Jacob in his blessing on Judah his son:

The sceptre shall not depart from Judah, nor the ruler's staff from between his feet, until Shiloh come; and unto him shall the obedience of the peoples be.
—Genesis 49:10

Hearsay had it that when the members of the Sanhedrin found themselves deprived of their right over life and death, a general consternation took possession of them, for "they covered their heads with ashes, and their bodies with sackcloth, and cried out: "Woe unto us, for the Scepter has departed from Judah and the Messiah has not come.'"[129]

In the meanwhile the child Jesus had grown like a young plant. At the age of twelve He was seen in the temple courts among the teachers listening and asking questions, and all who heard Him were amazed at His understanding and His answers. He grew in wisdom and stature, and in favor with God and men, and at the adult age of thirty He came from Nazareth of Galilee, and was baptized by his younger cousin John the Baptist, the son of Zacharias and Elizabeth, in the River Jordan (Mark 1:9–11). Anointed by the Holy Spirit He was led into the wilderness to be tempted by Satan. He rebutted Satan's deceptive and enticing propositions by citing the Holy Scriptures. Then at the age of ca. 30 He launched His public ministry. Opening the scroll of the prophet Isaiah, He read the words:

The Spirit of the Lord Jehovah is upon me; because Jehovah hath anointed me to preach good tidings unto the meek; he hath sent me to bind up the broken-hearted, to proclaim liberty to the captives, and the opening of the prison to them that are bound; to proclaim the year of Jehovah's favor, and the day of vengeance of our God; to comfort all that mourn.

—Isaiah 61:1–2

The eyes of all who were in the synagogue were fixed on Him when, after a slight pause, he added: *"Today… this scripture is fulfilled in your ears"* (Luke 4:21). Then for three years He went about with His twelve disciples urging His hearers to "seek the Kingdom of God and His righteousness."

Authoritatively, convincingly, and with great power He preached the good news of the Gospel to the brokenhearted, proclaimed liberty to the captives, and opened the prison to those who are entangled in sin. A large portion of His public teaching consisted of parables as in His "Sermon on the Mount," and when he was asked privately, He talked about His coming demise (Matthew 16:21; 20:17–19; Mark 8:31; 9:31; Luke 9:22;18:31–3; 24:46 ; John 2:19–22), the frightening signs of the times, the end of the age (Matthew 24:3–44; Mark 13:3–36; Luke 21:7–36), and of false Messiahs rising up and performing great signs and wonders to deceive many (Matthew 24:4,5–26; Mark 13:6–22; Luke 21:8; 2 Corinthians 11:4). He healed those afflicted with various diseases and torments: epileptics, paralytics, lepers, the blind, and many more, even raising from the dead Lazarus

---

[129] Babylonian Talmud. San. Chronicles 4. fol. 37, recto, quoted by Rabbi Rachmon.

of Bethany the brother of Mary and Martha. However, when He claimed to be the Son of God, and moreover had the audacity to drive money-changers from the temple courts, He enraged the teachers of the law and the Pharisees.

He was blasphemed, spied upon, plotted against, and questioned by pious-looking phylactery- carrying-rabbis carrying Scriptures in small leather cases fastened to their foreheads, or below the elbow, and He would say to them:

Ye search the scriptures, because ye think that in them ye have eternal life; and these are they which bear witness of me; and ye will not come to me, that ye may have life.

—John 5:39–40

Following His last Passover, when instituting the Lord's Supper, He took bread and blessed it and broke it, and gave it to His disciples and said: *"Take, eat; this is my body"* (Matthew 26:26). Then He took the cup, and gave thanks, and gave it to them, saying: *"Drink ye all of it; for this is my blood of the covenant, which is poured out for many unto remission of sins"* (Matthew 26:27–28; see also Luke 22:30). He was referring to the shedding of His own blood on the cross which would achieve human redemption by the removal of sins, and make possible eternal life for penitent sinners who by faith would place their trust in His blood-atoning work. Then He was betrayed by one of His own disciples Judas, the son of Simon surnamed Iscariot (from Kriot), for thirty pieces of silver and a kiss. One may speculate that when Judas Iscariot approached with a multitude to arrest Jesus in the Garden of Gethsemane, Jesus could have asked His heavenly Father to give Him more than twelve legions of angels to protect Him, but had He done so, He would have undone the redemptive plan and purpose of God the Father as promised by the holy prophets. Had He indeed done so: *"How then should the scriptures be fulfilled, that thus it must be?"* (Matthew 26:54)

Having been arrested Jesus was brought before the Jewish high priest Joseph Caiaphas (ca. A.D. 27–36) to be examined.[130] He was tried and condemned by the Sanhedrin, and then brought before the Roman Governor Pontius Pilate (A.D. 26–36/7) who sent Him to Herod Antipas (ca. 20 B.C.-A.D. 39). Then He was

---

130 According to Flavius Josephus (ca. A.D. 37–?100) and Eusebius Pamphilus (ca. A.D. 264–340) there were four high priests in succession during the ministry of Jesus, each holding the office for one year: Annas, Ismael (the son of Baphi), Eleazar (the son of Annas), Simon (the son of Camithus), and Josephus, surnamed Caiaphas.

handed over to Roman soldiers who mockingly threw a purple robe around Him, placed a crown of thorns on His head, and put what looked like a scepter in His hand. Cruelly they maltreated Him, for they thought it incredible that He could be who He claimed to be, the "One" whom the prophets from Moses to Malachi had spoken of. They made Him carry His own cross to Golgotha the place of His execution, and there, by the determinate counsel and foreknowledge of God (Acts 2:23) they crucified Him like a transgressor between two malefactors.[131] Being forsaken by His heavenly Father, He cried: *"Eloi, Eloi, lama sabachthani? which is, being interpreted, My God, my God, why hast thou forsaken me?"* (Mark 15:34; see also Psalm 22:1), and bearing the full weight of our transgressions the "Anointed One of God," as prophesied by Daniel, was "cut off, but not for Himself," for He died in our place an offering for sin. As commented by one writer:

> Once Christ had volunteered to be the Lamb of God, laden with our sins… God made Christ accursed for the sin He bore. Yet it was done for us. He took what justice demanded from us. This 'for us' aspect of the Cross is what displays the majesty of its grace, wrath and mercy. It is too astounding to fathom.[132]

On the cross above His head they nailed an inscription in letters of Greek, Latin and Hebrew: *"Jesus of Nazareth, the King of the Jews"* (John 19:19; see also Luke 23:38).

By His death full payment was finally made for our redemption. As explained by one well-known theologian:

> It is the plain doctrine of Scripture that Christ saves us neither by the mere exercise of power, nor by His doctrine, nor by His example, nor by the moral influence which He exerted, nor by any subjective influence on His people, whether natural or mystical, but as a satisfaction to divine justice, as an expiation for sin, and as a ransom from the curse

---

131 Although the Jews wanted to see Jesus crucified, they did not have the legal authority. When Pontius Pilate, Roman Prefect of Judea (ca. A.D. 26–33/36) in the reign of Emperor Tiberius (ca. A.D. 14–37), instructed them to judge Jesus according to their law, they replied: "It is not lawful for us to put any man to death." Babylonian Talmud. San. Chronicles 4. fol. 37, recto, quoted by Rabbi Rachmon.

132 R. C. Sproul. The Holiness of God (Tyndale House Publishers, Inc., Carol Stream, Illinois, 1985, 1998), 132–133.

and authority of the law, thus reconciling us to God by making it consistent with His perfection to exercise mercy towards sinners.[133]

As the mob cried *"His blood be on us, and on our children"* (Matthew 27:25), the veil between the two portions of the tabernacle that separated the Holy of Holies from the rest of the tabernacle was rent in two. It was finished. The old covenant of works was superseded by the new covenant of grace. By His sacrificial death He had executed the purpose of God, fulfilled the Old Testament types and prophesies, satisfied the law in the room of guilty sinners, and procured for believers eternal redemption and blessings for the ages to come. That the Scriptures should be fulfilled He was buried by Joseph of Arimathea, and three days later on the first day of the week He was raised bodily from the grave, the first begotten of the dead. Following His resurrection He revealed Himself to Mary Magdalene, to Simon, who is called Peter, and to the eleven disciples and said:

> *These are my words which I spake unto you, while I was yet with you, that all things must needs be fulfilled, which are written in the law of Moses, and the prophets, and the psalms, concerning me. Then opened he their mind, that they might understand the scriptures.*
>
> —Luke 24:44–45[134]

Again following the resurrection when two disciples Cleophas and his friend were traveling on the road to Emmaus near Jerusalem the resurrected Christ drew near to them and said:

> *O foolish men, and slow of heart to believe in all that the prophets have spoken! Behooved it not the Christ to suffer these things, and to enter into his glory? And beginning from Moses and from all the prophets, he interpreted to them in all the scriptures the things concerning himself.*
>
> —Luke 24:25–27

In response to their supposed questions Jesus may have talked about His pre-incarnation-existence with the Father, interpreted Old Testament types,

---

133   Hodge. Systematic Theology.
134   *"…and all the things that are written through the prophets shall be accomplished unto the Son of man."* (Luke 18:31).

symbols and epiphanies pointing to His incarnation and final exaltation,[135] for the two disciples afterwards could but say:

> *Was not our heart burning within us, while he spake to us in the way, while he opened to us the scriptures?*
> —Luke 24:32
> (see also Job 19:25–27)

Perhaps Cleophas and his friend experienced a yearning not unlike that felt by the ancient Patriarch Job, who had once said:

> *But as for me I know that my Redeemer liveth, and at last he will stand up upon the earth: and after my skin, even this body, is destroyed, then without my flesh shall I see God; whom I, even I, shall see, on my side, and mine eyes shall behold, and not as a stranger. My heart is consumed within me.*
> —Job 19:25–27

Now before the resurrected Jesus ascended to heaven He endowed the disciples with the promised Holy Spirit (Acts 1:4–5,8; 2:1–4) and commissioned His disciples, saying:

> *All authority hath been given unto me in heaven and on earth. Go ye therefore, and make disciples of all the nations, baptizing them into the name of the Father and of the Son and of the Holy Spirit: teaching them to observe all things whatsoever I commanded you: and lo, I am with you always, even unto the end of the world.*
> —Matthew 28:18–20[136]

---

[135] In the various life-histories of the patriarchs are theophanies (Gk. Theos phaino), or pre-incarnate appearances of Christ. Appellations such as "The Angel of the Lord," "The Angel of God," "My Angel," and "the Angel of His presence," all seemingly refer to the pre-incarnate Son of God. In addition, many persons in the books of Moses appear to serve as types of the incarnate Christ, for in their lives, similarities of actions, circumstances and events, they appear to foreshadow, portray, figure, or typify traits, circumstances and events in the life of Christ the Antitype.

[136] For the Great Commission see Matthew 28:18–20; Mark 16:15–18; Acts 1:8. The prophet Ezekiel tells us that the awesome responsibility of end-time believers (or watchmen) is to warn unbelievers (Ezekiel 33:1–7).

The Church Age

After His disciples had received the indwelling and enabling Holy Spirit, Jesus ascended to heaven, and is now interceding for His own who constitute the true Church. His crucifixion and ascension eliminated the need for the royal genealogy that was interrupted on the deportation of King Jehoiachin in 597 B.C. As prophesied He will at the times of restitution of all things descend bodily a second time in order to reign in perpetuity over David's covenanted kingdom.

Now Emperor Tiberius (Tiberius Claudius Nero Caesar) (ca. A.D. 14–37) placed Judea under the control of Roman Prefects, the most prominent from a Christian perspective being Pontius Pilate (ca. A.D. 26–33/36), in whose reign Jesus Christ was crucified and bodily resurrected from the dead by the power of God.[137] Then following the demise first of the Emperor Gaius Caligula (Gaius Caesar Germanicus) (ca. A.D. 37–41) and then of Claudius (Tiberius Claudius Nero Germanicus) (ca. A.D. 41–54), Herod Agrippa I (ca. 11 B.C.-A.D. 44), the son of Aristobolus and Bernice, was nominated to be king of the Jews. Agrippa I put to death James the Elder and cast the apostle Peter into prison. A few years later Agrippa I died of the same repulsive illness that had killed Herod I his grandfather (Acts 12:21–23). He was followed by Herod Agrippa II (ca. A.D. 48–73), son of Herod Agrippa I and Cypros, in whose reign Porcius Festus (ca. A.D. 60–62) and Lucceius Albinus (ca. A.D. 62–64) were Roman procurators of Judea. When the province in A.D. 66 was troubled by renewed revolts started by Jewish zealots against Gessius Florus (ca. A.D. 64–66) then the Roman procurator of Judea, Emperor Nero (Claudius Nero Caesar) (ca. A.D. 54–68) sent his general Titus Flavius Vespasianus (Sr.) to Judea to deal with the insurrection. Following Nero's suicide Titus Flavius Vespasianus (Sr.) (ca. A.D. 69–79) became emperor of Rome, and in the second year of his reign he ordered his same- named son Titus to invade Palestine from Syria with three legions to deal with the insurrection. In A.D. 70–71 Jerusalem was assaulted, the temple was pillaged, and Bezaleel's ancient lampstand of pure gold carried away (Exodus 37:1,17–24).[138] What transpired had been foretold years earlier by Jesus:

---

137 Approximate dates of Roman Prefects of Judea in the lifetime of Jesus Christ: Coponius (ca. 6 B.C.-A.D.9); Marcus Ambibulus (ca. A.D. 9–12); Annius Rufus (ca. A.D. 12–15); Valerius Gratus (ca. A.D. 15–26), and Pontius Pilate (ca. A.D. 26–33/36).

138 See the cover image of the Menorah taken from the Jerusalem Temple by the soldiers of Titus.

> *For the days shall come upon thee, when thine enemies shall cast up a bank about thee, and compass thee round, and keep thee in on every side, and shall dash thee to the ground, and thy children within thee; and they shall not leave in thee one stone upon another; because thou knewest not the time of thy visitation.*
>
> —Luke 19:43–44

Using siege ramps the Romans breached the walls of the city, set Herod's temple on fire, and utterly destroyed the city. The terrible devastation of the city, its citizens, and their temple was witnessed by the Jewish historian Joseph ben Matthias (ca. A.D. 37–100), commonly known as Flavius Josephus. In his account of the event he carefully notes:

> As for the house, God had for certain long ago doomed it to the fire; and now that fatal day was come, according to the revolution of ages: it was the tenth day of the month Lous, [Ab=July/August] upon which it was formerly burnt by the king of Babylon [Nebuchadnezzar II]... However, one cannot wonder at the accuracy of this period thereto relating; for the same month and day were now observed, as I said before, wherein the holy house was burnt formerly by the Babylonians. Now the number of years that passed from its first foundation, which was laid by King Solomon, till this its destruction, which happened in the second year of the reign of Vespasian, are collected to be one thousand one hundred and thirty, besides seven months and fifteen days; and from the second building of it, which was done by Haggai, in the second year of Cyrus the king, till its destruction under Vespasian, there were six hundred and thirty-nine years and forty-five days.[139]

As importantly noted by one commentator, the "Seventy-Weeks Prophesy" of Daniel should have been deeply disturbing to the Jews for two reasons:

> First, it clearly teaches that the Messiah had to come before the Temple was destroyed in A.D. 70... Second, the prophesy clearly teaches that a terrible time of tribulation for the Jews still lies ahead.[140]

---

139 Flavius Josephus. The Wars of the Jews. IV. 5 and 8 in Josephus. Complete Works (Kregel Publications, Grand Rapids, Michigan 49503), pp. 580b-581b.

140 D. Reagan. Daniel's 70 Weeks of Years. http://www.raptureready.com/featured/reagan/dr31.html.

The Church Age

By-passers beholding the ruined Jerusalem temple could only look in astonishment and ask: *"Why hath Jehovah done thus unto this land, and to this house?"* (2 Chronicles 7:21)

Then from the crowd might have been heard someone answering:

Because they forsook Jehovah, the God of their fathers, who brought them forth out of the land of Egypt, and laid hold on other gods, and worshipped them, and served them: therefore hath he brought all this evil upon them.
—2 Chronicles 7:22

With the total destruction of the Jerusalem temple, "the elaborate ritual of sacrifice inaugurated fourteen hundred years before at Mt. Sinai came to a crashing end."[141]

Jewish resistance to Rome however continued with the defiant Zealots commanded by Eleazar ben Ja'ir (Ya'ir) operating from the almost unassailable fortress of Masada built by Herod south of Jerusalem. Between A.D. 72–73 the Roman general Lucius Flavius Silva (ca. A.D. 40–?) led his legion X Fretensis and auxiliaries against the mountain plateau of Masada occupied by extremist Jewish rebels called the Sicarii, a splinter group of the Jewish Zealots. A ramp was built, and with a battering ram mounted on top of a siege tower the Romans relentlessly attacked, breached the walls and took the Masada fortress - only to find that the Sicarii had all taken their own lives. Thereafter in A.D. 79, following the death of Emperor Vespasian (Titus Flavius Vespasianus, Sr.), his same- named son Titus (Titus Flavius Vespasianus, Jr.) (ca. A.D. 79–81) became Emperor. As for Lucius Flavius Silva he remained as governor of Judea for eight years from ca. A.D. 73 to A.D. 81 when he became a victim in the reign of terror of the Emperor Domitian (ca. A.D. 81–96). Throughout the years of hardship following the great destruction of the Holy City and it's temple, those Jews and Christians who by hiding had survived their Roman persecutors were dispersed throughout Judea and beyond the borders of their homeland. Within fifty years of the demise of the last Apostle, splits and divisions, as testified by the apostle John (3 John 9–10), had fragmented the visible church (3 John 9–10) in Asia Minor. As indicated by the Apostle John in the Book of Revelation, the Christian church in Ephesus had become a loveless church (Revelation 2:1–11), the church in Smyrna had become

---

[141] W. Varner. Messiah (AuthorHouse, Bloomington, Indiana, 2004).

a persecuted church (Revelation 2:8–11), the church in Pergamos had become a compromising church (Revelation 2:12–17), the church of Thyatira had become corrupt (Revelation 2:18–29), and the church of Sardis had become dead (Revelation 3:1–6). Of the remaining two churches in Asia Minor, only the church in Philadelphia had remained faithful (Revelation 3:7–13) while the church in Laodicea had become lukewarm (Revelation 3:14–22).[142]

Near the end of Emperor Hadrian's reign (ca. A.D. 117–138), the Roman army was again faced with a major anti-Roman militant messianic rebellion in Judea led by Simon Bar Kokhba (ca. A.D. 132–135), a self-proclaimed Messiah.

> The Romans inflamed the Jews of Judea by attempting to erects a shrine to Jupiter, supreme Roman God, on the site of the Temple at Jerusalem and by issuing decrees against circumcision and public instruction of Jewish Law.[143]

The Bar Kokhba rebellion was short-lived, and crushed by the Roman General Sextus Julius Severus (ca. A.D. 132–136) at Bethar southwest of Jerusalem. During this time the finest Torah scholar Rabbi Yehudah HaNasi (ca. A.D. 135–220), the son of Rabbi Shimon Ben Gamliel II, resettled in Babylon in the Persian Empire, where with other scholars he committed himself to the enormous task of writing down in Hebrew the Oral Torah as transmitted by previous generations from the time of Moses. The end result, finished in ca. A.D. 190, was the Mishna containing the sayings of the rabbis who lived from ca 100 B.C.-A.D.200. Following the completion of the Mishna, further discussions eventually led to the writing of the Jerusalem Talmud or Palestinian Talmud (ca. A.D. 400) and the authoritative Babylonian Talmud (ca. A.D. 500). Throughout these years much time was spent studying and discussing the available Rabbinic literature. Materials were collected from the non-legal portions of the Talmud and Midrash such as history, parables, proverbs and folklore, and arranged into a compendium known as the Sefer Ha-Aggadah (The Book of Legends) containing, as stated by William

---

142 The seven churches addressed in Revelation 2 and 3 represent types of churches in all ages. The message to Laodicea may perhaps represent the last age of the church before the Second Coming of Jesus Christ.

143 Kohn, G. C. Dictionary of Wars. Revised ed. (New Work: Checkmark Books, 1999), 52.

Braude, the translator, "whatever the imaginations can invent... to teach man the ways of God."[144]

The first Christian Roman Emperor Constantine I, the Great (ca. A.D. 305–337), sought to eradicate paganism by prohibiting pagan sacrifices, and by building churches. He involved himself enthusiastically in the theological controversies of his time, and as a result Christians, wedded to the state began to compromise their Christian testimony. Recognized as the official religion of the empire, the church for the next ten centuries of the Middle Ages, ruled supreme, and developed new doctrines, ceremonies and feasts.[145] From the time of the conversion of Constantine I to Christianity, most Roman emperors were largely indifferent to Judaism, and the Jews for a while continued to retain all the privileges granted by former Seleucid and Roman emperors. Of these privileges, the main one was that Jews could not be forced to perform any task which violated their religious convictions.

An interesting report by the Roman historian Ammianus Marcellinus (ca. A.D. 325–395) has it that the Roman Emperor Flavius Claudius Julianus (ca. A.D. 361–363), also known as Julian I the Apostate, vainly tried to restore the temple at Jerusalem, which had been destroyed almost three centuries earlier.

> Eager to extend the memory of his reign by great works, he planned at vast cost to restore the once splendid temple at Jerusalem which after many mortal combats during the siege by Vespasian and later by Titus had barely been stormed. He has entrusted the speedy performance of this work to Alypius of Antioch [fl. A.D. 350–360], who had once been vice-prefect of Britain. But, though this Alypius pushed the work on with vigor, aided by the governor of the province, terrifying balls of flame kept bursting forth near the foundations of the temple, and made the place inaccessible to the workmen, some of whom were burned to

---

[144] Modern translations in English: Hayim Nahman Bialik and Yehoshua Hana Ravnitzky, eds. The Book of Legends. Sefer Ha-Aggadah. Legends from the Talmud and Midrash (Schocken Books, New York, 1992). See also Ephraime E. Urbach. The Sages. Their concepts and beliefs (Harvard Univ. Press, Cambridge, Massachusetts and London, 1987).

[145] Henry Bettenson, editor. Documents of the Christian Church (Oxford University Press, London, 1963), 2nd edition, Section XI, pp. 258–281. Bettenson's book deals with the doctrines of: Papal infallibility, invocation of saints, veneration of images and relics, place of purgatory, granting and the use of indulgences, immaculate conception and the assumption of the Virgin Mary, celibacy of the clergy, and transubstantiation.

death; and since in this way the element persistently repelled them, the enterprise halted.[146]

Thereafter in A.D. 613, another Jewish revolt against the Byzantine Emperor Heraclitus (ca. A.D. 610–641) climaxed a year later in the conquest of Jerusalem by the Persians (Sassanians) under Khosrau II (Khusro II) (ca. A.D. 591–628), son of Hormuz IV (ca. A.D. 579–590). As noted by the Muslim historian Abdullah Yusuf'Ali in his chronology:

> The city was burnt and pillaged, the Christians were massacred, the churches were burnt, the burial place of Christ was insulted, and many relics, including the true cross on which Christians believed that Christ had been crucified were carried away to Persia. The priests of the Persian religion celebrated an exultant triumph over the priests of Christ. In this pillage and massacre the Persians were assisted by crowds of Jews, who were discontented with the Christian domination, and the Pagan Arabs to whom any opportunity of plunder and destruction was in itself welcome.[147]

Israel remained under Byzantine control until ca. A.D. 638 when the successors of Muhammed (ca. A.D. 570–632) occupied Palestine: first by Caliph Omar I (Umar I) (ca. A.D. 637–644) of the Medina Caliphate (ca. A.D. 637–661), then by Abd-al-Malik (ca. A.D. 685–705) and Omar II (ca. A.D. 717–720) of the Damascus Omayyad Caliphate (ca. A.D. 661–750), and finally by Harun-al-Rashid (ca. A.D. 786–809) of the Baghdad Abbasid Caliphate (ca. A.D. 750–1072). The Islamic forces initially conquered Spain in A.D. 711 when the Umayyad Caliphate, led by Al Ghadiqi, advanced northward toward Gaul and into France, and between Tours and Poitiers were opposed and defeated by the Frankish statesman Charles Martel (ca. 686–741 B.C.), who drove the invaders back through Spain to North Africa. Thereafter Palestine fell under the rule of the Seljuk Turks (ca. A.D. 1072–1099), first under Malik-shah (ca. A.D. 1072–1092), and then under Barki-yarrok (ca. A.D. 1094–1099). Throughout these years of Islamic conquest true Christianity virtually disappeared in Palestine. In A.D. 1099 at the Council

---

146 Ammianus Marcellinus. Vol. II. Book XXIII. I.2–3 in Loeb Classical Library (LCL).
147 Abdullah Yusuf'Ali., tr. First Contact of Islam with World Movements (Appendix VIII.14), in The Holy Qur'an (Brentwood, Maryland: Amana Corporation, 1989), 1028. New Revised Edition.

of Piacenza, Pope Urban II (ca. A.D. 1088–1099) called on Christian warriors to deliver Jerusalem from Muslim domination and issued a summons to the First Crusade (ca. A.D. 1095–1099) led by Peter the Hermit (ca. A.D. 1050–1115) and Walter the Penniless (dead ca. A.D. 1096). A larger princes' crusade followed to Palestine then controlled by the Fatimids of Egypt, and on to Jerusalem where in the name of Christ and pope they murdered thousands of Muslims and Jews:

> The crusaders, maddened by so great a victory after such sufferings, rushed through the streets and into the houses and mosques killing all that they met, men, women and children alike. All that afternoon and all through the night the massacre continued... The massacre at Jerusalem profoundly impressed all the world. No one can say how many victims it involved; but it emptied Jerusalem of its Moslem and Jewish inhabitants.[148]

Impiously the crusaders took possession of the throne of David, and Godfrey of Bouillon (ca. A.D. 1058–1100) assumed the title "King of Jerusalem," a designation also taken by a long line of hereditary or elected claimants. Between A.D. 1099 and A.D. 1291, interrupted by the sixteen-year rule of Saladin (Salah al-Din Al-Ayyubi) (ca. A.D. 1187–1193), Jerusalem was besieged and taken, and the crusaders defeated. The defeat of the crusaders provoked additional European crusades. Jerusalem fell to the Saracens in A.D. 1244, and by A.D. 1260 the Mongols under Genghis Khan (A.D. 1190–1227) briefly swept over the Near East to meet their defeat at Ain Jalut at the hands of Baybars I (Baibars I) (ca. A.D. 1260–1277) then the Mamluk Sultan of Egypt, who subsequently, in A.D. 1291? fought the Crusader states in Palestine and expelled the remaining crusaders. Thereafter the Ottoman Sultans, initially under Suleiman I the Magnificent (ca. A.D. 1520–1566), occupied Palestine. Ottoman control lasted until World War I (ca. A.D. 1914–1918) when they were driven from much of the eastern Mediterranean region by the British Empire.

Over the centuries from the fall of Jerusalem in 70 A.D. to the end of World War I, Hebrew history had become the history of the Jewish Diaspora. Centers of Judaism outside Israel shifted from country to country as Jews increasingly became victims of violent anti-Semitism. They became "an astonishment, a proverb, and

---

[148] S. Runciman. A History of the Crusades: The First Crusade and the Foundation of the Kingdom of Jerusalem. (The Folio Society, London, 1994), I. 231–238.

a byword among all nations" where they had fled, or been driven (Deuteronomy 28:37). Repressive laws were enacted to limit their rights, and to distance Catholicism from Judaism.[149] Jews were ordered to wear yellow badges and special hats, coerced to attend forced baptisms and conversion sermons.[150] Synagogues were closed and Jewish writings confiscated and burned. Moreover they were frequently attacked by anti-Semitic riots, tortured, and forcibly expelled, or exterminated by the powers that be.[151] Between A.D. 1939–1941, it must have seemed to the prisoners in German Nazi concentration camps that all the curses of Deuteronomy had "come upon the Jews and overtaken them" (Deuteronomy 28:15–20).

Freed from Ottoman control, Palestine in the meanwhile had become an international zone. The "Balfour Declaration" of A.D. 1917 supported the Zionist concept of a national Jewish home in Palestine, and by A.D. 1922 the "Mandate Declaration" was approved by the League of Nations (A.D. 1919–1946). Following World War II (A.D. 1939–1945), and the establishment of the United Nations (A.D. 1945–present), Israel in A.D. 1948 finally became an independent Jewish State. This was followed in A.D. 1967 by the restoration of Jerusalem. However since the land currently is not the land promised to the Patriarch Abraham, the Jews await the prophesied final end-time restoration.[152]

The first modern-day Prime Minister of Israel was David Ben-Gurion (A.D. 1948–1954; 1955–1963). Since then Israel has been served by seventeen Prime Ministers. Of these Levi Eshkol (A.D. 1963–1969) died in office, Yitzhak Rabin (A.D. 1974–1977; 1992–1995) was assassinated, Ariel Sharon (A.D. 2001–2006) was deemed unable to exercise his office due to a severe stroke, and Shimon Peres (A.D. 2007–2014) died from a major stroke. The Prime Minister currently serving Israel is Benjamin Netanyahu (A.D. 1996–1999; 2009–2015; 2015– ?). Although surrounded by hostile nations and often engaged in war with these, Israel has resisted, and survived, the determined political and militant efforts of Muslim Sunni and Shiite governments to eradicate Israel from Palestine and from the face of the earth. Israel has been attacked by Fatah (A.D. 2006–present) and by Hamas (A.D. 1987–present) from within, by Persian backed Hezbollah (A.D. 1982–present)

---

149 P. Halsall. Medieval Source Book: Legislation Affecting the Jew from 300 to 800 CE (www.fordham.edu/halsall/source/300-800-lawa-jews.html).

150 Seaver, J. E. The Persecution of the Jews in the Roman Empire (300-428). Humanistic Studies, No.30 (Lawrence, Kansas: Univ. of Kansas Press., 1952), 84-85.

151 Mattis Kantor. Codex Judaica. Chronological Index of Jewish History (Zichron Press, New York, 2005), 393 pp.

152 Genesis 15:18; Kings 4:21.

and ISIS (Islamic State of Iraq and Syria)(1999–present) from without.[153] Nations formerly supportive of Israel have used the United Nations (A.D. 1945–present) as a forum to undermine God's design for Israel, and even the staunchest supporters of Israel may yet fail in their covenant commitments to Israel as they become increasingly secularized. Mindful perhaps of the words of the prophet Ezekiel, who spoke of the destruction of nations that sought to destroy Israel, one Bible scholar comments:

> History has borne out the fact that nations which have persecuted Israel, even when that very persecution was in fulfillment of God's discipline, have been punished for dealing with Abraham's seed.[154]

No weapon that is formed against thee shall prosper; and every tongue that shall rise against thee in judgment thou shalt condemn. This is the heritage of the servants of Jehovah, and their righteousness which is of me, saith Jehovah. (Isaiah 54:17).

---

[153] Deep-seated hatred towards Israel may plausibly be rooted in the unholy jealousy and coveting of Ishmael, the son of Abraham and the Egyptian bond-woman Hagar, Sarah's maid. Ishmael the firstborn of Abraham was denied what God covenanted to Isaac the son of Abraham and Sarah (Genesis 17:19–20; Galatians 4:22–31). The land of Israel promised to Abraham's lineage (Genesis 26:3–4) became a continuous source of friction between Jews and Arabs and will one day ignite the great battle of God called Armageddon as foretold by the prophet Zechariah (Zechariah 12:2–9; Revelation 16:16).

[154] J. Dwight Pentecost. Things to Come. A Study in Biblical Eschatology (Dunham Publishing Company, 1958; Epub Edition 2010), 135. See Deut. 30:7.

Chapter Eight

DAY OF THE LORD

Biblical eschatology deals with a still future end-time effort by the enemies of God to utterly destroy Israel. It is not within the scope of this book to deal extensively with matters of biblical eschatology, and only a brief overview of this evil effort to utterly destroy the Jewish people may cautiously be attempted.[155] Seven years prior to the Second Coming of Jesus Christ with power and great glory, a conglomerate of ten European nations will gain world domination, and enter into a seven year covenant with Israel. Its political and military ruler Gog is referred to as *"the man of sin"* and *"the lawless one"* (2 Thessalonians 2:3, 8). As foretold in the second half of Daniel's "Seventy-Weeks Prophesy:

> *And he shall make a firm covenant with many for one week: and in the midst of the week he shall cause the sacrifice and the oblation to cease; and upon the wing of abominations shall come one that maketh desolate; and even unto the full end, and that determined, shall wrath be poured out upon the desolate.*
>
> —Daniel 9:27

Deceptively the man of lawlessness will appear to abide by the covenant for the first three and a half years, and during that time there will be a measure of peace allowing Orthodox Jews time to build anew their temple, and renew their ancient sacrificial worship. Toward the end of the first three and a half years, and at the beginning of the next three and a half years, the seven year covenant with

---

155 Biblical eschatology, the church doctrine of the last things, has endured much at the hands of interpreters. Opinions differ as to the anticipated timing of the second advent, or Second Coming of Christ; the timing of the translation of the church into the Lord's presence; the timing of the tribulation period (pre-tribulation, mid-tribulation, and post-tribulation), and the timing of the millennial period (a-millennial, pre-millennial, mid-millennial, and post-millennial). J. Dwight Pentecost. Things to Come. A Study in Biblical Eschatology (Dunham Publishing Company, 1958; Epub Edition 2010.

Israel will be broken, and like an oncoming swarm of locusts the army of the anti-Christ will come from the north, invade the "Glorious Land" and, like the legions of Titus centuries before, trample the holy city of Jerusalem underfoot (Zechariah 12:2–9; 14:1–3; Ezekiel 38:15–16). The city shall be taken, the houses rifled, and the women ravished. Half of the city will go into captivity, but the remnant of the people shall not be cut off from the city (Zechariah 14:2). The rebuilt Jewish temple will be desecrated, and the daily sacrifices aborted. The lawless ruler, endowed by Satan with power, signs, lying wonders and all unrighteous deception, will establish himself as the object of worship *"so that he sitteth in the temple of God, setting himself forth as God"* (2 Thessalonians 2:4). The "abomination that causes desolation" will be set up, and then those of the true church who make a profession of faith in Christ, including Abraham's spiritual seed, will be miraculously transported into the Lord's presence.[156] Most Jews throughout the ages have not been prepared to recognize Jesus as the Christ, the promised Seed of the woman. As many Jews still do, they have believed that Messiah, the anticipated king and deliverer prophesied in the Old Testament, could not have come, for important messianic prophesies had not been fulfilled. Their Messiah, they argued, was not yet on the throne of David; the Kingdom of David was not yet restored; the exiles of the diaspora scattered throughout the world had not yet been fully re-gathered to Israel; the Jerusalem temple had not yet been built; peace in the world had not yet been established; and Israel had not yet been delivered from her many enemies. They were looking for an earthly kingdom, and expected that their Messiah would come as a strong warrior-prince like King David. They did not expect that what they were looking for was imminent.

Those of the unbelieving portion of the visible church together with unbelievers in the nation of Israel, i.e., Abraham's physical seed, will go into the tribulation period that follows. The tribulation period will be a dreadful time of trials referred to as "the Seventieth-Week," the "Great Tribulation," and the time of "Jacob's Trouble" (Jeremiah 30:7; Daniel 12:1; Zechariah 13:8). It will be a time of judgments, the opening of seals, the sounding of trumpets, and the outpouring of seven golden bowls full of the wrath of God (Revelation 6:1–17; 8:1–9; 9:1–21; 11:15; 15:1–8; 16:1–21). It will be a time of economic and political

---

156 The importance of the doctrine of the Second Coming of Christ is indicated by what the Bible teaches. The Second Coming of Christ is mentioned 318 times in the 266 chapters of the New Testament and it occupies one in every twenty-five verses from Matthew to Revelation. R. A. Torrey. What the Bible Teaches (Fleming H. Revell Company, 1898–1933), pp. 195–222.

distress, a time of devastation and desolation, and a time attended by frightening cosmic disturbances and changes in the normal order of nature culminating in the eschatological final Battle of Armageddon. At the end of the seven-year broken covenant, the nations that have chosen to follow the world ruler and his cohorts will be defeated by Christ at His Second Coming to restore David's kingdom, and Christ the King will make His enemies His footstool, and they will suffer the outpouring of His wrath.

However, it is important to realize, *"It is not for you to know times or seasons, which the Father hath set within his own authority"* (Acts 1:7; see also Matthew 24:27). Indeed no one can know the day and hour of the Second Coming, or the return of Christ, referred to as "the day of the Lord."

> *But of that day and hour knoweth no one, not even the angels of heaven, neither the Son, but the Father only.*
>
> —Matthew 24:36
> (see also Matthew 24:42–44, 1 Thessalonians 5:2)

What can be said with absolute certainty is that the end, according to the prophetic words of Jesus, will be much like the days of Noah, for as the days of Noah were:

> *So shall be the coming of the Son of man. For as in those days which were before the flood they were eating and drinking, marrying and giving in marriage, until the day that Noah entered into the ark, and they knew not until the flood came, and took them all away; so shall be the coming of the Son of man. Then shall two men be in the field; one is taken, and one is left: two women shall be grinding at the mill; one is taken, and one is left.*
>
> —Matthew 24:37–41

The ones taken will be translated into the Lord's presence to reign with Christ who will descend in clouds to exercise His dominion over the earth, and inaugurate a universal kingdom of peace and tranquility (Daniel 7:13–14).[157] The government will be upon His shoulders, and as prophesied in Daniel's "Seventy-Weeks Prophesy," God at that time will

---

[157] In Daniel's vision of the Ancient of Days *"there came with the clouds of heaven one like unto a son of man"* (Daniel 7:13).

> *finish transgression, and to make an end of sins, and to make reconciliation for iniquity, and to bring in everlasting righteousness, and to seal up vision and prophecy, and to anoint the most holy.*
> —Daniel 9:24

Christ, the righteous Branch, will rule from David's throne in fulfillment of the Davidic covenant (Acts 2:29–36; Amos 9:11–12), Satan will be bound for a time, and the earth will experience peace and prosperity (Revelation 20:1–7). These events will mark the end of "the present age of grace" as well as the end of "the times of the Gentiles" which began with the capture of Jerusalem in 605 B.C. by King Nebuchadnezzar II and his Babylonian armies. It marks the termination of our present historical order and introduces a new order discontinuous with the present course of history.[158] It also mark the onset of a millennium of a thousand years with the nation of Israel reinstated and restored under a new covenant in priestly communion and blessing as the light of the world. As prophesied by the prophet Amos:

> *In that day will I raise up the tabernacle of David that is fallen, and close up the breaches thereof; and I will raise up its ruins, and I will build it as in the days of old; that they may possess the remnant of Edom [from the Septuagint, "mankind"], and all the nations that are called by my name, saith Jehovah that doeth this.*
> —Amos 9:11–12
> (see also Acts 15:16–17)

The old covenants of works and grace will be replaced by an unbreakable New Covenant with the house of Israel and with the house of Judah:

> *not according to the covenant that I made with their fathers in the day that I took them by the hand to bring them out of the land of Egypt; which my covenant they brake, although I was a husband unto them, saith Jehovah. But this is the covenant that I will make with the house of Israel after those days, saith Jehovah: I will put my law in their inward parts, and in their heart will I write it; and I will be their God, and they shall be my people.*
> —Jeremiah 31:32–33

---

158 S. B. Ferguson, D. F. Wright, and J. I. Packer. Editors. New Dictionary of Theology (Inter-Varsity Press, Illinois, U.S.A.), 228b–231b; 428a–430a.

As explained by the prophet Ezekiel the new covenant will fulfill all the Old Testament promises to Israel:

> *For I will take you from among the nations, and gather you out of all the countries, and will bring you into your own land. And I will sprinkle clean water upon you, and ye shall be clean: from all your filthiness, and from all your idols, will I cleanse you. A new heart also will I give you, and a new spirit will I put within you; and I will take away the stony heart out of your flesh, and I will give you a heart of flesh. And I will put my Spirit within you, and cause you to walk in my statutes, and ye shall keep mine ordinances, and do them. And ye shall dwell in the land that I gave to your fathers; and ye shall be my people, and I will be your God.*
>
> —Ezekiel 36:24–28
> (see also Ezekiel 37:21–22, Jeremiah 32:36 – 39, and Hebrews 8:10)

Part III
Prophesies
Fulfilled

Chapter Nine

THE PROPHESIES OF THE OLD TESTAMENT[159]

The secret things belong unto Jehovah our God; but the things that are revealed belong unto us and to our children for ever...

—Deuteronomy 29:29

As witnessed by Matthew, Mark, and Luke, Jesus came to fulfill the Law and the Prophets. He said to his disciples:

Think not that I came to destroy the law or the prophets: I came not to destroy, but to fulfil. For verily I say unto you, Till heaven and earth pass away, one jot or one tittle shall in no wise pass away from the law, till all things be accomplished.

—Matthew 5:17–18

Indeed, "[t]he Son of man goeth, even as it is written of him... But all this is come to pass, that the scriptures of the prophets might be fulfilled" (Matthew 26:24, 56).

Verily I say unto you, This generation shall not pass away, until all these things be accomplished. Heaven and earth shall pass away: but my words shall not pass away.

—Mark 13:30–31

...all the things that are written through the prophets shall be accomplished unto the Son of man.

—Luke 18:31

---

[159] All biblical prophecy pertaining to past, present, and still future events are marked in the text that follows as foreordained, and thus fulfilled "even as is written."

Part Three: Prophecies Fulfilled

...all things which are written may be fulfilled.

—Luke 21:22

Verily I say unto you, This generation shall not pass away, till all things be accomplished. Heaven and earth shall pass away: but my words shall not pass away.

—Luke 21:32–33

And he said unto them, These are my words which I spake unto you, while I was yet with you, that all things must needs be fulfilled, which are written in the law of Moses, and the prophets, and the psalms, concerning me.

—Luke 24:44

Although Moses had expressed the hope that *"all Jehovah's people were prophets, that Jehovah would put his Spirit upon them!"* (Numbers 11:29), he also said that the prophets who presume to speak for God must be measured by what comes to pass and what does not come to pass:

But the prophet, that shall speak a word presumptuously in my name, which I have not commanded him to speak, or that shall speak in the name of other gods, that same prophet shall die. And if thou say in thy heart, How shall we know the word which Jehovah hath not spoken? when a prophet speaketh in the name of Jehovah, if the thing follow not, nor come to pass, that is the thing which Jehovah hath not spoken: the prophet hath spoken it presumptuously, thou shalt not be afraid of him.

—Deuteronomy 18:20–22

The apostles John, Paul and Peter all urged the believers not to be beguiled by false prophets, but to examine the spirits whether they are of God, for many untaught and unstable corrupt or twist to their own destruction the Word of God (2 Peter 3:16).

Beloved, believe not every spirit, but prove the spirits, whether they are of God; because many false prophets are gone out into the world. Hereby know ye the Spirit of God: every spirit that confesseth that Jesus Christ is come in the flesh is of God: and every spirit that confesseth not Jesus is not of God: and this is the spirit of the antichrist...

—1 John 4:1–3[160]

Again the Apostle Paul warns believers:

Take heed lest there shall be any one that maketh spoil of you through his philosophy and vain deceit, after the tradition of men, after the rudiments of the world, and not after Christ...

—Colossians 2:8

As for the interpretation of prophesy the Apostle Peter tells us to carefully heed the sure word of God as a light that shines in a dark place:

And we have the word of prophecy made more sure; whereunto ye do well that ye take heed, as unto a lamp shining in a dark place, until the day dawn, and the day-star arise in your hearts: knowing this first, that no prophecy of scripture is of private interpretation. For no prophecy ever came by the will of man: but men spake from God, being moved by the Holy Spirit.

—2 Peter 1:20–21

---

[160] To the church of Ephesus Christ says: "*I know thy works, and thy toil and patience, and that thou canst not bear evil men, and didst try them that call themselves apostles, and they are not, and didst find them false*" (Revelation 2:2).

Chapter Ten
PROPHECIES IN GENESIS

1. Messiah: The "Seed of the woman" shall bruise Satan's head.

...I will put enmity between thee and the woman, and between thy seed and her seed: he shall bruise thy head, and thou shalt bruise his heel.

—Genesis 3:15

Prophesy fulfilled: As the fall of mankind was set in motion through Eve, so redemption will come through woman. It will be the "Seed of the woman that is virgin born without the agency of man."[161]

Behold, the virgin shall be with child, and shall bring forth a son, and they shall call his name Immanuel; which is, being interpreted, God with us.

—Matthew 1:23[162]

...but when the fulness of the time came, God sent forth his Son, born of a woman, born under the law, that he might redeem them that were under the law, that we might receive the adoption of sons.

—Galatians 4:4–5

---

[161] H. H. Halley. Finding Jesus in the Old Testament (Excerpt from Halley's Bible Handbook), pp. 4–5; Halley's Bible Handbook with the New International Version (Zondervan, Grand Rapids, Michigan, 2000), 667–668, etc.

[162] But *"when the fulness of the time came, God sent forth his Son, born of a woman, born under the law"* (Galatians 4:4).

Part Three: Prophecies Fulfilled

2. Messiah: His blood-sacrifice is foreshadowed in Abel's offering.

And in process of time it came to pass, that Cain brought of the fruit of the ground an offering unto Jehovah. And Abel, he also brought of the firstlings of his flock and of the fat thereof. And Jehovah had respect unto Abel and to his offering: but unto Cain and to his offering he had not respect.

—Genesis 4:3–5

Prophesy fulfilled:

...to Jesus the mediator of a new covenant, and to the blood of sprinkling that speaketh better than that of Abel.

—Hebrews 12:24

3. Messiah: He shall bless all nations in Abraham's Seed.

...I will bless them that bless thee, and him that curseth thee will I curse: and in thee shall all the families of the earth be blessed.

—Genesis 12:3[163]

...seeing that Abraham shall surely become a great and mighty nation, and all the nations of the earth shall be blessed in him...

—Genesis 18:18

Prophesy fulfilled:

The book of the generation of Jesus Christ, the son of David, the son of Abraham.

—Matthew 1:1

(see also Mark 12:35)

The Apostles Matthew, Luke and Paul all write about the covenant blessings which God made with the descendants of Abraham:

---

[163] Genesis 17:7; 18:18; 22:18; 28:14.

Ye are the sons of the prophets, and of the covenant which God made with your fathers, saying unto Abraham, and in thy seed shall all the families of the earth be blessed.

—Acts 3:25[164]

4. Messiah: He is blessed in Isaac's seed.

And God said, Nay, but Sarah thy wife shall bear thee a son; and thou shalt call his name Isaac: and I will establish my covenant with him for an everlasting covenant for his seed after him.

—Genesis 17:19

…in all that Sarah saith unto thee, hearken unto her voice; for in Isaac shall thy seed be called.

—Genesis 21:12

Prophesy fulfilled:

…the son of Jacob, the son of Isaac, the son of Abraham, the son of Terah, the son of Nahor…

—Luke 3:34

For they are not all Israel, that are of Israel: neither, because they are Abraham's seed, are they all children: but, In Isaac shall thy seed be called. That is, it is not the children of the flesh that are children of God; but the children of the promise are reckoned for a seed. For this is a word of promise, According to this season will I come, and Sarah shall have a son.

—Romans 9:6–9

By faith Abraham, being tried, offered up Isaac: yea, he that had gladly received the promises was offering up his only begotten son; even he to whom it was said, In Isaac shall thy seed be called: accounting that God is able to raise up, even from the dead

—Hebrews 11:17–19

---

[164] Galatians 3:16; Hebrews 2:16,18.

Part Three: Prophecies Fulfilled

5. Messiah: He is foreshadowed in Melchizedek the king of Salem.

And Melchizedek king of Salem brought forth bread and wine: and he was priest of God Most High. And he blessed him, and said, Blessed be Abram of God Most High, possessor of heaven and earth: and blessed be God Most High, who hath delivered thine enemies into thy hand. And he gave him a tenth of all.

—Genesis 14:18–20

Jehovah hath sworn, and will not repent: thou art a priest for ever after the order of Melchizedek.

—Psalms 110:4

Prophesy fulfilled:

So Christ also glorified not himself to be made a high priest, but he that spake unto him, Thou art my Son, this day have I begotten thee: as he saith also in another place, Thou art a priest for ever after the order of Melchizedek.

—Hebrews 5:5–6

...to whom also Abraham divided a tenth part of all (being first, by interpretation, King of righteousness, and then also King of Salem, which is, King of peace; without father, without mother, without genealogy, having neither beginning of days nor end of life, but made like unto the Son of God), abideth a priest continually.

—Hebrews 7:2–3

6. Messiah: He is foreshadowed in Abraham's offering of Isaac his only son.

And Abraham stretched forth his hand, and took the knife to slay his son. And the angel of Jehovah called unto him out of heaven, and said, Abraham, Abraham: and he said, Here am I. And he said, Lay not thy hand upon the lad, neither do thou anything unto him; for now I know that thou fearest God, seeing thou hast not withheld thy son, thine only son, from me. And Abraham lifted up his eyes, and looked, and, behold, behind him a ram caught in the thicket by his horns: and Abraham went and took the ram, and offered him up for a burnt-offering in the stead of his son.

—Genesis 22:10–13

Prophesy fulfilled: The Apostle John tells us that God, like Abraham, *"gave his only begotten Son"* (John 3:16), whom He also raised from the dead (John 2:22). The author of the Epistle of Hebrews writes:

> *By faith Abraham, being tried, offered up Isaac: yea, he that had gladly received the promises was offering up his only begotten son; even he to whom it was said, In Isaac shall thy seed be called: accounting that God is able to raise up, even from the dead; from whence he did also in a figure receive him back.*
>
> —Hebrews 11:17–19

Abraham full of faith believed that God would raise up Isaac from the dead. When he was ready to leave for the sacrifice he said to his two young men with them:

> *Abide ye here with the ass, and I and the lad will go yonder; and we will worship, and come again to you.*
>
> —Genesis 22:5

7. Mesiah: Shall bless all nations in Jacob's Seed.

> *…sojourn in this land, and I will be with thee, and will bless thee; for unto thee, and unto thy seed, I will give all these lands, and I will establish the oath which I sware unto Abraham thy father; and I will multiply thy seed as the stars of heaven, and will give unto thy seed all these lands; and in thy seed shall all the nations of the earth be blessed; because that Abraham obeyed my voice, and kept my charge, my commandments, my statutes, and my laws.*
>
> —Genesis 26:3–5

The promise to Abraham is reconfirmed to Jacob in a dream at Bethel:

> *And, behold, Jehovah stood above it, and said, I am Jehovah, the God of Abraham thy father, and the God of Isaac: the land whereon thou liest, to thee will I give it, and to thy seed; and thy seed shall be as the dust of the earth, and thou shalt spread abroad to the west, and to the east, and to the north, and to the south: and in thee and in thy seed shall all the families of the earth be blessed.*
>
> —Genesis 28:13–14

Part Three: Prophecies Fulfilled

8. Messiah: He is foreshadowed as Shiloh of the Seed of Judah.

The sceptre shall not depart from Judah, nor the ruler's staff from between his feet, until Shiloh come; and unto him shall the obedience of the peoples be.
—Genesis 49:10

Prophesy fulfilled: Shiloh, a type of Christ, shall descend from the tribe of Judah.

Weep not; behold, the Lion that is of the tribe of Judah, the Root of David, hath overcome to open the book and the seven seals thereof.
—Revelation 5:5

Chapter Eleven

PROPHECIES IN EXODUS

1. Messiah: His bones were not broken.

In one house shall it be eaten; thou shalt not carry forth aught of the flesh abroad out of the house; neither shall ye break a bone thereof.
—Exodus 12:46[165]

Prophesy fulfilled:

The soldiers therefore came, and brake the legs of the first, and of the other that was crucified with him: but when they came to Jesus, and saw that he was dead already, they brake not his legs…
—John 19:32–33

---

[165] Numbers 9:12; Psalm 34:19–20.

Chapter Twelve
PROPHESIES IN NUMBERS

1. Messiah: He is lifted up like Moses's bronze serpent.

And Jehovah sent fiery serpents among the people, and they bit the people; and much people of Israel died... And Jehovah said unto Moses, Make thee a fiery serpent, and set it upon a standard: and it shall come to pass, that every one that is bitten, when he seeth it, shall live. And Moses made a serpent of brass, and set it upon the standard: and it came to pass, that if a serpent had bitten any man, when he looked unto the serpent of brass, he lived.

—Numbers 21:6, 8–9

Prophesy fulfilled: Moses's bronze serpent is connected by the Apostle John with the redemptive work of the resurrected Christ:

And no one hath ascended into heaven, but he that descended out of heaven, even the Son of man, who is in heaven. And as Moses lifted up the serpent in the wilderness, even so must the Son of man be lifted up; that whosoever believeth may in him have eternal life.

—John 3:13–15

And I, if I be lifted up from the earth, will draw all men unto myself.

—John 12:32

When the bronze symbol became an idol to the people, King Hezekiah (ca. 727–697 B.C.) of Judah had the bronze serpent destroyed (2 Kings 18:4).

Part Three: Prophecies Fulfilled

2. Messiah: He will rise like the Star and Scepter out of Jacob.

I see him, but not now; I behold him, but not nigh: there shall come forth a star out of Jacob, and a sceptre shall rise out of Israel... And out of Jacob shall one have dominion...

—Numbers 24:17, 19

Prophesy fulfilled: The prophesies and doctrines of Baalam the seer (Numbers 22–24) are referred to in the Apostle John's letter to the compromising Church in Pergamos (Revelation 2:14). Baalam refused to curse and denounce Israel for Balak the king of Moab, for he perceived in the far distance him who out of Jacob should one day have dominion (Numbers 23:7–10).

Chapter Thirteen
Prophesies in Deuteronomy

1. Messiah: He will be a prophet like Moses.

Jehovah thy God will raise up unto thee a prophet from the midst of thee, of thy brethren, like unto me; unto him ye shall hearken; according to all that thou desiredst of Jehovah thy God in Horeb in the day of the assembly, saying, Let me not hear again the voice of Jehovah my God, neither let me see this great fire any more, that I die not. And Jehovah said unto me, They have well said that which they have spoken. I will raise them up a prophet from among their brethren, like unto thee; and I will put my words in his mouth, and he shall speak unto them all that I shall command him. And it shall come to pass, that whosoever will not hearken unto my words which he shall speak in my name, I will require it of him.
—Deuteronomy 18:15–19

Prophesy fulfilled:

Moses indeed said, A prophet shall the Lord God raise up unto you from among your brethren, like unto me; to him shall ye hearken in all things whatsoever he shall speak unto you. And it shall be, that every soul that shall not hearken to that prophet, shall be utterly destroyed from among the people.
—Acts 3:22–23

This is that Moses, who said unto the children of Israel, A prophet shall God raise up unto you from among your brethren, like unto me.
—Acts 7:37

Philip findeth Nathanael, and saith unto him, We have found him, of whom Moses in the law, and the prophets, wrote, Jesus of Nazareth, the son of Joseph.
—John 1:45

Part Three: Prophecies Fulfilled

Wherefore, holy brethren, partakers of a heavenly calling, consider the Apostle and High Priest of our confession, even Jesus; who was faithful to him that appointed him, as also was Moses in all his house. For he hath been counted worthy of more glory than Moses, by so much as he that built the house hath more honor than the house. For every house is builded by some one; but he that built all things is God. And Moses indeed was faithful in all his house as a servant, for a testimony of those things which were afterward to be spoken; but Christ as a son, over his house; whose house are we, if we hold fast our boldness and the glorying of our hope firm unto the end.

—Hebrews 3:1–6

The Apostle John quotes Jesus as saying:

For if ye believed Moses, ye would believe me; for he wrote of me. But if ye believe not his writings, how shall ye believe my words?

—John 5:46–47

Moreover, in the parable of the Rich man and Lazarus as recorded by the Apostle Luke, the rich man in Hades seeing Abraham afar off implores him to send Lazarus to warn his brothers about his place of torment. But Abraham directing the rich man's attention to Moses replies:

They have Moses and the prophets; let them hear them... If they hear not Moses and the prophets, neither will they be persuaded, if one rise from the dead.

—Luke 16:29, 31

2. Messiah: He was accursed of God and hanged on a tree.

And if a man have committed a sin worthy of death, and he be put to death, and thou hang him on a tree; his body shall not remain all night upon the tree, but thou shalt surely bury him the same day; for he that is hanged is accursed of God.

—Deuteronomy 21:22–23

Prophesy fulfilled:

Prophesies in Deuteronomy

The Jews therefore, because it was the Preparation, that the bodies should not remain on the cross upon the sabbath (for the day of that sabbath was a high day), asked of Pilate that their legs might be broken, and that they might be taken away.

—John 19:31

3. Messiah: The Rock who begot them, is not remembered by the people.

Of the Rock that begat thee thou art unmindful, and hast forgotten God that gave thee birth.

—Deuteronomy 32:18

The words which the rebellious children of Israel heard did not profit them, not being mixed with faith.[166] Moses said to the children of Israel:

Ye have seen all that Jehovah did before your eyes in the land of Egypt unto Pharaoh, and unto all his servants, and unto all his land; the great trials which thine eyes saw, the signs, and those great wonders: but Jehovah hath not given you a heart to know, and eyes to see, and ears to hear, unto this day.

—Deuteronomy 29:2–4

Prophesy fulfilled:

That which Israel seeketh for, that he obtained not; but the election obtained it, and the rest were hardened: according as it is written, God gave them a spirit of stupor, eyes that they should not see, and ears that they should not hear, unto this very day.

—Romans 11:7–8[167]

---

166 Hebrews 4:2; Romans 16:25–26; 2 Corinthians 3:13–14.
167 Romans 11:25; II Corinthians 3:15–16.

Chapter Fourteen
PROPHESIES IN JOSHUA

1. Messiah: He is the Captain of the Lord's host.

From the beginning the success of Israel's military campaign in Canaan was not due exclusively to Joshua and the might of his army. Prior to the commencement of his campaign when he was still by Jericho and lifted up his eyes:

> ...*behold, there stood a man [a theophany] over against him with his sword drawn in his hand: and Joshua went unto him, and said unto him, Art thou for us, or for our adversaries? And he said, Nay; but as prince of the host of Jehovah am I now come. And Joshua fell on his face to the earth, and did worship, and said unto him, What saith my lord unto his servant? And the prince of Jehovah's host said unto Joshua, Put off thy shoe from off thy foot; for the place whereon thou standest is holy. And Joshua did so.*
> —Joshua 5:13–15[168]

Prophesy fulfilled: The "Commander of the army of the Lord" is here seen as a type of Christ, the Captain of our salvation.

---

[168] Joshua 5:13–15. Moses at the burning bush in Horeb, the mountain of God, was told by God: "Take your sandals off your feet, for the place where you stand is holy ground." (Exodus 3:5).

Chapter Fifteen
PROPHESIES IN JUDGES

1. Messiah: He is called a Nazarene.

for, lo, thou shalt conceive, and bear a son; and no razor shall come upon his head; for the child shall be a Nazirite unto God from the womb: and he shall begin to save Israel out of the hand of the Philistines. Then the woman came and told her husband, saying, A man of God came unto me, and his countenance was like the countenance of the angel of God, very terrible; and I asked him not whence he was, neither told he me his name: but he said unto me, Behold, thou shalt conceive, and bear a son; and now drink no wine nor strong drink, and eat not any unclean thing; for the child shall be a Nazirite unto God from the womb to the day of his death.

—Judges 13:5–7

Prophesy fulfilled:

...and came and dwelt in a city called Nazareth; that it might be fulfilled which was spoken through the prophets, that he should be called a Nazarene.

—Matthew 2:23

Chapter Sixteen
PROPHESIES IN JOB

1. Messiah: He shall be seen as the promised Redeemer at the resurrection.

But as for me I know that my Redeemer liveth, and at last he will stand up upon the earth: and after my skin, even this body, is destroyed, then without my flesh shall I see God; whom I, even I, shall see, on my side, and mine eyes shall behold, and not as a stranger. My heart is consumed within me.
—Job 19:25–27

As for me, I shall behold thy face in righteousness; I shall be satisfied, when I awake, with beholding thy form.
—Psalm 17:15

Prophesy fulfilled:

Beloved, now are we children of God, and it is not yet made manifest what we shall be. We know that, if he shall be manifested, we shall be like him; for we shall see him even as he is.
—1 John 3:2

Chapter Seventeen

PROPHESIES IN PSALMS

David composed a number of Psalms, many pointing prophetically to the coming of the promised Messiah of Israel, the "Seed of the woman." When the power of prophesy came upon him he would say: "The Spirit of the Lord spoke by me, and his word was on my tongue."[169] At such moments of inspiration David composed the Messianic Psalms applicable to Jesus Christ and expounded in the New Testament.[170]

1. Messiah: He was counseled against by kings and rulers of the earth.

Why do the nations rage, and the peoples meditate a vain thing? The kings of the earth set themselves, and the rulers take counsel together, against Jehovah, and against his anointed, saying, Let us break their bonds asunder, and cast away their cords from us.

—Psalm 2:1–3

Prophesy fulfilled:

who by the Holy Spirit, by the mouth of our father David thy servant, didst say, Why did the Gentiles rage, and the peoples imagine vain things? The kings of the earth set themselves in array, and the rulers were gathered together, against the Lord, and against his Anointed: for of a truth in this city against thy holy Servant Jesus, whom thou didst anoint, both Herod and Pontius Pilate, with the Gentiles

---

[169] 2 Samuel 23:1–2.
[170] Wilson, T. E. The Messianic Psalms. Gospel Folio Press (Grand Rapids: MI, 1997). "Sometimes a whole Psalm applies to Christ (Psalm 22), sometimes a paragraph (Psalm 40:6–10), sometimes several verses (Psalm 69:4,9,21), sometimes a single verse (Psalm 41:9)."

and the peoples of Israel, were gathered together, to do whatsoever thy hand and thy council foreordained to come to pass.

—Acts 4:25–28

2. Messiah: He is revealed as the Son of God.

I will tell of the decree: Jehovah said unto me, Thou art my son; this day have I begotten thee. Ask of me, and I will give thee the nations for thine inheritance, and the uttermost parts of the earth for thy possession.

—Psalm 2:7–8

David ends the Psalm by directing attention to the consequence of refusing God's Son:

Kiss [submit to] the son, lest he be angry, and ye perish in the way, for his wrath will soon be kindled. Blessed are all they that take refuge in him.

—Psalm 2:12

Prophesy fulfilled: Matthew, Mark, Luke, John, Peter and the author of Hebrews all identify Jesus as the Son, the beloved Son, the Son of the Blessed, the Son of Man, the Son of the highest, and the only beloved Son:

…and lo, a voice out of the heavens, saying, This is my beloved Son, in whom I am well pleased.

—Matthew 3:17

Thou art the Christ, the Son of the living God.

—Matthew 16:16

…and a voice came out of the heavens, Thou art my beloved Son, in thee I am well pleased.

—Mark 1:11

And there came a cloud overshadowing them: and there came a voice out of the cloud, This is my beloved Son: hear ye him.

—Mark 9:7

Again the high priest asked him, and saith unto him, Art thou the Christ, the Son of the Blessed? And Jesus said, I am: and ye shall see the Son of man sitting at the right hand of Power, and coming with the clouds of heaven.

—Mark 14:61–62

He shall be great, and shall be called the Son of the Most High: and the Lord God shall give unto him the throne of his father David: and he shall reign over the house of Jacob for ever; and of his kingdom there shall be no end… And the angel answered and said unto her, The Holy Spirit shall come upon thee, and the power of the Most High shall overshadow thee: wherefore also the holy thing which is begotten shall be called the Son of God.

—Luke 1:32–33, 35

…and the Holy Spirit descended in a bodily form, as a dove, upon him, and a voice came out of heaven, Thou art my beloved Son; in thee I am well pleased.

—Luke 3:22

And a voice came out of the cloud, saying, This is my Son, my chosen: hear ye him.

—Luke 9:35

…God hath fulfilled the same unto our children, in that he raised up Jesus; as also it is written in the second psalm, Thou art my Son, this day have I begotten thee.

—Acts 13:33

For God so loved the world, that he gave his only begotten Son, that whosoever believeth on him should not perish, but have eternal life.

—John 3:16

She saith unto him, Yea, Lord: I have believed that thou art the Christ, the Son of God, even he that cometh into the world.

—John 11:27

…his Son, who was born of the seed of David according to the flesh, who was declared to be the Son of God with power, according to the spirit of holiness, by the resurrection from the dead.

—Romans 1:3–4

Part Three: Prophecies Fulfilled

For unto which of the angels said he at any time, Thou art my Son, This day have I begotten thee? and again, I will be to him a Father, and he shall be to me a Son?... but of the Son he saith, Thy throne, O God, is for ever and ever; and the sceptre of uprightness is the sceptre of thy kingdom.
—Hebrews 1:5, 8

For he received from God the Father honor and glory, when there was borne such a voice to him by the Majestic Glory, This is my beloved Son, in whom I am well pleased...
—2 Peter 1:17

...that which we have seen and heard declare we unto you also, that ye also may have fellowship with us: yea, and our fellowship is with the Father, and with his Son Jesus Christ...
—1 John 1:3

Herein was the love of God manifested in us, that God hath sent his only begotten Son into the world that we might live through him. Herein is love, not that we loved God, but that he loved us, and sent his Son to be the propitiation for our sins.
—1 John 4:9–10

And we know that the Son of God is come, and hath given us an understanding, that we know him that is true, and we are in him that is true, even in his Son Jesus Christ. This is the true God, and eternal life.
—1 John 5:20

3. Messiah: The Son of David will be praised by babes.

Out of the mouth of babes and sucklings hast thou established strength...
—Psalm 8:2

Prophesy fulfilled: On the triumphal entry into Jerusalem Jesus was surrounded by children singing: "Hosanna to the Son of David."[171] It was an expression understood to refer to the promised Messiah who would fulfill the ancient prophesy

---

171 Matthew 21:14–16. In verse 9, as Jesus made his triumphal entry into Jerusalem, "the multitude who went before and those who followed cried out: *"Hosanna to the son of David: Blessed is he that cometh in the name of the Lord; Hosanna in the highest."*

of the Seed of David.[172] The chief priests and scribes did not believe Jesus to be the promised Messiah, and accusingly they said to him: "Do you hear what these are saying?" Repeating the words of the Psalmist, Jesus replied:

I thank thee, O Father, Lord of heaven and earth, that thou didst hide these things from the wise and understanding, and didst reveal them unto babes...

—Matthew 11:25

And Jesus saith unto them, Yea: did ye never read, Out of the mouth of babes and sucklings thou hast perfected praise?

—Matthew 21:16

In that same hour he rejoiced in the Holy Spirit, and said, I thank thee, O Father, Lord of heaven and earth, that thou didst hide these things from the wise and understanding, and didst reveal them unto babes: yea, Father; for so it was well-pleasing in thy sight.

—Luke 10:21

4. Messiah: He did not to see corruption, but was resurrected from the dead.

Therefore my heart is glad, and my glory rejoiceth: my flesh also shall dwell in safety. For thou wilt not leave my soul to Sheol; neither wilt thou suffer thy holy one to see corruption.

—Psalm 16:9–10

Prophesy fulfilled: That David spoke of the resurrected Messiah is confirmed by the Apostles Mark, Luke and John.

And he saith unto them, Be not amazed: ye seek Jesus, the Nazarene, who hath been crucified: he is risen; he is not here: behold, the place where they laid him!

—Mark 16:6

He is not here, but is risen: remember how he spake unto you when he was yet in Galilee, saying that the Son of man must be delivered up into the hands of sinful men, and be crucified, and the third day rise again.

—Luke 24:6–7

---

[172] 2 Samuel 7:14–16; Romans 1:3; 2 Tim. 2:8.

Part Three: Prophecies Fulfilled

I beheld the Lord always before my face; for he is on my right hand, that I should not be moved: therefore my heart was glad, and my tongue rejoiced; moreover my flesh also shall dwell in hope: because thou wilt not leave my soul unto Hades, neither wilt thou give thy Holy One to see corruption... he foreseeing this spake of the resurrection of the Christ, that neither was he left unto Hades, nor did his flesh see corruption. This Jesus did God raise up, whereof we all are witnesses.

—Acts 2:25–27, 31–32

And we bring you good tidings of the promise made unto the fathers, that God hath fulfilled the same unto our children, in that he raised up Jesus; as also it is written in the second psalm, Thou art my Son, this day have I begotten thee. And as concerning that he raised him up from the dead, now no more to return to corruption, he hath spoken on this wise, I will give you the holy and sure blessings of David. Because he saith also in another psalm, Thou wilt not give thy Holy One to see corruption. For David, after he had in his own generation served the counsel of God, fell asleep, and was laid unto his fathers, and saw corruption: but he whom God raised up saw no corruption.

—Acts 13:32–37

For as yet they knew not the scripture, that he must rise again from the dead.

—John 20:9

...Christ died for our sins according to the scriptures; and that he was buried; and that he hath been raised on the third day according to the scriptures.

—1 Corinthians 15:3–4

5. Messiah: He was forsaken by God the Father.

My God, my God, why hast thou forsaken me? Why art thou so far from helping me, and from the words of my groaning?

—Psalm 22:1

Prophesy fulfilled: The same words were spoken by Jesus on the cross:

And about the ninth hour Jesus cried with a loud voice, saying, Eli, Eli, lama sabachthani? that is, My God, my God, why hast thou forsaken me?... And Jesus cried again with a loud voice, and yielded up his spirit.
—Matthew 27:46, 50

And at the ninth hour Jesus cried with a loud voice, Eloi, Eloi, lama sabachthani? which is, being interpreted, My God, my God, why hast thou forsaken me?... And Jesus uttered a loud voice, and gave up the ghost.
—Mark 15:34, 37

In their separate accounts of the sufferings of Jesus on the cross the Apostles Matthew and John write that *"these things came to pass, that the scripture might be fulfilled"* (John 19:36; see also John 19:28)" and *"that it might be fulfilled which was spoken through the prophet [Isaiah]..."* (Matthew 27:35).

Yet it pleased Jehovah to bruise him; he hath put him to grief: when thou shalt make his soul an offering for sin, he shall see his seed, he shall prolong his days, and the pleasure of Jehovah shall prosper in his hand. He shall see of the travail of his soul, and shall be satisfied: by the knowledge of himself shall my righteous servant justify many; and he shall bear their iniquities.
—Isaiah 53:10–11

6. Messiah: He was mocked, ridiculed by the priests, scribes and elders

All they that see me laugh me to scorn: they shoot out the lip, they shake the head, saying, commit thyself unto Jehovah; let him deliver him: let him rescue him, seeing he delighteth in him.
—Psalm 22:7–8

Prophesy fulfilled:

And they platted a crown of thorns and put it upon his head, and a reed in his right hand; and they kneeled down before him, and mocked him, saying, Hail, King of the Jews! And they spat upon him, and took the reed and smote him on the head. And when they had mocked him, they took off from him the robe, and put on him his garments, and led him away to crucify him.
—Matthew 27:29–31

Part Three: Prophecies Fulfilled

In like manner also the chief priests mocking him, with the scribes and elders, said, He saved others; himself he cannot save. He is the King of Israel; let him now come down from the cross, and we will believe on him. He trusteth on God; let him deliver him now, if he desireth him: for he said, I am the Son of God.
—Matthew 27:41–43

And they clothe him with purple, and platting a crown of thorns, they put it on him; and they began to salute him, Hail, King of the Jews! And they smote his head with a reed, and spat upon him, and bowing their knees worshipped him. And when they had mocked him, they took off from him the purple, and put on him his garments. And they lead him out to crucify him.
—Mark 15:17–20

For he shall be delivered up unto the Gentiles, and shall be mocked, and shamefully treated, and spit upon...
—Luke 18:32

And the men that held Jesus mocked him, and beat him.
—Luke 22:63

And the people stood beholding. And the rulers also scoffed at him, saying, He saved others; let him save himself, if this is the Christ of God, his chosen. And the soldiers also mocked him, coming to him, offering him vinegar...
—Luke 23:35–36

7. Messiah: He suffered many things on the cross and was set at nought.

Psalm 22 deals with the physical suffering endured by Messiah, *"how is it written of the Son of man, that he should suffer many things and be set at nought?"* (Mark 9:12)

I am poured out like water, and all my bones are out of joint: my heart is like wax; it is melted within me. My strength is dried up like a potsherd; and my tongue cleaveth to my jaws; and thou hast brought me into the dust of death. For dogs have compassed me: a company of evil-doers have inclosed me; they pierced my

Prophesies in Psalms

hands and my feet. I may count all my bones. They look and stare upon me; they part my garments among them, and upon my vesture do they cast lots.

—Psalm 22:14–18[173]

The physical and mental sufferings described by David precisely match the sufferings of Jesus as recorded in the Gospels.

8. Messiah: His hands, feet and side were pierced.

They pierced my hands and my feet.

—Psalm 22:16

Prophesy fulfilled:

...howbeit one of the soldiers with a spear pierced his side, and straightway there came out blood and water.

—John 19:34[174]

When following the resurrection Jesus appeared to His disciples he said to them:

See my hands and my feet, that it is I myself: handle me, and see; for a spirit hath not flesh and bones, as ye behold me having.

—Luke 24:39

Addressing the disciple Thomas, called Didymus, Jesus said:

Reach hither thy finger, and see my hands; and reach hither thy hand, and put it into my side: and be not faithless, but believing. Thomas answered and said unto him, My Lord and my God. Jesus saith unto him, Because thou hast seen me, thou hast believed: blessed are they that have not seen, and yet have believed.

—John 20:27–29

In reference to the Second Coming of Jesus, the Apostle John writes:

---

[173] Elsewhere in Psalm 69:21 David writes: "My strength is dried up like a potsherd; and my tongue cleaves to my jaws; and you have brought me into the dust of death."

[174] The issuing of blood and water may refer to the leakage of pleural and pericardial fluids.

> *And again another scripture saith, They shall look on him whom they pierced.*
> —John 19:37

> *Behold, he cometh with the clouds; and every eye shall see him, and they that pierced him.*
> —Revelation 1:7

9. Messiah: His garments were parted and soldiers cast lots for them.

> *They part my garments among them, and upon my vesture do they cast lots.*
> —Psalm 22:18

Prophesy fulfilled: The Apostles Matthew, Mark, Luke and John all write about the parting of Christ's garments: *"And when they had crucified him, they parted his garments among them, casting lots"* (Matthew 27:35).

> *And they crucify him, and part his garments among them, casting lots upon them, what each should take.*
> —Mark 15:24

> *And Jesus said, Father, forgive them; for they know not what they do. And parting his garments among them, they cast lots.*
> —Luke 23:34

> *The soldiers therefore, when they had crucified Jesus, took his garments and made four parts, to every soldier a part; and also the coat: now the coat was without seam, woven from the top throughout. They said therefore one to another, Let us not rend it, but cast lots for it, whose it shall be: that the scripture might be fulfilled, which saith, They parted my garments among them, and upon my vesture did they cast lots. These things therefore the soldiers did.*
> —John 19:23–25

10. Messiah: He is the good shepherd and the chief shepherd.

The opening verse of this Psalm reveals Messiah as the shepherd who cares for and leads his sheep.

Prophesies in Psalms

Jehovah is my shepherd; I shall not want.

—Psalm 23:1

Other Psalms of David speak about God's people as sheep, and of God as the shepherd (Psalm 79:13; 95:7; 100:3).

Prophesy fulfilled:

I am the good shepherd: the good shepherd layeth down his life for the sheep. He that is a hireling, and not a shepherd, whose own the sheep are not, beholdeth the wolf coming, and leaveth the sheep, and fleeth, and the wolf snatcheth them, and scattereth them: he fleethbecause he is a hireling, and careth not for the sheep. I am the good shepherd; and I know mine own, and mine own know me, even as the Father knoweth me, and I know the Father; and I lay down my life for the sheep. And other sheep I have, which are not of this fold: them also I must bring, and they shall hear my voice; and they shall become one flock, one shepherd.

—John 10:11–16

Those chosen to shepherd the flock of God are instructed by the Apostle Peter to follow the example of the Lord Jesus, the Chief Shepherd.

Tend the flock of God which is among you, exercising the oversight, not of constraint, but willingly, according to the will of God; nor yet for filthy lucre, but of a ready mind; neither as lording it over the charge allotted to you, but making yourselves ensamples to the flock. And when the chief Shepherd shall be manifested, ye shall receive the crown of glory that fadeth not away.

—1 Peter 5:2–4

11. Messiah: His last words on the cross before He gave up His Spirit to God.

Into thy hand I commend my spirit: thou hast redeemed me, O Jehovah, thou God of truth.

—Psalm 31:5

Prophesy fulfilled:

And Jesus, crying with a loud voice, said, Father, into thy hands I commend my spirit: and having said this, he gave up the ghost.

—Luke 23:46

Part Three: Prophecies Fulfilled

12. Messiah: His bones were not broken.

Many are the afflictions of the righteous; but Jehovah delivereth him out of them all. He keepeth all his bones: not one of them is broken.
—Psalm 34:19–20

Prophesy fulfilled: The Apostle John connects these verses from the Psalm with Jesus when he writes: "they broke not His legs."

The Jews therefore, because it was the Preparation, that the bodies should not remain on the cross upon the sabbath (for the day of that sabbath was a high day), asked of Pilate that their legs might be broken, and that they might be taken away. The soldiers therefore came, and brake the legs of the first, and of the other that was crucified with him: but when they came to Jesus, and saw that he was dead already, they brake not his legs: howbeit one of the soldiers with a spear pierced his side, and straightway there came out blood and water. And he that hath seen hath borne witness, and his witness is true: and he knoweth that he saith true, that ye also may believe. For these things came to pass, that the scripture might be fulfilled, A bone of him shall not be broken.
—John 19:31–36

The bones of Christ our Passover and Pascal lamb, were left unbroken like the bones of the Passover lamb mentioned by Moses:

In one house shall it be eaten; thou shalt not carry forth aught of the flesh abroad out of the house; neither shall ye break a bone thereof.
—Exodus 12:46

…they shall leave none of it unto the morning, nor break a bone thereof…
—Numbers 9:12

13. Messiah: Like a dumb man He opened not his mouth when charged falsely.

Unrighteous witnesses rise up; they ask me of things that I know not. They reward me evil for good, to the bereaving of my soul.
—Psalm 35:11–12

My lovers and my friends stand aloof from my plague; and my kinsmen stand afar off. They also that seek after my life lay snares for me; and they that seek my hurt speak mischievous things, and meditate deceits all the day long. But I, as a deaf man, hear not; and I am as a dumb man that openeth not his mouth. Yea, I am as a man that heareth not, and in whose mouth are no reproofs.

—Psalm 38:11–14

Prophesy fulfilled: The Apostles Matthew and Mark write that when accused by false witnesses, who deliberately misconstrued what Jesus had actually said about the temple of His body, He held His peace.

And the high priest stood up, and said unto him, Answerest thou nothing? what is it which these witness against thee? But Jesus held his peace. And the high priest said unto him, I adjure thee by the living God, that thou tell us whether thou art the Christ, the Son of God. Jesus saith unto him, Thou hast said: nevertheless I say unto you, Henceforth ye shall see the Son of man sitting at the right hand of Power, and coming on the clouds of heaven.

—Matthew 26:62–64

And when he was accused by the chief priests and elders, he answered nothing. Then saith Pilate unto him, Hearest thou not how many things they witness against thee? And he gave him no answer, not even to one word: insomuch that the governor marvelled greatly.

—Matthew 27:12–14

Now the chief priests and the whole council sought witness against Jesus to put him to death; and found it not. For many bare false witness against him, and their witness agreed not together. And there stood up certain, and bare false witness against him, saying, We heard him say, I will destroy this temple that is made with hands, and in three days I will build another made without hands. And not even so did their witness agree together. And the high priest stood up in the midst, and asked Jesus, saying, Answerest thou nothing? what is it which these witness against thee? But he held his peace, and answered nothing.

—Mark 14:55–61

And the chief priests accused him of many things. And Pilate again asked him, saying, Answerest thou nothing? behold how many things they accuse thee of. But Jesus no more answered anything; insomuch that Pilate marvelled.

—Mark 15:3–5

Now when Herod saw Jesus, he was exceeding glad: for he was of a long time desirous to see him, because he had heard concerning him; and he hoped to see some miracle done by him. And he questioned him in many words; but he answered him nothing.

—Luke 23:8–9

14. Messiah: He delighted to fulfill the will of God.

Sacrifice and offering thou hast no delight in; mine ears hast thou opened: burnt-offering and sin-offering hast thou not required. Then said I, Lo, I am come; in the roll of the book it is written of me: I delight to do thy will, O my God; yea, thy law is within my heart.

—Psalm 40:6–8

Prophesy fulfilled:

Jesus saith unto them, My meat is to do the will of him that sent me, and to accomplish his work.

—John 4:34

Wherefore when he cometh into the world, he saith, Sacrifice and offering thou wouldest not, but a body didst thou prepare for me; in whole burnt offerings and sacrifices for sin thou hadst no pleasure: then said I, Lo, I am come (In the roll of the book it is written of me) to do thy will, O God.

—Hebrew 10:5–7

Prophesies in Psalms

15. Messiah: He was betrayed by a friend.

Yea, mine own familiar friend, in whom I trusted, who did eat of my bread, hath lifted up his heel against me.

—Psalm 41:9[175]

For it was not an enemy that reproached me; then I could have borne it: neither was it he that hated me that did magnify himself against me; then I would have hid myself from him: but it was thou, a man mine equal, my companion, and my familiar friend. We took sweet counsel together; we walked in the house of God with the throng.

—Psalm 55:12–14

When he is judged, let him come forth guilty; and let his prayer be turned into sin. Let his days be few; and let another take his office.

—Psalm 109:7–8

Prophesy fulfilled: The betrayal of Jesus is referred to by the Apostles Matthew, Mark, Luke and John who all identify the betrayer as Judas Iscariot:

Then one of the twelve, who was called Judas Iscariot, went unto the chief priests, and said, What are ye willing to give me, and I will deliver him unto you? And they weighed unto him thirty pieces of silver. And from that time he sought opportunity to deliver him unto them.

—Matthew 26:14–16

...and as they were eating, he said, Verily I say unto you, that one of you shall betray me. And they were exceeding sorrowful, and began to say unto him every one, Is it I, Lord? And he answered and said, He that dipped his hand with me in the dish, the same shall betray me. The Son of man goeth, even as it is written of him: but woe unto that man through whom the Son of man is betrayed! good were it for that man if he had not been born. And Judas, who betrayed him, answered and said, Is it I, Rabbi? He saith unto him, Thou hast said.

—Matthew 26:21–25

---

[175] Perhaps a reference to David's friend Ahithophel (2 Samuel 15:12) who deserted David for Absalom and who later hanged himself (2 Samuel 17:1–23), like Judas Iscariot (Matthew 27:5).

Part Three: Prophecies Fulfilled

Now he that betrayed him gave them a sign, saying, Whomsoever I shall kiss, that is he: take him. And straightway he came to Jesus, and said, Hail, Rabbi; and kissed him.

—Matthew 26:48–49

Then Judas, who betrayed him, when he saw that he was condemned, repented himself, and brought back the thirty pieces of silver to the chief priests and elders, saying, I have sinned in that I betrayed innocent blood. But they said, What is that to us? see thou to it. And he cast down the pieces of silver into the sanctuary, and departed; and he went away and hanged himself.

—Matthew 27:3–5

For the Son of man goeth, even as it is written of him: but woe unto that man through whom the Son of man is betrayed! good were it for that man if he had not been born.

—Mark 14:21

And Satan entered into Judas who was called Iscariot, being of the number of the twelve. And he went away, and communed with the chief priests and captains, how he might deliver him unto them.

—Luke 22:3–4

For the Son of man indeed goeth, as it hath been determined: but woe unto that man through whom he is betrayed!

—Luke 22:22

While he yet spake, behold, a multitude, and he that was called Judas, one of the twelve, went before them; and he drew near unto Jesus to kiss him. But Jesus said unto him, Judas, betrayest thou the Son of man with a kiss?

—Luke 22:47–48

I speak not of you all: I know whom I have chosen: but that the scripture may be fulfilled, He that eateth my bread lifted up his heel against me... Verily, verily, I say unto you, that one of you shall betray me.

—John 13:18, 21

While I was with them, I kept them in thy name which thou hast given me: and I guarded them, and not one of them perished, but the son of perdition; that the scripture might be fulfilled.

—John 17:12

Brethren, it was needful that the scripture should be fulfilled, which the Holy Spirit spake before by the mouth of David concerning Judas, who was guide to them that took Jesus. For he was numbered among us, and received his portion in this ministry... For it is written in the book of Psalms [109:7–8], Let his habitation be made desolate, and let no man dwell therein:

and, His office let another take.

—Acts 1:16–17,20[176]

16. Messiah: His kingdom is forever a right scepter.

Thy throne, O God, is for ever and ever: a sceptre of equity is the sceptre of thy kingdom. Thou hast loved righteousness, and hated wickedness: therefore God, thy God, hath anointed thee with the oil of gladness above thy fellows.

—Psalm 45:6–7

Prophesy fulfilled:

...but of the Son he saith, Thy throne, O God, is for ever and ever; and the sceptre of uprightness is the sceptre of thy kingdom. Thou hast loved righteousness, and hated iniquity; therefore God, thy God, hath anointed thee with the oil of gladness above thy fellows.

—Hebrews 1:8–9

17. Messiah: He ascended on high.

Thou hast ascended on high, thou hast led away captives; thou hast received gifts among men, yea, among the rebellious also, that Jehovah God might dwell with them.

—Psalm 68:18

---

[176] Acts 1:25 speaks of *"this ministry and apostleship from which Judas fell."*

Part Three: Prophecies Fulfilled

Prophesy fulfilled:

So then the Lord Jesus, after he had spoken unto them, was received up into heaven, and sat down at the right hand of God.
—Mark 16:19

And it came to pass, while he blessed them, he parted from them, and was carried up into heaven.
—Luke 24:51

And when he had said these things, as they were looking, he was taken up; and a cloud received him out of their sight. And while they were looking stedfastly into heaven as he went, behold two men stood by them in white apparel; who also said, Ye men of Galilee, why stand ye looking into heaven? this Jesus, who was received up from you into heaven, shall so come in like manner as ye beheld him going into heaven.
—Acts 1:9–11

Wherefore he saith, When he ascended on high, he led captivity captive, and gave gifts unto men.
—Ephesians 4:8

Christ ascended to heaven like the prophets Enoch and Elijah (Genesis 5:22–24; 2 Kings 2:11–12), but not in the same manner.

18. Messiah: He was hated without a cause.

They that hate me without a cause are more than the hairs of my head: they that would cut me off, being mine enemies wrongfully, are mighty.
—Psalm 69:4

Let not them that are mine enemies wrongfully rejoice over me; neither let them wink with the eye that hate me without a cause. For they speak not peace; but they devise deceitful words against them that are quiet in the land. Yea, they opened their mouth wide against me; they said, Aha, aha, our eye hath seen it. Thou hast seen it, O Jehovah; keep not silence: O Lord, be not far from me.
—Psalm 35:19–22

They have compassed me about also with words of hatred, and fought against me without a cause. For my love they are my adversaries: but I give myself unto prayer.
—Psalm 109:3–4

Prophesy fulfilled:

If I had not done among them the works which none other did, they had not had sin: but now have they both seen and hated both me and my Father. But this cometh to pass, that the word may be fulfilled that is written in their law, They hated me without a cause.
—John 15:24–25

19. Messiah: His zeal for the Lord's House.

I am become a stranger unto my brethren, and an alien unto my mother's children. For the zeal of thy house hath eaten me up; and the reproaches of them that reproach thee are fallen upon me.
—Psalm 69:8–9

My zeal hath consumed me, because mine adversaries have forgotten thy words.
—Psalm 119:139

Prophesy fulfilled: The Apostle John report that the disciples later recalled the words of David as applied to Jesus.

His disciples remembered that it was written, Zeal for thy house shall eat me up.
—John 2:17

20. Messiah: He was given vinegar to drink.

They gave me also gall for my food; and in my thirst they gave me vinegar to drink.
—Psalm 69:21

Prophesy fulfilled: Matthew, Mark, Luke and John all apply this passage to Jesus:

Part Three: Prophecies Fulfilled

...they gave him wine to drink mingled with gall: and when he had tasted it, he would not drink... And straightway one of them ran, and took a sponge, and filled it with vinegar, and put it on a reed, and gave him to drink.
—Matthew 27:34, 48

And they offered him wine mingled with myrrh: but he received it not.
—Mark 15:23

And one ran, and filling a sponge full of vinegar, put it on a reed, and gave him to drink, saying, Let be; let us see whether Elijah cometh to take him down.
—Mark 15:36

And the soldiers also mocked him, coming to him, offering him vinegar...
—Luke 23:36

After this Jesus, knowing that all things are now finished, that the scripture might be accomplished, saith, I thirst. There was set there a vessel full of vinegar: so they put a sponge full of the vinegar upon hyssop, and brought it to his mouth. When Jesus therefore had received the vinegar, he said, It is finished: and he bowed his head, and gave up his spirit.
—John 19:28–30

21. Messiah: He is presented with gifts and Kings will bow before Him.

The kings of Tarshish and of the isles shall render tribute: the kings of Sheba and Seba shall offer gifts. Yea, all kings shall fall down before him; all nations shall serve him... And they shall live; and to him shall be given of the gold of Sheba: and men shall pray for him continually; they shall bless him all the day long.
—Psalm 72:10–11, 15

Prophesy fulfilled and pending: When Christ was born, wise Magi from the East brought gifts of gold, frankincense and myrrh.

Now when Jesus was born in Bethlehem of Judaea in the days of Herod the king, behold, Wise-men from the east came to Jerusalem, saying, Where is he that is born King of the Jews? for we saw his star in the east, and are come to worship him... And they came into the house and saw the young child with Mary his mother; and they fell down and worshipped him; and opening their treasures they offered unto him gifts, gold and frankincense and myrrh.

—Matthew 2:1–2, 11

22. Messiah: He spoke the Wisdom of God in parables.

I will open my mouth in a parable; I will utter dark sayings of old, which we have heard and known, and our fathers have told us. We will not hide them from their children, telling to the generation to come the praises of Jehovah, and his strength, and his wondrous works that he hath done.

—Psalm 78:2–4

Prophesy fulfilled: The Apostles Matthew and Mark write that Jesus taught in parables, and John tells us that He taught in parables and in proverbs:

And he spake to them many things in parables...

—Matthew 13:3

Therefore speak I to them in parables; because seeing they see not, and hearing they hear not, neither do they understand. And unto them is fulfilled the prophecy of Isaiah [6:9–10], which saith, By hearing ye shall hear, and shall in no wise understand; and seeing ye shall see, and shall in no wise perceive: for this people's heart is waxed gross, and their ears are dull of hearing, and their eyes they have closed; lest haply they should perceive with their eyes, and hear with their ears, and understand with their heart, and should turn again, and I should heal them.

—Matthew 13:13–15

All these things spake Jesus in parables unto the multitudes; and without a parable spake he nothing unto them: that it might be fulfilled which was spoken through the prophet [Psalm 78:6–2], saying, I will open my mouth in parables; I will utter things hidden from the foundation of the world.

—Matthew 13:34–35

And with many such parables spake he the word unto them, as they were able to hear it; and without a parable spake he not unto them: but privately to his own disciples he expounded all things.

—Mark 4:33–34

Part Three: Prophecies Fulfilled

And he began to speak unto them in parables.

—Mark 12:1

These things have I spoken unto you in dark sayings: the hour cometh, when I shall no more speak unto you in dark sayings, but shall tell you plainly of the Father.

—John 16:25

23. Messiah: The Son of David His kingdom will be established forever.

I have made a covenant with my chosen, I have sworn unto David my servant: thy seed will I establish for ever, and build up thy throne to all generations.

—Psalm 89:3–4

I also will make him my first-born, the highest of the kings of the earth. My lovingkindness will I keep for him for evermore; and my covenant shall stand fast with him.

—Psalm 89:27–28

My covenant will I not break, nor alter the thing that is gone out of my lips. Once have I sworn by my holiness: I will not lie unto David: his seed shall endure for ever, ad his throne as the sun before me. It shall be established for ever as the moon, and as the faithful witness in the sky.

—Psalms 89:34–37

Prophesy fulfilled: The Apostles Matthew, Mark and Luke all report that the people believed Jesus to be the Son of David.

And as Jesus passed by from thence, two blind men followed him, crying out, and saying, Have mercy on us, thou son of David.

—Matthew 9:27

And all the multitudes were amazed, and said, Can this be the son of David?

—Matthew 12:23

And behold, a Canaanitish woman came out from those borders, and cried, saying, Have mercy on me, O Lord, thou son of David.

—Matthew 15:22

And behold, two blind men sitting by the way side, when they heard that Jesus was passing by, cried out, saying, Lord, have mercy on us, thou son of David.

—Matthew 20:30

And the multitudes that went before him, and that followed, cried, saying, Hosanna to the son of David: Blessed is he that cometh in the name of the Lord; Hosanna in the highest… But when the chief priests and the scribes saw the wonderful things that he did, and the children that were crying in the temple and saying, Hosanna to the son of David; they were moved with indignation…

—Matthew 21:9, 15

And Jesus answered and said, as he taught in the temple, How say the scribes that the Christ is the son of David?

—Mark 12:35

And he cried, saying, Jesus, thou son of David, have mercy on me. And they that went before rebuked him, that he should hold his peace: but he cried out the more a great deal, Thou son of David, have mercy on me.

—Luke 18:38–39

24. Messiah: He was tempted by the Devil.

There shall no evil befall thee, neither shall any plague come nigh thy tent. For he will give his angels charge over thee, to keep thee in all thy ways. They shall bear thee up in their hands, lest thou dash thy foot against a stone.

—Psalm 91:10–12

Prophesy fulfilled:

Then the devil taketh him into the holy city; and he set him on the pinnacle of the temple, and saith unto him, If thou art the Son of God, cast thyself down: for it is written, He shall give his angels charge concerning thee: and, On their hands they shall bear thee up, lest haply thou dash thy foot against a stone.

—Matthew 4:5–6

25. Messiah: The preexistent and pre-incarnate Son is the Creator and His years will have no end.

Part Three: Prophecies Fulfilled

Of old didst thou lay the foundation of the earth; and the heavens are the work of thy hands. They shall perish, but thou shalt endure; yea, all of them shall wax old like a garment; as a vesture shalt thou change them, and they shall be changed: but thou art the same, and thy years shall have no end.

—Psalm 102:25–27

Prophesy fulfilled: The Apostles John and Paul, and the author of The Epistle to the Hebrews, all attribute the creative act to the Word, the pre-incarnate Christ, the Son of God.

In the beginning was the Word, and the Word was with God, and the Word was God. The same was in the beginning with God. All things were made through him; and without him was not anything made that hath been made.

—John 1:1–3

He was in the world, and the world was made through him, and the world knew him not.

—John 1:10

…yet to us there is one God, the Father, of whom are all things, and we unto him; and one Lord, Jesus Christ, through whom are all things, and we through him.

—I Corinthians. 8:6

…for in him were all things created, in the heavens and upon the earth, things visible and things invisible, whether thrones or dominions or principalities or powers; all things have been created through him, and unto him.

—Colossians 1:16

God, having of old time spoken unto the fathers in the prophets by divers portions and in divers manners, hath at the end of these days spoken unto us in his Son, whom he appointed heir of all things, through whom also he made the worlds… Thou, Lord, in the beginning didst lay the foundation of the earth, and the heavens are the works of thy hands: they shall perish; but thou continuest: and they all shall wax old as doth a garment; and as a mantle shalt thou roll them up, as a garment, and they shall be changed: but thou art the same, and thy years shall not fail.

—Hebrews 1:1–2, 10–12

Unto me, who am less than the least of all saints, was this grace given, to preach unto the Gentiles the unsearchable riches of Christ; and to make all men see what is the dispensation of the mystery which for ages hath been hid in God who created all things.
—Ephesians 3:8–9

And to the angel of the church in Laodicea write: these things saith the Amen, the faithful and true witness, the beginning of the creation of God...
—Revelation 3:14

Worthy art thou, our Lord and our God, to receive the glory and the honor and the power: for thou didst create all things, and because of thy will they were, and were created.
—Revelation 4:11

26. Messiah: He became a reproach.

I am become also a reproach unto them: when they see me, they shake their head.
—Psalm 109:25

Prophesy fulfilled:

And they that passed by railed on him, wagging their heads...
—Matthew 27:39

27. Messiah: He will be seated at the right hand of the Father.

Jehovah saith unto my Lord, Sit thou at my right hand, until I make thine enemies thy footstool.
—Psalm 110:1

Prophesy fulfilled:

The Lord said unto my Lord, Sit thou on my right hand, till I put thine enemies underneath thy feet?
—Matthew 22:44

Part Three: Prophecies Fulfilled

So then the Lord Jesus, after he had spoken unto them, was received up into heaven, and sat down at the right hand of God.

—Mark 16:19

For David himself saith in the book of Psalms, the Lord said unto my Lord, Sit thou on my right hand, till I make thine enemies the footstool of thy feet.

—Luke 20:42–43

But from henceforth shall the Son of man be seated at the right hand of the power of God. And they all said, Art thou then the Son of God? And he said unto them, Ye say that I am.

—Luke 22:69–70

For David ascended not into the heavens: but he saith himself, the Lord said unto my Lord, Sit thou on my right hand, till I make thine enemies the footstool of thy feet.

—Acts 2:34–35

Him did God exalt with his right hand to be a Prince and a Saviour, to give repentance to Israel, and remission of sins. And we are witnesses of these things; and so is the Holy Spirit, whom God hath given to them that obey him.

—Acts 5:31–32

But he [Philip], being full of the Holy Spirit, looked up stedfastly into heaven, and saw the glory of God, and Jesus standing on the right hand of God, and said, Behold, I see the heavens opened, and the Son of man standing on the right hand of God.

—Acts 7:55–56

Elsewhere the Apostle Paul refers to the ascension of Christ, and of Christ being seated at the right hand of God:

…who is he that condemneth? It is Christ Jesus that died, yea rather, that was raised from the dead, who is at the right hand of God, who also maketh intercession for us.

—Romans 8:34

...which he wrought in Christ, when he raised him from the dead, and made him to sit at his right hand in the heavenly places, far above all rule, and authority, and power, and dominion, and every name that is named, not only in this world, but also in that which is to come: and he put all things in subjection under his feet, and gave him to be head over all things to the church, which is his body, the fulness of him that filleth all in all.

—Ephesians 1:20–23

If then ye were raised together with Christ, seek the things that are above, where Christ is, seated on the right hand of God.

—Colossians 3:1

...who being the effulgence of his glory, and the very image of his substance, and upholding all things by the word of his power, when he had made purification of sins, sat down on the right hand of the Majesty on high.

—Hebrews 1:3

Now in the things which we are saying the chief point is this: We have such a high priest, who sat down on the right hand of the throne of the Majesty in the heavens...

—Hebrews 8:1

...but he, when he had offered one sacrifice for sins for ever, sat down on the right hand of God.

—Hebrews 10:12

...looking unto Jesus the author and perfecter of our faith, who for the joy that was set before him endured the cross, despising shame, and hath sat down at the right hand of the throne of God.

—Hebrews 12:2

...[Christ] who is on the right hand of God, having gone into heaven; angels and authorities and powers being made subject unto him.

—1 Peter 3:22

28. Messiah: A priest of God Most High after the order of Melchizedek.

Part Three: Prophecies Fulfilled

> *Jehovah hath sworn, and will not repent: Thou art a priest for ever after the order of Melchizedek.*
>
> —Psalms 110:4

Abraham's encounter with Melchizedek of Salem, the priest of God Most High, took place following Lot's captivity and rescue. He met up with Melchizedek of Salem (a type of Jesus Christ) of whom Moses writes:

> *And Melchizedek king of Salem brought forth bread and wine: and he was priest of God Most High. And he blessed him, and said, Blessed be Abram of God Most High, possessor of heaven and earth: and blessed be God Most High, who hath delivered thine enemies into thy hand. And he gave him a tenth of all.*
>
> —Genesis 14:18–20

Prophesy fulfilled: The author of Hebrews has much to say about this Melchizedek, king of Salem:

> *So Christ also glorified not himself to be made a high priest, but he that spake unto him, Thou art my Son, this day have I begotten thee: as he saith also in another place, Thou art a priest for ever after the order of Melchizedek... named of God a high priest after the order of Melchizedek.*
>
> —Hebrews 5:5–6, 10

> *...whither as a forerunner Jesus entered for us, having become a high priest for ever after the order of Melchizedek.*
>
> —Hebrews 6:20

> *For this Melchizedek, king of Salem, priest of God Most High, who met Abraham returning from the slaughter of the kings and blessed him, to whom also Abraham divided a tenth part of all (being first, by interpretation, King of righteousness, and then also King of Salem, which is, King of peace; without father, without mother, without genealogy, having neither beginning of days nor end of life, but made like unto the Son of God), abideth a priest continually.*
>
> —Hebrews 7:1–3

> *And what we say is yet more abundantly evident, if after the likeness of Melchizedek there ariseth another priest, who hath been made, not after the law of a carnal*

commandment, but after the power of an endless life: for it is witnessed of him, Thou art a priest for ever after the order of Melchizedek.

—Hebrews 7:15–17

29. Messiah: He was the rejected stone that became the Head cornerstone.

The stone which the builders rejected is become the head of the corner... Blessed be he that cometh in the name of Jehovah...

—Psalm 118:22, 26
(see also Isaiah 28:16)

Prophesy fulfilled:

Jesus saith unto them, Did ye never read in the scriptures, the stone which the builders rejected, the same was made the head of the corner; this was from the Lord, and it is marvellous in our eyes?

—Matthew 21:42

Have ye not read even this scripture: The stone which the builders rejected, the same was made the head of the corner; this was from the Lord, and it is marvellous in our eyes?

—Mark 12:10–11

But he looked upon them, and said, What then is this that is written, the stone which the builders rejected, the same was made the head of the corner? Every one that falleth on that stone shall be broken to pieces; but on whomsoever it shall fall, it will scatter him as dust

—Luke 20:17–18

So then ye are no more strangers and sojourners, but ye are fellow-citizens with the saints, and of the household of God, being built upon the foundation of the apostles and prophets, Christ Jesus himself being the chief corner stone; in whom each several building, fitly framed together, groweth into a holy temple in the Lord; in whom ye also are builded together for a habitation of God in the Spirit.

—Ephesians 2:19–22

...unto whom coming, a living stone, rejected indeed of men, but with God elect, precious, ye also, as living stones, are built up a spiritual house, to be a

holy priesthood, to offer up spiritual sacrifices, acceptable to God through Jesus Christ. Because it is contained in scripture, Behold, I lay in Zion a chief corner stone, elect, precious: and he that believeth on him shall not be put to shame. For you therefore that believe is the preciousness: but for such as disbelieve, The stone which the builders rejected, the same was made the head of the corner; and, A stone of stumbling, and a rock of offence; for they stumble at the word, being disobedient: whereunto also they were appointed.

—1 Peter 2:4–8

30. Messiah: The Seed of David will sit on the throne of His father David.

Jehovah hath sworn unto David in truth; he will not turn from it: of the fruit of thy body will I set upon thy throne. If thy children will keep my covenant and my testimony that I shall teach them, their children also shall sit upon thy throne for evermore.

—Psalm 32:11–12

Prophesy fulfilled: King David understood that God, by the covenant promises given to the earlier Patriarchs, had guaranteed that the "Seed of the woman," the Lord's Messiah, would be a descendant of David and arise as an everlasting anointed Prophet, Priest, and King to sit on the throne of David. This is confirmed by the Apostle Luke who writes:

And behold, thou shalt conceive in thy womb, and bring forth a son, and shalt call his name Jesus. He shall be great, and shall be called the Son of the Most High: and the Lord God shall give unto him the throne of his father David: and he shall reign over the house of Jacob for ever; and of his kingdom there shall be no end.

—Luke 1:31–33

Brethren, I may say unto you freely of the patriarch David, that he both died and was buried, and his tomb is with us unto this day. Being therefore a prophet, and knowing that God had sworn with an oath to him, that of the fruit of his loins he would set one upon his throne; he foreseeing this spake of the resurrection of the Christ, that neither was he left unto Hades, nor did his flesh see corruption. This Jesus did God raise up, whereof we all are witnesses.

—Acts 2:29–32

And when he had removed him, he raised up David to be their king; to whom also he bare witness and said, I have found David the son of Jesse, a man after my heart, who shall do all my will. Of this man's seed hath God according to promise brought unto Israel a Saviour, Jesus.

—Acts 13:22–23

Elsewhere Jesus is referred to as *"the son of David"* (Matthew 1:1), *"born of the seed of David according to the flesh"* (Romans 1:3), and as *"the root and the offspring of David, the bright, the morning star"* (Revelation 22:16).

Chapter Eighteen
PROPHESIES IN PROVERBS

1. Messiah: He will be called the Son of God.

Who hath ascended up into heaven, and descended? Who hath gathered the wind in his fists? Who hath bound the waters in his garment? Who hath established all the ends of the earth? What is his name, and what is his son's name, if thou knowest?

—Proverbs 30:4

Prophesy fulfilled: The Apostles Matthew, Mark, Luke and Paul all identify the Son as Jesus:

...and lo, a voice out of the heavens, saying, This is my beloved Son, in whom I am well pleased.

—Matthew 3:17

And Simon Peter answered and said, Thou art the Christ, the Son of the living God.

—Matthew 16:16

While he was yet speaking, behold, a bright cloud overshadowed them: and behold, a voice out of the cloud, saying, This is my beloved Son, in whom I am well pleased; hear ye him.

—Matthew 17:5

...and a voice came out of the heavens, Thou art my beloved Son, in thee I am well pleased.

—Mark 1:11

And the angel answered and said unto her, The Holy Spirit shall come upon thee, and the power of the Most High shall overshadow thee: wherefore also the holy thing which is begotten shall be called the Son of God.
—Luke 1:35

…and the Holy Spirit descended in a bodily form, as a dove, upon him, and a voice came out of heaven, Thou art my beloved Son; in thee I am well pleased.
—Luke 3:22

For he received from God the Father honor and glory, when there was borne such a voice to him by the Majestic Glory, This is my beloved Son, in whom I am well pleased…
—2 Peter 1:17

For unto which of the angels said he at any time, Thou art my Son, this day have I begotten thee? and again, I will be to him a Father, and he shall be to me a Son?
—Hebrews 1:5

Although the religious leaders did not recognize Jesus as the son of God, Satan and his demons did. The Apostle Luke writes that Satan recognized Jesus as the Son of God (Luke 4:3). One unclean demon cried out with a loud voice, saying, *"I know thee who thou art, the Holy One of God"* (Luke 4:34). Other demons cried, *"Thou art the Son of God. And rebuking them, he suffered them not to speak, because they knew that he was the Christ"* (Luke 4:41). Still another demon, when he saw Jesus, cried out with a loud voice saying, *"What have we to do with thee, thou Son of God"* (Matthew 8:29).

Chapter Nineteen

PROPHESIES IN ISAIAH

1. Messiah: He will rebuild the Lord's house and all nations shall flow to it.

And it shall come to pass in the latter days, that the mountain of Jehovah's house shall be established on the top of the mountains, and shall be exalted above the hills; and all nations shall flow unto it. And many peoples shall go and say, Come ye, and let us go up to the mountain of Jehovah, to the house of the God of Jacob; and he will teach us of his ways, and we will walk in his paths: for out of Zion shall go forth the law, and the word of Jehovah from Jerusalem.

—Isaiah 2:2–3

Prophesy to be fulfilled:

After these things I will return, and I will build again the tabernacle of David, which is fallen; and I will build again the ruins thereof, and I will set it up: that the residue of men may seek after the Lord, and all the Gentiles, upon whom my name is called…

—Acts 15:16–17
(see also Amos 9:11–12)

Who shall ascend into the hill of Jehovah? And who shall stand in his holy place? He that hath clean hands, and a pure heart.

—Psalm 24:3–4

Only those Jews and Gentiles who by faith have been accounted righteous may ascend the Mountain of the Lord of hosts, the Holy Mountain (Zechariah 8:3).

Part Three: Prophecies Fulfilled

2. Messiah: He is the Branch of the Lord.

In that day shall the branch of Jehovah be beautiful and glorious, and the fruit of the land shall be excellent and comely for them that are escaped of Israel. And it shall come to pass, that he that is left in Zion, and he that remaineth in Jerusalem, shall be called holy, even every one that is written among the living in Jerusalem.

—Isaiah 4:2–3

Prophesy to be fulfilled: Isaiah writes of the expected blessings that Messiah, the "Branch of the Lord," will bestow on that day on his holy people in Zion and Jerusalem.

3. Messiah: He was unheeded by His people.

And he said, Go, and tell this people, Hear ye indeed, but understand not; and see ye indeed, but perceive not. Make the heart of this people fat, and make their ears heavy, and shut their eyes; lest they see with their eyes, and hear with their ears, and understand with their heart, and turn again, and be healed.

—Isaiah 6:9–10

Prophesy fulfilled:

And the disciples came, and said unto him, Why speakest thou unto them in parables? And he answered and said unto them, Unto you it is given to know the mysteries of the kingdom of heaven, but to them it is not given... And unto them is fulfilled the prophecy of Isaiah, which saith, By hearing ye shall hear, and shall in no wise understand; and seeing ye shall see, and shall in no wise perceive: for this people's heart is waxed gross, and their ears are dull of hearing, and their eyes they have closed; lest haply they should perceive with their eyes, and hear with their ears, and understand with their heart, and should turn again, and I should heal them.

—Matthew 10:10–11, 14–15

Well spake the Holy Spirit through Isaiah the prophet unto your fathers, saying, Go thou unto this people, and say, By hearing ye shall hear, and shall in no wise understand; and seeing ye shall see, and shall in no wise perceive...

—Acts 28:25–26

Prophesies in Isaiah

4. Messiah: He was born of a Virgin and given honorific titles.

Therefore the Lord himself will give you a sign: behold, a virgin shall conceive, and bear a son, and shall call his name Immanuel.

—Isaiah 7:14

For unto us a child is born, unto us a son is given; and the government shall be upon his shoulder: and his name shall be called Wonderful, Counsellor, Mighty God, Everlasting Father, Prince of Peace. Of the increase of his government and of peace there shall be no end, upon the throne of David, and upon his kingdom, to establish it, and to uphold it with justice and with righteousness from henceforth even for ever. The zeal of Jehovah of hosts will perform this.

—Isaiah 9:6–7

Prophesy fulfilled:

Now all this is come to pass, that it might be fulfilled which was spoken by the Lord through the prophet, saying, Behold, the virgin shall be with child, and shall bring forth a son, and they shall call his name Immanuel; which is, being interpreted, God with us.

—Matthew 1:22–23

...for there is born to you this day in the city of David a Saviour, who is Christ the Lord.

—Luke 2:11

Now in the sixth month the angel Gabriel was sent from God unto a city of Galilee, named Nazareth, to a virgin betrothed to a man whose name was Joseph, of the house of David; and the virgin's name was Mary.

—Luke 1:26–27

The Apostle John speaks of the birth of Jesus as the incarnation of the pre-existing Word (Logos).

And the Word became flesh, and dwelt among us (and we beheld his glory, glory as of the only begotten from the Father), full of grace and truth.

—John 1:14

Part Three: Prophecies Fulfilled

5. Messiah: He is the stone of stumbling and rock of offense.

Jehovah of hosts, him shall ye sanctify; and let him be your fear, and let him be your dread. And he shall be for a sanctuary; but for a stone of stumbling and for a rock of offence to both the houses of Israel, for a gin and for a snare to the inhabitants of Jerusalem. And many shall stumble thereon, and fall, and be broken, and be snared, and be taken.

—Isaiah 8:13–15

Prophesy fulfilled: The Apostles Luke, Paul and Peter identify Jesus as the rejected stone prophesied by David and by the Prophet Isaiah.

But he looked upon them, and said, What then is this that is written, the stone which the builders rejected, the same was made the head of the corner? Every one that falleth on that stone shall be broken to pieces; but on whomsoever it shall fall, it will scatter him as dust.

—Luke 20:17–18

But they cried out all together, saying, Away with this man, and release unto us Barabbas...

—Luke 23:18

He came unto his own, and they that were his own received him not.

—John 1:11

He is the stone which was set at nought of you the builders, which was made the head of the corner. And in none other is there salvation: for neither is there any other name under heaven, that is given among men, wherein we must be saved.

—Acts 4:11–12

...Israel, following after a law of righteousness, did not arrive at that law. Wherefore? Because they sought it not by faith, but as it were by works. They stumbled at the stone of stumbling; even as it is written, Behold, I lay in Zion a stone of stumbling and a rock of offence: and he that believeth on him shall not be put to shame.

—Romans 9:31–33

Seeing that Jews ask for signs, and Greeks seek after wisdom: but we preach Christ crucified, unto Jews a stumblingblock, and unto Gentiles foolishness; but unto them that are called, both Jews and Greeks, Christ the power of God, and the wisdom of God. Because the foolishness of God is wiser than men; and the weakness of God is stronger than men.

—1 Corinthians 1:22–25

...unto whom coming, a living stone, rejected indeed of men, but with God elect, precious, ye also, as living stones, are built up a spiritual house, to be a holy priesthood, to offer up spiritual sacrifices, acceptable to God through Jesus Christ. Because it is contained in scripture, Behold, I lay in Zion a chief corner stone, elect, precious: and he that believeth on him shall not be put to shame. For you therefore that believe is the preciousness: but for such as disbelieve, The stone which the builders rejected, the same was made the head of the corner; and, A stone of stumbling, and a rock of offence; for they stumble at the word, being disobedient: whereunto also they were appointed.

—1 Peter 2:4–8

6. Messiah: He is a shining Light to the Gentiles.

But there shall be no gloom to her that was in anguish. In the former time he brought into contempt the land of Zebulun and the land of Naphtali; but in the latter time hath he made it glorious, by the way of the sea, beyond the Jordan, Galilee of the nations. The people that walked in darkness have seen a great light: they that dwelt in the land of the shadow of death, upon them hath the light shined.

—Isaiah 9:1–2

I, Jehovah, have called thee in righteousness, and will hold thy hand, and will keep thee, and give thee for a covenant of the people, for a light of the Gentiles; to open the blind eyes, to bring out the prisoners from the dungeon, and them that sit in darkness out of the prison-house.

—Isaiah 42:6–7

I will also give thee for a light to the Gentiles, that thou mayest be my salvation unto the end of the earth.

—Isaiah 49:6

Part Three: Prophecies Fulfilled

Prophesy fulfilled: The Apostles Matthew and Luke associate Isaiah 9:1–2 with the onset of the preaching ministry of Jesus:

> ...and leaving Nazareth, he came and dwelt in Capernaum, which is by the sea, in the borders of Zebulun and Naphtali: that it might be fulfilled which was spoken through Isaiah the prophet, saying, The land of Zebulun and the land of Naphtali, toward the sea, beyond the Jordan, Galilee of the Gentiles, the people that sat in darkness saw a great light, and to them that sat in the region and shadow of death, to them did light spring up. From that time began Jesus to preach, and to say, Repent ye; for the kingdom of heaven is at hand.
> —Matthew 4:13–17

> For mine eyes have seen thy salvation, which thou hast prepared before the face of all peoples; a light for revelation to the Gentiles, and the glory of thy people Israel.
> —Luke 2:30–32

> In him was life; and the life was the light of men. And the light shineth in the darkness.
> —John 1:4–5

> Again therefore Jesus spake unto them, saying, I am the light of the world: he that followeth me shall not walk in the darkness, but shall have the light of life.
> —John 8:12

> For so hath the Lord commanded us, saying, I have set thee for a light of the Gentiles, that thou shouldest be for salvation unto the uttermost part of the earth. And as the Gentiles heard this, they were glad, and glorified the word of God: and as many as were ordained to eternal life believed.
> —Acts 13:47–48

> ...that the Christ must suffer, and how that he first by the resurrection of the dead should proclaim light both to the people and to the Gentiles.
> —Acts 26:23

7. Messiah: His government will be forever.

> Of the increase of his government and of peace there shall be no end, upon the throne of David, and upon his kingdom, to establish it, and to uphold it with

Prophesies in Isaiah

justice and with righteousness from henceforth even for ever. The zeal of Jehovah of hosts will perform this.

—Isaiah 9:7

Prophesy to be fulfilled: Luke writes that he will reign over the house of Jacob forever, and of His kingdom there will be no end.

He shall be great, and shall be called the Son of the Most High: and the Lord God shall give unto him the throne of his father David: and he shall reign over the house of Jacob for ever; and of his kingdom there shall be no end.

—Luke 1:32–33

8. Messiah: He will gather the dispersed of Judah, and draw the Gentiles.

And it shall come to pass in that day, that the Lord will set his hand again the second time to recover the remnant of his people, that shall remain, from Assyria, and from Egypt, and from Pathros, and from Cush, and from Elam, and from Shinar, and from Hamath, and from the islands of the sea. And he will set up an ensign for the nations, and will assemble the outcasts of Israel, and gather together the dispersed of Judah from the four corners of the earth.

—Isaiah 11:11–12

Prophesy to be fulfilled:

And again, Isaiah saith, There shall be the root of Jesse, and he that ariseth to rule over the Gentiles; on him shall the Gentiles hope.

—Romans 15:12

9. Messiah: He shall sit on the throne of David and judge righteously.

And a throne shall be established in lovingkindness; and one shall sit thereon in truth, in the tent of David, judging, and seeking justice, and swift to do righteousness.

—Isaiah 16:5

Prophesy to be fulfilled:

He shall be great, and shall be called the Son of the Most High: and the Lord God shall give unto him the throne of his father David: and he shall reign over the house of Jacob for ever; and of his kingdom there shall be no end.
—Luke 1:32–33

10. Messiah: He will swallow up death in Victory and the dead shall rise.

He hath swallowed up death for ever; and the Lord Jehovah will wipe away tears from off all faces; and the reproach of his people will he take away from off all the earth: for Jehovah hath spoken it. And it shall be said in that day, Lo, this is our God; we have waited for him, and he will save us: this is Jehovah; we have waited for him, we will be glad and rejoice in his salvation.
—Isaiah 25:8–9

Thy dead shall live; my dead bodies shall arise. Awake and sing, ye that dwell in the dust; for thy dew is as the dew of herbs, and the earth shall cast forth the dead.
—Isaiah 26:19

Prophesy to be fulfilled: In his letter to the Corinthian church the Apostle Paul provides the following account of the future bodily resurrection of the dead in Christ:

So also is the resurrection of the dead. It is sown in corruption; it is raised in incorruption: it is sown in dishonor; it is raised in glory: it is sown in weakness; it is raised in power: it is sown a natural body; it is raised a spiritual body. If there is a natural body, there is also a spiritual body... Behold, I tell you a mystery: We all shall not sleep, but we shall all be changed, in a moment, in the twinkling of an eye, at the last trump: for the trumpet shall sound, and the dead shall be raised incorruptible, and we shall be changed. For this corruptible must put on incorruption, and this mortal must put on immortality.
—1 Corinthians 15:42–44, 51–53[177]

---

[177] *"...who shall fashion anew the body of our humiliation, that it may be conformed to the body of his glory, according to the working whereby he is able even to subject all things unto himself"* (Philippians 3:21).

Prophesies in Isaiah

11. Messiah: He will deliver and purge Jacob of iniquity.

...when the Lord shall have washed away the filth of the daughters of Zion, and shall have purged the blood of Jerusalem from the midst thereof, by the spirit of justice, and by the spirit of burning. And Jehovah will create over the whole habitation of mount Zion, and over her assemblies, a cloud and smoke by day, and the shining of a flaming fire by night; for over all the glory shall be spread a covering.

—Isaiah 4:4–5

Therefore by this shall the iniquity of Jacob be forgiven, and this is all the fruit of taking away his sin: that he maketh all the stones of the altar as chalkstones that are beaten in sunder, so that the Asherim and the sun-images shall rise no more.

—Isaiah 27:9

Prophesy to be fulfilled:

...and so all Israel shall be saved: even as it is written, There shall come out of Zion the Deliverer; he shall turn away ungodliness from Jacob: and this is my covenant unto them, when I shall take away their sins.

—Romans 11:26–27

...whose fan is in his hand, and he will thoroughly cleanse his threshing-floor; and he will gather his wheat into the garner, but the chaff he will burn up with unquenchable fire.

—Matthew 3:12

Gather up first the tares, and bind them in bundles to burn them; but gather the wheat into my barn.

—Matthew 13:30

12. Messiah: He is the foundation stone, stone of stumbling and chief corner stone.

As in Isaiah chapter 4 Messiah is again referred to as the foundation stone, and stumbling stone, a chief corner stone, and a rock of offense:

...therefore thus saith the Lord Jehovah, Behold, I lay in Zion for a foundation a stone, a tried stone, a precious corner-stone of sure foundation: he that believeth shall not be in haste. And I will make justice the line, and righteousness the

plummet; and the hail shall sweep away the refuge of lies, and the waters shall overflow the hiding-place.
—Isaiah 28:16–17

Prophesy fulfilled:

He is the stone which was set at nought of you the builders, which was made the head of the corner. And in none other is there salvation: for neither is there any other name under heaven, that is given among men, wherein we must be saved.
—Acts 4:11–12

...but Israel, following after a law of righteousness, did not arrive at that law. Wherefore? Because they sought it not by faith, but as it were by works. They stumbled at the stone of stumbling; even as it is written, Behold, I lay in Zion a stone of stumbling and a rock of offence: and he that believeth on him shall not be put to shame.
—Romans 9:31–33

Because it is contained in scripture, Behold, I lay in Zion a chief corner stone, elect, precious: And he that believeth on him shall not be put to shame. For you therefore that believe is the preciousness: but for such as disbelieve, The stone which the builders rejected, the same was made the head of the corner; and,

A stone of stumbling, and a rock of offence; for they stumble at the word, being disobedient: whereunto also they were appointed.
—1 Peter 2:6–8

13. Messiah: He is honored by the people, but not with their hearts.

And the Lord said, Forasmuch as this people draw nigh unto me, and with their mouth and with their lips do honor me, but have removed their heart far from me, and their fear of me is a commandment of men which hath been taught them; therefore, behold, I will proceed to do a marvellous work among this people, even a marvellous work and a wonder; and the wisdom of their wise men shall perish, and the understanding of their prudent men shall be hid.
—Isaiah 29:13–14

Prophesy fulfilled:

Ye hypocrites, well did Isaiah prophesy of you, saying, This people honoreth me with their lips; but their heart is far from me. But in vain do they worship me, teaching as their doctrines the precepts of men.

—Matthew 15:7–9

And he said unto them, Well did Isaiah prophesy of you hypocrites, as it is written, This people honoreth me with their lips, but their heart is far from me. But in vain do they worship me, teaching as their doctrines the precepts of men. Ye leave the commandment of God, and hold fast the tradition of men. And he said unto them, Full well do ye reject the commandment of God, that ye may keep your tradition.

—Mark. 7:6–9

14. Messiah: His miraculous healing ministry is revealed.

And in that day shall the deaf hear the words of the book, and the eyes of the blind shall see out of obscurity and out of darkness.

—Isaiah 29:18

Say to them that are of a fearful heart, Be strong, fear not: behold, your God will come with vengeance, with the recompense of God; he will come and save you. Then the eyes of the blind shall be opened, and the ears of the deaf shall be unstopped. Then shall the lame man leap as a hart, and the tongue of the dumb shall sing.

—Isaiah 35:4–6

Prophesy fulfilled:

And Jesus answered and said unto them, Go and tell John the things which ye hear and see: the blind receive their sight, and the lame walk, the lepers are cleansed, and the deaf hear, and the dead are raised up, and the poor have good tidings preached to them. And blessed is he, whosoever shall find no occasion of stumbling in me.

—Matthew 11:4–6[178]

---

[178] Matthew 4:24; 9:35.

Go and tell John the things which ye have seen and heard; the blind receive their sight, the lame walk, the lepers are cleansed, and the deaf hear, the dead are raised up, the poor have good tidings preached to them.
—Luke 7:22

Witnesses to the miraculous acts of Jesus were astonished beyond measure, saying, that a great Prophet had risen among them, and that God had visited His people. Others said, *"He hath done all things well; he maketh even the deaf to hear, and the dumb to speak"* (Mark 7:37).

15. Messiah: He will be preceded by a Messenger preparing the way for Him.

The voice of one that crieth, Prepare ye in the wilderness the way of Jehovah; make level in the desert a highway for our God. Every valley shall be exalted, and every mountain and hill shall be made low; and the uneven shall be made level, and the rough places a plain: and the glory of Jehovah shall be revealed, and all flesh shall see it together; for the mouth of Jehovah hath spoken it.
—Isaiah 40:3–5

Go through, go through the gates; prepare ye the way of the people; cast up, cast up the highway; gather out the stones; lift up an ensign for the peoples. Behold, Jehovah hath proclaimed unto the end of the earth, Say ye to the daughter of Zion, Behold, thy salvation cometh; behold, his reward is with him, and his recompense before him.
—Isaiah 62:10–11

Prophesy fulfilled: The messenger whom Jesus tells us *"is more than a prophet"* (Matthew 11:9) or *"much more than a prophet"* (Luke 7:26) is identified as John the Baptist by the Apostles Matthew, Mark, Luke and John.

And in those days cometh John the Baptist, preaching in the wilderness of Judaea, saying, Repent ye; for the kingdom of heaven is at hand. For this is he that was spoken of through Isaiah the prophet [40:3], saying, The voice of one crying in the wilderness, make ye ready the way of the Lord, make his paths straight.
—Matthew 3:1–3

Prophesies in Isaiah

But wherefore went ye out? to see a prophet? Yea, I say unto you, and much more than a prophet. This is he, of whom it is written, Behold, I send my messenger before thy face, who shall prepare thy way before thee. Verily I say unto you, Among them that are born of women there hath not arisen a greater than John the Baptist: yet he that is but little in the kingdom of heaven is greater than he.

—Matthew 11:9–11

Even as it is written in Isaiah the prophet, Behold, I send my messenger before thy face, who shall prepare thy way; the voice of one crying in the wilderness, make ye ready the way of the Lord, make his paths straight.

—Mark 1:2–3

And he [John the Baptist] shall go before his face in the spirit and power of Elijah, to turn the hearts of the fathers to the children, and the disobedient to walk in the wisdom of the just; to make ready for the Lord a people prepared for him.

—Luke 1:17[179]

Yea and thou, child, shalt be called the prophet of the Most High: for thou shalt go before the face of the Lord to make ready his ways; to give knowledge of salvation unto his people in the remission of their sins...

—Luke 1:76–77

...as it is written in the book of the words of Isaiah the prophet, The voice of one crying in the wilderness, make ye ready the way of the Lord, make his paths straight. Every valley shall be filled, and every mountain and hill shall be brought low; and the crooked shall become straight, and the rough ways smooth; and all flesh shall see the salvation of God.

—Luke 3:4–6

But what went ye out to see? a prophet? Yea, I say unto you, and much more than a prophet. This is he of whom it is written, Behold, I send my messenger before thy face, who shall prepare thy way before thee. I say unto you, Among them that

---

[179] Jesus told the multitudes *"And if ye are willing to receive it, this [John the Baptist] is Elijah, that is to come"* (Matthew 11:14). *"And his disciples asked him, saying, Why then say the scribes that Elijah must first come? And he answered and said, Elijah indeed cometh, and shall restore all things: but I say unto you, that Elijah is come already, and they knew him not, but did unto him whatsoever they would"* (Matthew 17:10–13). Elijah appeared with Moses at the Transfiguration of Jesus (Matthew 17:1–4).

are born of women there is none greater than John: yet he that is but little in the kingdom of God is greater than he.

—Luke 7:26–28

He said, I am the voice of one crying in the wilderness, Make straight the way of the Lord, as said Isaiah the prophet.

—John 1:23

16. Messiah: He is the compassionate shepherd who leads His sheep.

He will feed his flock like a shepherd, he will gather the lambs in his arm, and carry them in his bosom, and will gently lead those that have their young.

—Isaiah 40:11

Prophesy fulfilled:

Jesus therefore said unto them again, Verily, verily, I say unto you, I am the door of the sheep. All that came before me are thieves and robbers: but the sheep did not hear them. I am the door; by me if any man enter in, he shall be saved, and shall go in and go out, and shall find pasture. The thief cometh not, but that he may steal, and kill, and destroy: I came that they may have life, and may have it abundantly. I am the good shepherd: the good shepherd layeth down his life for the sheep.

—John 10:7–11

17. Messiah: He is the First (Alpha) the Beginning, and the Last (Omega) End.

Who hath wrought and done it, calling the generations from the beginning? I, Jehovah, the first, and with the last, I am he.

—Isaiah 41:4

Thus saith Jehovah, the King of Israel, and his Redeemer, Jehovah of hosts: I am the first, and I am the last; and besides me there is no God.

—Isaiah 44:6

Prophesy fulfilled:

I am the Alpha and the Omega, saith the Lord God, who is and who was and who is to come, the Almighty... write in a book and send it to the seven churches: unto Ephesus, and unto Smyrna, and unto Pergamum, and unto Thyatira, and unto Sardis, and unto Philadelphia, and unto Laodicea.

—Revelation 1:8, 11

And when I saw him, I fell at his feet as one dead. And he laid his right hand upon me, saying, Fear not; I am the first and the last, and the Living one; and I was dead, and behold, I am alive for evermore, and I have the keys of death and of Hades.

—Revelation 1:17–18

And to the angel of the church in Smyrna write: These things saith the first and the last, who was dead, and lived again...

—Revelation 2:8

And to the angel of the church in Laodicea write: These things saith the Amen, the faithful and true witness, the beginning of the creation of God...

—Revelation 3:14

We give thee thanks, O Lord God, the Almighty, who art and who wast; because thou hast taken thy great power, and didst reign.

—Revelation 11:17

And he said unto me, They are come to pass. I am the Alpha and the Omega, the beginning and the end. I will give unto him that is athirst of the fountain of the water of life freely.

—Revelation 21:6

I am the Alpha and the Omega, the first and the last, the beginning and the end.

—Revelation 22:13

18. Messiah: The servant is given for a covenant and light to the Gentiles.

I, Jehovah, have called thee in righteousness, and will hold thy hand, and will keep thee, and give thee for a covenant of the people, for a light of the Gentiles; to open the blind eyes, to bring out the prisoners from the dungeon, and them that sit

in darkness out of the prison-house. I am Jehovah, that is my name; and my glory will I not give to another, neither my praise unto graven images.
—Isaiah 42:6–8

Messiah is again referred to by Isaiah as a Servant and a light to the Gentiles."

...yea, he saith, It is too light a thing that thou shouldest be my servant to raise up the tribes of Jacob, and to restore the preserved of Israel: I will also give thee for a light to the Gentiles, that thou mayest be my salvation unto the end of the earth. Thus saith Jehovah, the Redeemer of Israel, and his Holy One, to him whom man despiseth, to him whom the nation abhorreth, to a servant of rulers: Kings shall see and arise; princes, and they shall worship; because of Jehovah that is faithful, even the Holy One of Israel, who hath chosen thee.
—Isaiah 49:6–7

Prophesy fulfilled:

...that it might be fulfilled which was spoken through Isaiah the prophet, saying, Behold, my servant whom I have chosen; my beloved in whom my soul is well pleased: I will put my Spirit upon him, and he shall declare judgment to the Gentiles... and in his name shall the Gentiles hope.
—Matthew 12:17–18, 21

When the Christ-child was presented in the temple to the devout Simeon who was waiting for the Consolation of Israel, Simeon took the child in his arms, and blessing God he said:

Now lettest thou thy servant depart, Lord, According to thy word, in peace; for mine eyes have seen thy salvation, which thou hast prepared before the face of all peoples; a light for revelation to the Gentiles, and the glory of thy people Israel.
—Luke 2:29–32

For so hath the Lord commanded us, saying, I have set thee for a light of the Gentiles, that thou shouldest be for salvation unto the uttermost part of the earth.
—Acts 13:47

Prophesies in Isaiah

19. Messiah: He was brutally beaten and spat upon.

I gave my back to the smiters, and my cheeks to them that plucked off the hair; I hid not my face from shame and spitting.
—Isaiah 50:6

Prophesy fulfilled:

Then did they spit in his face and buffet him: and some smote him with the palms of their hands, saying, Prophesy unto us, thou Christ: who is he that struck thee?
—Matthew 26:67–68

And they spat upon him, and took the reed and smote him on the head.
—Matthew 27:30

And some began to spit on him, and to cover his face, and to buffet him, and to say unto him, Prophesy: and the officers received him with blows of their hands.
—Mark 14:65

20. Messiah: The Servant shall be exalted and extolled, and be very high.

Behold, my servant shall deal wisely, he shall be exalted and lifted up, and shall be very high. Like as many were astonished at thee (his visage was so marred more than any man, and his form more than the sons of men), so shall he sprinkle many nations; kings shall shut their mouths at him: for that which had not been told them shall they see; and that which they had not heard shall they understand.
—Isaiah 52:13–15

Prophesy fulfilled:

Wherefore also God highly exalted him, and gave unto him the name which is above every name; that in the name of Jesus every knee should bow, of things in heaven and things on earth and things under the earth, and that every tongue should confess that Jesus Christ is Lord, to the glory of God the Father.
—Philippians 2:9–11

Part Three: Prophecies Fulfilled

21. Messiah: He was not believed.

Who hath believed our message? and to whom hath the arm of Jehovah been revealed?

—Isaiah 53:1

Prophesy fulfilled:

But though he had done so many signs before them, yet they believed not on him: that the word of Isaiah the prophet might be fulfilled, which he spake, Lord, who hath believed our report? And to whom hath the arm of the Lord been revealed? For this cause they could not believe, for that Isaiah said again, He hath blinded their eyes, and he hardened their heart; lest they should see with their eyes, and perceive with their heart, and should turn, and I should heal them. These things said Isaiah, because he saw his glory; and he spake of him.

—John 12:37–41

But they did not all hearken to the glad tidings. For Isaiah saith, Lord, who hath believed our report?

—Romans 10:16

22. Messiah: The Servant was a Man of sorrows, despised and rejected.

He was despised, and rejected of men; a man of sorrows, and acquainted with grief: and as one from whom men hide their face he was despised; and we esteemed him not.

—Isaiah 53:3

Thus saith Jehovah, the Redeemer of Israel, and his Holy One, to him whom man despiseth, to him whom the nation abhorreth, to a servant of rulers: Kings shall see and arise; princes, and they shall worship; because of Jehovah that is faithful, even the Holy One of Israel, who hath chosen thee.

—Isaiah 49:7

Prophesy fulfilled:

He was in the world, and the world was made through him, and the world knew him not. He came unto his own, and they that were his own received him not.

—John 1:10–11

Jesus himself said:

Verily I say unto you, No prophet is acceptable in his own country.

—Luke 4:24

And Jesus said unto him, The foxes have holes, and the birds of the heaven have nests; but the Son of man hath not where to lay his head.

—Luke 9:58

23. Messiah: His blood sacrifice was for all of mankind.

…so shall he sprinkle many nations; kings shall shut their mouths at him: for that which had not been told them shall they see; and that which they had not heard shall they understand.

—Isaiah 52:15

Prophesy fulfilled: The Apostles Paul and John attribute the forgiveness of sins to the sprinkling of the shed blood of Jesus on the cross.

Much more then, being now justified by his blood, shall we be saved from the wrath of God through him.

—Romans 5:9

…in whom we have our redemption through his blood, the forgiveness of our trespasses, according to the riches of his grace…

—Ephesians 1:7

But now in Christ Jesus ye that once were far off are made nigh in the blood of Christ. For he is our peace, who made both one, and brake down the middle wall of partition, having abolished in his flesh the enmity, even the law of commandments contained in ordinances; that he might create in himself of the two one new man, so making peace.

—Ephesians 2:13–15

Part Three: Prophecies Fulfilled

...in whom we have our redemption, the forgiveness of our sins... and through him to reconcile all things unto himself, having made peace through the blood of his cross; through him, I say, whether things upon the earth, or things in the heavens. And you, being in time past alienated and enemies in your mind in your evil works, yet now hath he reconciled in the body of his flesh through death, to present you holy and without blemish and unreproveable before him...

—Colossians 1:14, 20–22

...but if we walk in the light, as he is in the light, we have fellowship one with another, and the blood of Jesus his Son cleanseth us from all sin.

—1 John 1:7

Unto him that loveth us, and loosed us from our sins by his blood; and he made us to be a kingdom, to be priests unto his God and Father; to him be the glory and the dominion for ever and ever. Amen.

—Revelation 1:5–6

24. Messiah: His atoning sacrifice was willed by God.

Yet it pleased Jehovah to bruise him; he hath put him to grief: when thou shalt make his soul an offering for sin, he shall see his seed, he shall prolong his days, and the pleasure of Jehovah shall prosper in his hand. He shall see of the travail of his soul, and shall be satisfied...

—Isaiah 53:10–11

Prophesy fulfilled:

Ye men of Israel, hear these words: Jesus of Nazareth, a man approved of God unto you by mighty works and wonders and signs which God did by him in the midst of you, even as ye yourselves know; him, being delivered up by the determinate counsel and foreknowledge of God, ye by the hand of lawless men did crucify and slay: whom God raised up, having loosed the pangs of death: because it was not possible that he should be holden of it.

—Acts 2:22–24

25. Messiah: He bore our iniquities, and by His stripes we are healed.

Surely he hath borne our griefs, and carried our sorrows; yet we did esteem him stricken, smitten of God, and afflicted. But he was wounded for our transgressions, he was bruised for our iniquities; the chastisement of our peace was upon him; and with his stripes we are healed.

—Isaiah 53:4–5

He shall see of the travail of his soul, and shall be satisfied: by the knowledge of himself shall my righteous servant justify many; and he shall bear their iniquities. Therefore will I divide him a portion with the great, and he shall divide the spoil with the strong; because he poured out his soul unto death, and was numbered with the transgressors: yet he bare the sin of many, and made intercession for the transgressors.

—Isaiah 53:11–12

Prophesy fulfilled: The Apostles Paul, Peter, John and the author of Hebrews all emphasize that Christ died and bore our sins.

...even as the Son of man came not to be ministered unto, but to minister, and to give his life a ransom for many.

—Matthew 20:28

Him who knew no sin he made to be sin on our behalf; that we might become the righteousness of God in him.

—2 Corinthians 5:21

...who gave himself for our sins, that he might deliver us out of this present evil world, according to the will of our God and Father...

—Galatians 1:4

...who his own self bare our sins in his body upon the tree, that we, having died unto sins, might live unto righteousness; by whose stripes ye were healed.

—1 Peter 2:24

...but now once at the end of the ages hath he been manifested to put away sin by the sacrifice of himself... so Christ also, having been once offered to bear the sins

of many, shall appear a second time, apart from sin, to them that wait for him, unto salvation.

—Hebrews 9:26, 28

…and he is the propitiation for our sins; and not for ours only, but also for the whole world.

—1 John 2:2

Herein is love, not that we loved God, but that he loved us, and sent his Son to be the propitiation for our sins.

—1 John. 4:10

26. Messiah: He took upon Himself our sins and infirmities.

He was despised, and rejected of men; a man of sorrows, and acquainted with grief: and as one from whom men hide their face he was despised; and we esteemed him not.

Surely he hath borne our griefs, and carried our sorrows; yet we did esteem him stricken, smitten of God, and afflicted. But he was wounded for our transgressions, he was bruised for our iniquities; the chastisement of our peace was upon him; and with his stripes we are healed. All we like sheep have gone astray; we have turned every one to his own way; and Jehovah hath laid on him the iniquity of us all.

—Isaiah 53:3–6

Prophesy fulfilled: Matthew writes that what Isaiah prophesied was fulfilled, and the apostle Peter tells us that Christ submitted to the wrath of a holy God so that we should live to righteousness and be healed.

…that it might be fulfilled which was spoken through Isaiah the prophet, saying, Himself took our infirmities, and bare our diseases.

—Matthew 8:17

For while we were yet weak, in due season Christ died for the ungodly… But God commendeth his own love toward us, in that, while we were yet sinners, Christ died for us.

—Romans 5:6, 8

...who his own self bare our sins in his body upon the tree, that we, having died unto sins, might live unto righteousness; by whose stripes ye were healed.

—1 Peter 2:24

27. Messiah: He remained silent and did not answer his accusers.

He was oppressed, yet when he was afflicted he opened not his mouth; as a lamb that is led to the slaughter, and as a sheep that before its shearers is dumb, so he opened not his mouth.

—Isaiah 53:7

Prophesy fulfilled: When Jesus was wrongly accused He remained silent before the high priest, chief priests, governor and witnesses:

And the high priest stood up, and said unto him, Answerest thou nothing? what is it which these witness against thee? But Jesus held his peace.

—Matthew 26:62–63

Now Jesus stood before the governor: and the governor asked him, saying, Art thou the King of the Jews? And Jesus said unto him, Thou sayest. And when he was accused by the chief priests and elders, he answered nothing. Then saith Pilate unto him, Hearest thou not how many things they witness against thee? And he gave him no answer, not even to one word: insomuch that the governor marvelled greatly.

—Matthew 27:11–14

And the chief priests accused him of many things. And Pilate again asked him, saying, Answerest thou nothing? behold how many things they accuse thee of. But Jesus no more answered anything; insomuch that Pilate marvelled.

—Mark 15:3–5

28. Messiah: He was cut off and led like a lamb to the slaughter.

By oppression and judgment he was taken away; and as for his generation, who among them considered that he was cut off out of the land of the living for the transgression of my people to whom the stroke was due?

—Isaiah 53:8

Part Three: Prophecies Fulfilled

The prophet Daniel writes that "Messiah the Prince" after sixty-two weeks would be "cut off but not for Himself (Daniel 9:25).

Prophesy fulfilled:

Him who knew no sin he made to be sin on our behalf; that we might become the righteousness of God in him.

—2 Corinthians 5:21

The Apostle Luke provides the following account of the Ethiopian eunuch in the employ of Candace (?), the queen of Ethiopia, who had come to Jerusalem and was returning to Ethiopia in his chariot.[180]

And Philip ran to him, and heard him reading Isaiah the prophet, and said, Understandest thou what thou readest? And he said, How can I, except some one shall guide me? And he besought Philip to come up and sit with him. Now the passage of the scripture which he was reading was this, He was led as a sheep to the slaughter; and as a lamb before his shearer is dumb, so he openeth not his mouth: in his humiliation his judgment was taken away: his generation who shall declare? For his life is taken from the earth. And the eunuch answered Philip, and said, I pray thee, of whom speaketh the prophet this? of himself, or of some other?

—Acts 8:30–34

Continuing at this Scripture Philip preached Jesus to the eunuch, and expounded unto him the way of God more perfectly, showing by the scriptures that Jesus was Christ.

29. Messiah: He would die with the wicked and be buried with the rich.

And they made his grave with the wicked, and with a rich man in his death; although he had done no violence, neither was any deceit in his mouth.

—Isaiah 53:9

Prophesy fulfilled:

And when even was come, there came a rich man from Arimathaea, named Joseph, who also himself was Jesus' disciple: this man went to Pilate, and asked for

---

180 Acts 8:28–38.

the body of Jesus. Then Pilate commanded it to be given up. And Joseph took the body, and wrapped it in a clean linen cloth, and laid it in his own new tomb, which he had hewn out in the rock: and he rolled a great stone to the door of the tomb, and departed.

—Matthew 27:57–60

And when even was now come, because it was the Preparation, that is, the day before the sabbath, there came Joseph of Arimathaea, a councillor of honorable estate, who also himself was looking for the kingdom of God; and he boldly went in unto Pilate, and asked for the body of Jesus. And Pilate marvelled if he were already dead: and calling unto him the centurion, he asked him whether he had been any while dead. And when he learned it of the centurion, he granted the corpse to Joseph. And he bought a linen cloth, and taking him down, wound him in the linen cloth, and laid him in a tomb which had been hewn out of a rock; and he rolled a stone against the door of the tomb.

—Mark 15:42–46

And behold, a man named Joseph, who was a councillor, a good and righteous man (he had not consented to their counsel and deed), a man of Arimathaea, a city of the Jews, who was looking for the kingdom of God: this man went to Pilate, and asked for the body of Jesus. And he took it down, and wrapped it in a linen cloth, and laid him in a tomb that was hewn in stone, where never man had yet lain.

—Luke 23:50–53

And after these things Joseph of Arimathaea, being a disciple of Jesus, but secretly for fear of the Jews, asked of Pilate that he might take away the body of Jesus: and Pilate gave him leave. He came therefore, and took away his body. And there came also Nicodemus, he who at the first came to him by night, bringing a mixture of myrrh and aloes, about a hundred pounds. So they took the body of Jesus, and bound it in linen cloths with the spices, as the custom of the Jews is to bury. Now in the place where he was crucified there was a garden; and in the garden a new tomb wherein was never man yet laid. There then because of the Jews' Preparation (for the tomb was nigh at hand) they laid Jesus.

—John 19:38–42

Part Three: Prophecies Fulfilled

And when they had fulfilled all things that were written of him, they took him down from the tree, and laid him in a tomb. But God raised him from the dead...
—Acts 13:29–30

30. Messiah: He was crucified with transgressors and interceded for them.

Therefore will I divide him a portion with the great, and he shall divide the spoil with the strong; because he poured out his soul unto death, and was numbered with the transgressors: yet he bare the sin of many, and made intercession for the transgressors.
—Isaiah 53:12

Prophesy fulfilled:

And there were also two others, malefactors, led with him to be put to death. And when they came unto the place which is called the skull, there they crucified him, and the malefactors, one on the right hand and the other on the left. And Jesus said, Father, forgive them; for they know not what they do.
—Luke 23:32–34

Then are there crucified with him two robbers, one on the right hand and one on the left.
—Matthew 27:38

And with him they crucify two robbers; one on his right hand, and one on his left. So the scripture was fulfilled, which saith, And he was reckoned with transgressors.
—Mark 15:27–28

31. Messiah: He will make a new and everlasting covenant with the people.

Incline your ear, and come unto me; hear, and your soul shall live: and I will make an everlasting covenant with you, even the sure mercies of David. Behold, I have given him for a witness to the peoples, a leader and commander to the peoples. Behold, thou shalt call a nation that thou knowest not; and a nation that knew not thee shall run unto thee, because of Jehovah thy God, and for the Holy One of Israel; for he hath glorified thee.
—Isaiah 55:3–5

And as for me, this is my covenant with them, saith Jehovah: my Spirit that is upon thee, and my words which I have put in thy mouth, shall not depart out of thy mouth, nor out of the mouth of thy seed, nor out of the mouth of thy seed's seed, saith Jehovah, from henceforth and for ever.

—Isaiah 59:21

Prophesy fulfilled:

...and so all Israel shall be saved: even as it is written, There shall come out of Zion the Deliverer; he shall turn away ungodliness from Jacob: and this is my covenant unto them, when I shall take away their sins.

—Romans 11:26–27

For finding fault with them, he saith, Behold, the days come, saith the Lord, that I will make a new covenant with the house of Israel and with the house of Judah; not according to the covenant that I made with their fathers in the day that I took them by the hand to lead them forth out of the land of Egypt; for they continued not in my covenant, and I regarded them not, saith the Lord. For this is the covenant that I will make with the house of Israel after those days, saith the Lord; I will put my laws into their mind, and on their heart also will I write them: and I will be to them a God, and they shall be to me a people... For I will be merciful to their iniquities, and their sins will I remember no more. In that he saith, A new covenant, he hath made the first old. But that which is becoming old and waxeth aged is nigh unto vanishing away.

—Hebrew 8:8–10, 12–13

32. Messiah: He calls the temple of God a house of prayer.

...even them will I bring to my holy mountain, and make them joyful in my house of prayer: their burnt-offerings and their sacrifices shall be accepted upon mine altar; for my house shall be called a house of prayer for all peoples...

—Isaiah 56:7

Prophesy fulfilled:

...and he saith unto them, It is written, My house shall be called a house of prayer: but ye make it a den of robbers.

—Matthew 21:13

And he taught, and said unto them, Is it not written, My house shall be called a house of prayer for all the nations? but ye have made it a den of robbers.

—Mark 11:17

And he entered into the temple, and began to cast out them that sold, saying unto them, It is written, And my house shall be a house of prayer: but ye have made it a den of robbers.

—Luke 19:46

33. Messiah: He is our Intercessor, Mediator and Advocate.

And he saw that there was no man, and wondered that there was no intercessor: therefore his own arm brought salvation unto him; and his righteousness, it upheld him.

—Isaiah 59:16

Prophesy fulfilled:

What then is the law? It was added because of transgressions, till the seed should come to whom the promise hath been made; and it was ordained through angels by the hand of a mediator.

—Galatians 3:19

For there is one God, one mediator also between God and men, himself man, Christ Jesus...

—1 Timothy 2:5

Wherefore also he is able to save to the uttermost them that draw near unto God through him, seeing he ever liveth to make intercession for them.

—Hebrews 7:25

And for this cause he is the mediator of a new covenant, that a death having taken place for the redemption of the transgressions that were under the first covenant, they that have been called may receive the promise of the eternal inheritance.

—Hebrews 9:15

…to Jesus the mediator of a new covenant…

—Hebrews 12:24

My little children, these things write I unto you that ye may not sin. And if any man sin, we have an Advocate with the Father, Jesus Christ the righteous…

—1 John 2:1

34. Messiah: He is our Redeemer.

And a Redeemer will come to Zion, and unto them that turn from transgression in Jacob, saith Jehovah.

—Isaiah 59:20

Prophesy fulfilled:

…looking for the blessed hope and appearing of the glory of the great God and our Saviour Jesus Christ; who gave himself for us, that he might redeem us from all iniquity, and purify unto himself a people for his own possession, zealous of good works.

—Titus 2:13–14

35. Messiah: He shall be a revealing everlasting light to the people.

Arise, shine; for thy light is come, and the glory of Jehovah is risen upon thee. For, behold, darkness shall cover the earth, and gross darkness the peoples; but Jehovah will arise upon thee, and his glory shall be seen upon thee. And nations shall come to thy light, and kings to the brightness of thy rising.

—Isaiah 60:1–3

The sun shall be no more thy light by day; neither for brightness shall the moon give light unto thee: but Jehovah will be unto thee an everlasting light, and thy God thy glory.

—Isaiah 60:19

Prophesy fulfilled:

For mine eyes have seen thy salvation, which thou hast prepared before the face of all peoples; a light for revelation to the Gentiles, and the glory of thy people Israel.
—Luke 2:30–32

In him was life; and the life was the light of men. And the light shineth in the darkness; and the darkness apprehended it not.
—John 1:4–5

Again therefore Jesus spake unto them, saying, I am the light of the world: he that followeth me shall not walk in the darkness, but shall have the light of life.
—John 8:12

36. Messiah: His public earthly mission is revealed.

The Spirit of the Lord Jehovah is upon me; because Jehovah hath anointed me to preach good tidings unto the meek; he hath sent me to bind up the broken-hearted, to proclaim liberty to the captives, and the opening of the prison to them that are bound; to proclaim the year of Jehovah's favour...
—Isaiah 61:1–2

Prophesy fulfilled:

The Spirit of the Lord is upon me, Because he anointed me to preach good tidings to the poor: he hath sent me to proclaim release to the captives, and recovering of sight to the blind, to set at liberty them that are bruised, to proclaim the acceptable year of the Lord. And he closed the book, and gave it back to the attendant, and sat down: and the eyes of all in the synagogue were fastened on him. And he began to say unto them, To-day hath this scripture been fulfilled in your ears.
—Luke 4:18–21

The remainder of the prophesy in Isaiah was not read by Jesus, for that portion applies to His anticipated Second Coming:

...and the day of vengeance of our God; to comfort all that mourn; to appoint unto them that mourn in Zion, to give unto them a garland for ashes, the oil of joy for

mourning, the garment of praise for the spirit of heaviness; that they may be called trees of righteousness, the planting of Jehovah, that he may be glorified.

—Isaiah 61:2–3

37. Messiah: He will tread the winepress on the day of vengeance.

Who is this that cometh from Edom, with dyed garments from Bozrah? this that is glorious in his apparel, marching in the greatness of his strength? I that speak in righteousness, mighty to save. Wherefore art thou red in thine apparel, and thy garments like him that treadeth in the winevat? I have trodden the winepress alone; and of the peoples there was no man with me: yea, I trod them in mine anger, and trampled them in my wrath; and their lifeblood is sprinkled upon my garments, and I have stained all my raiment. For the day of vengeance was in my heart, and the year of my redeemed is come.

—Isaiah 63:1–4

Prophesy to be fulfilled:

And he is arrayed in a garment sprinkled with blood: and his name is called The Word of God... And out of his mouth proceedeth a sharp sword, that with it he should smite the nations: and he shall rule them with a rod of iron: and he treadeth the winepress of the fierceness of the wrath of God, the Almighty.

—Revelation 19:13, 15

Chapter Twenty
PROPHESIES IN JEREMIAH

1. Messiah: He provides rest for the soul.

Thus saith Jehovah, Stand ye in the ways and see, and ask for the old paths, where is the good way; and walk therein, and ye shall find rest for your souls: but they said, We will not walk therein.

—Jeremiah 6:16

As the cattle that go down into the valley, the Spirit of Jehovah caused them to rest: so didst thou lead thy people, to make thyself a glorious name.

—Isaiah 63:14

Prophesy fulfilled:

Take my yoke upon you, and learn of me; for I am meek and lowly in heart: and ye shall find rest unto your souls. For my yoke is easy, and my burden is light.

—Matthew 11:29–30

2. Messiah: He drives the robbers and moneychangers from the Temple.

Is this house, which is called by my name, become a den of robbers in your eyes? Behold, I, even I, have seen it, saith Jehovah.

—Jeremiah 7:11

Prophesy fulfilled:

And Jesus entered into the temple of God, and cast out all them that sold and bought in the temple, and overthrew the tables of the money-changers, and the

seats of them that sold the doves; and he saith unto them, It is written, My house shall be called a house of prayer: but ye make it a den of robbers.
—Matthew 21:12–13

And they come to Jerusalem: and he entered into the temple, and began to cast out them that sold and them that bought in the temple, and overthrew the tables of the money-changers, and the seats of them that sold the doves; and he would not suffer that any man should carry a vessel through the temple. And he taught, and said unto them, Is it not written, My house shall be called a house of prayer for all the nations? but ye have made it a den of robbers.
—Mark 11:15–17

And he entered into the temple, and began to cast out them that sold, saying unto them, It is written, And my house shall be a house of prayer: but ye have made it a den of robbers.
—Luke 19:45–46

And he found in the temple those that sold oxen and sheep and doves, and the changers of money sitting: and he made a scourge of cords, and cast all out of the temple, both the sheep and the oxen; and he poured out the changers' money, and overthrew their tables; and to them that sold the doves he said, Take these things hence; make not my Father's house a house of merchandise.
—John 2:14–16

3. Messiah: Is The Branch of Righteous and the Lord our Righteousness.

Behold, the days come, saith Jehovah, that I will raise unto David a righteous Branch, and he shall reign as king and deal wisely, and shall execute justice and righteousness in the land. In his days Judah shall be saved, and Israel shall dwell safely; and this is his name whereby he shall be called: Jehovah our righteousness.
—Jeremiah 23:5–6

In those days, and at that time, will I cause a Branch of righteousness to grow up unto David; and he shall execute justice and righteousness in the land. In those days shall Judah be saved, and Jerusalem shall dwell safely; and this is the name whereby she shall be called: Jehovah our righteousness. For thus saith Jehovah: David shall never want a man to sit upon the throne of the house of Israel; neither shall the priests the Levites want a man before me to offer burnt-offerings, and to burn meal-offerings, and to do sacrifice continually.

And the word of Jehovah came unto Jeremiah, saying, Thus saith Jehovah: If ye can break my covenant of the day, and my covenant of the night, so that there shall not be day and night in their season; then may also my covenant be broken with David my servant, that he shall not have a son to reign upon his throne; and with the Levites the priests, my ministers.

—Jeremiah 33:15–21

4. Messiah: The Massacre of the Innocents.

Thus saith Jehovah: A voice is heard in Ramah, lamentation, and bitter weeping, Rachel weeping for her children; she refuseth to be comforted for her children, because they are not. Thus saith Jehovah: Refrain thy voice from weeping, and thine eyes from tears; for thy work shall be rewarded, saith Jehovah; and they shall come again from the land of the enemy. And there is hope for thy latter end, saith Jehovah; and thy children shall come again to their own border.

—Jeremiah 31:15–17

Prophesy fulfilled: Rachel was weeping for the exiled tribes of Ephraim and Manasseh descended from her,[181] but Matthew thinks that the slaughter of all the male children of Bethlehem by King Herod fulfills Jeremiah's prophesy.

Then was fulfilled that which was spoken through Jeremiah the prophet, saying, A voice was heard in Ramah, weeping and great mourning, Rachel weeping for her children; and she would not be comforted, because they are not.

—Matthew 2:17–18

5. Messiah: He makes a the New Covenant with Israel and Judah.

Behold, the days come, saith Jehovah, that I will make a new covenant with the house of Israel, and with the house of Judah: not according to the covenant that I made with their fathers in the day that I took them by the hand to bring them out of the land of Egypt; which my covenant they brake, although I was a husband unto them, saith Jehovah. But this is the covenant that I will make with the house

---

[181] H. L. Ginsberg. The Book of Isaiah (The Jewish Publication Society of America, Philadelphia, 1973), 13a.

Part Three: Prophecies Fulfilled

of Israel after those days, saith Jehovah: I will put my law in their inward parts, and in their heart will I write it; and I will be their God, and they shall be my people. And they shall teach no more every man his neighbor, and every man his brother, saying, Know Jehovah; for they shall all know me, from the least of them unto the greatest of them, saith Jehovah: for I will forgive their iniquity, and their sin will I remember no more.

—Jeremiah 31:31–34
(see also Jeremiah 32:38–40)

Prophesy fulfilled: The Apostles Matthew, Luke, Paul and the author of Hebrews all refer to the New Covenant, comparing the old Sinaitic, or first covenant, to the new:

...for this is my blood of the covenant, which is poured out for many unto remission of sins.

—Matthew 26:28

And the cup in like manner after supper, saying, This cup is the new covenant in my blood, even that which is poured out for you.

—Luke 22:20

...and so all Israel shall be saved: even as it is written, There shall come out of Zion the Deliverer; he shall turn away ungodliness from Jacob: and this is my covenant unto them, when I shall take away their sins.

—Romans 11:26–27

Now this I say: A covenant confirmed beforehand by God, the law, which came four hundred and thirty years after, doth not disannul, so as to make the promise of none effect.

—Galatians 3:17

But now hath he obtained a ministry the more excellent, by so much as he is also the mediator of a better covenant, which hath been enacted upon better promises. For if that first covenant had been faultless, then would no place have been sought for a second. For finding fault with them, he saith, Behold, the days come, saith the Lord, that I will make a new covenant with the house of Israel and with the house of Judah; not according to the covenant that I made with their fathers in the

day that I took them by the hand to lead them forth out of the land of Egypt; for they continued not in my covenant, and I regarded them not, saith the Lord. For this is the covenant that I will make with the house of Israel after those days, saith the Lord; I will put my laws into their mind, and on their heart also will I write them: and I will be to them a God, and they shall be to me a people.
—Hebrews 8:6–10

This is the covenant that I will make with them after those days, saith the Lord: I will put my laws on their heart, and upon their mind also will I write them; then saith he, and their sins and their iniquities will I remember no more.
—Hebrews 10:16–17

Chapter Twenty-One

PROPHESIES IN EZEKIEL

1. Messiah: Is He whose right it is.

...thus saith the Lord Jehovah: Remove the mitre, and take off the crown; this shall be no more the same; exalt that which is low, and abase that which is high. I will overturn, overturn, overturn it: this also shall be no more, until he come whose right it is; and I will give it him.

—Ezekiel 21:26–27

Prophesy to be fulfilled: The apostle Luke elaborating on "He whose right it is," refers to the millennial reign when Christ will be given the throne of His father David:

He shall be great, and shall be called the Son of the Most High: and the Lord God shall give unto him the throne of his father David: and he shall reign over the house of Jacob for ever; and of his kingdom there shall be no end.

—Luke 1:32–33

2. Messiah: The Shepherd-prince shall gather and feed his flock with judgment.

For thus saith the Lord Jehovah: Behold, I myself, even I, will search for my sheep, and will seek them out. As a shepherd seeketh out his flock in the day that he is among his sheep that are scattered abroad, so will I seek out my sheep; and I will deliver them out of all places whither they have been scattered in the cloudy and dark day. And I will bring them out from the peoples, and gather them from the countries, and will bring them into their own land; and I will feed them upon the mountains of Israel, by the watercourses, and in all the inhabited places of the country. I will feed them with good pasture; and upon the mountains of the height of Israel shall their fold be: there shall they lie down in a good fold; and on fat

Part Three: Prophecies Fulfilled

pasture shall they feed upon the mountains of Israel. I myself will be the shepherd of my sheep, and I will cause them to lie down, saith the Lord Jehovah. I will seek that which was lost, and will bring back that which was driven away, and will bind up that which was broken, and will strengthen that which was sick: but the fat and the strong I will destroy; I will feed them in justice.

—Ezekiel 34:11–16

And I will set up one shepherd over them, and he shall feed them, even my servant David; he shall feed them, and he shall be their shepherd. And I, Jehovah, will be their God, and my servant David prince among them; I, Jehovah, have spoken it.

—Ezekiel 34:23–24

And my servant David shall be king over them; and they all shall have one shepherd: they shall also walk in mine ordinances, and observe my statutes, and do them. And they shall dwell in the land that I have given unto Jacob my servant, wherein your fathers dwelt; and they shall dwell therein, they, and their children, and their children's children, for ever: and David my servant shall be their prince for ever. Moreover I will make a covenant of peace with them; it shall be an everlasting covenant with them; and I will place them, and multiply them, and will set my sanctuary in the midst of them for evermore.

—Ezekiel 37:24–26

Prophecy to be fulfilled: The apostle John and the author of the Epistle of Hebrews both identify Jesus as the good shepherd, and the great shepherd.

And thou Bethlehem, land of Judah, art in no wise least among the princes of Judah: for out of thee shall come forth a governor, who shall be shepherd of my people Israel.

—Matthew 2:6

"I am the good shepherd…

—John 10:11

Now the God of peace, who brought again from the dead the great shepherd of the sheep with the blood of an eternal covenant, even our Lord Jesus, make you perfect in every good thing to do his will, working in us that which is well-pleasing in his sight, through Jesus Christ; to whom be the glory for ever and ever. Amen.

—Hebrews 13:20–21

Chapter Twenty-Two

PROPHESIES IN DANIEL

1. Messiah: Shall smite and break in pieces, and fill the whole earth.

As for this image, its head was of fine gold, its breast and its arms of silver, its belly and its thighs of brass, its legs of iron, its feet part of iron, and part of clay. Thou sawest till that a stone was cut out without hands, which smote the image upon its feet that were of iron and clay, and brake them in pieces. Then was the iron, the clay, the brass, the silver, and the gold, broken in pieces together, and became like the chaff of the summer threshing-floors; and the wind carried them away, so that no place was found for them: and the stone that smote the image became a great mountain, and filled the whole earth.

—Daniel 2:32–35

And in the days of those kings shall the God of heaven set up a kingdom which shall never be destroyed, nor shall the sovereignty thereof be left to another people; but it shall break in pieces and consume all these kingdoms, and it shall stand for ever. Forasmuch as thou sawest that a stone was cut out of the mountain without hands, and that it brake in pieces the iron, the brass, the clay, the silver, and the gold; the great God hath made known to the king what shall come to pass hereafter: and the dream is certain, and the interpretation thereof sure.

—Daniel 2:44–45

Prophesy fulfilled: Luke writes that the smiting stone (a type of Christ) will have dominion and will rule forever:

…and he shall reign over the house of Jacob for ever; and of his kingdom there shall be no end.

—Luke 1:33

He is the stone which was set at nought of you the builders, which was made the head of the corner. And in none other is there salvation: for neither is there any other name under heaven, that is given among men, wherein we must be saved.

—Acts 4:11–12

2. Messiah: He is like the Son of God in the furnace.

Then Nebuchadnezzar the king was astonished, and rose up in haste: he spake and said unto his counsellors, Did not we cast three men bound into the midst of the fire? They answered and said unto the king, True, O king. He answered and said, Lo, I see four men loose, walking in the midst of the fire, and they have no hurt; and the aspect of the fourth is like a son of the gods.

—Daniel 3:24–25

3. Messiah: He will come with the clouds of heaven, and be given dominion.

I saw in the night-visions, and, behold, there came with the clouds of heaven one like unto a son of man, and he came even to the ancient of days, and they brought him near before him. And there was given him dominion, and glory, and a kingdom, that all the peoples, nations, and languages should serve him: his dominion is an everlasting dominion, which shall not pass away, and his kingdom that which shall not be destroyed... And the kingdom and the dominion, and the greatness of the kingdoms under the whole heaven, shall be given to the people of the saints of the Most High: his kingdom is an everlasting kingdom, and all dominions shall serve and obey him.

—Daniel 7:13–14, 27

Prophesy to be fulfilled: Matthew, Mark, Luke and John all write about Christ ascending or descending in the clouds of heaven, and Jesus confirms that he will come and return in the clouds of heaven.

...and then shall appear the sign of the Son of man in heaven: and then shall all the tribes of the earth mourn, and they shall see the Son of man coming on the clouds of heaven with power and great glory. And he shall send forth his angels with a great sound of a trumpet, and they shall gather together his elect from the four winds, from one end of heaven to the other.

—Matthew 24:30–31

And the high priest stood up in the midst, and asked Jesus, saying, Answerest thou nothing? what is it which these witness against thee? But he held his peace, and answered nothing. Again the high priest asked him, and saith unto him, Art thou the Christ, the Son of the Blessed? And Jesus said, I am: and ye shall see the Son of man sitting at the right hand of Power, and coming with the clouds of heaven.
—Mark 14:60–62

...men fainting for fear, and for expectation of the things which are coming on the world: for the powers of the heavens shall be shaken. And then shall they see the Son of man coming in a cloud with power and great glory.
—Luke 21:26–27

And when he had said these things, as they were looking, he was taken up; and a cloud received him out of their sight. And while they were looking stedfastly into heaven as he went, behold two men stood by them in white apparel; who also said, Ye men of Galilee, why stand ye looking into heaven? this Jesus, who was received up from you into heaven, shall so come in like manner as ye beheld him going into heaven.
—Acts 1:9–11

For the Lord himself shall descend from heaven, with a shout, with the voice of the archangel, and with the trump of God: and the dead in Christ shall rise first; then we that are alive, that are left, shall together with them be caught up in the clouds, to meet the Lord in the air: and so shall we ever be with the Lord. Wherefore comfort one another with these words.
—1 Thessalonians 4:16–18

Behold, he cometh with the clouds; and every eye shall see him, and they that pierced him; and all the tribes of the earth shall mourn over him. Even so, Amen.
—Revelation 1:7

4. Messiah: His birth and death foretold.

Know therefore and discern, that from the going forth of the commandment to restore and to build Jerusalem unto the anointed one, the prince, shall be seven weeks, and threescore and two weeks: it shall be built again, with street and moat, even in troublous times. And after the threescore and two weeks shall the anointed one be cut off, and shall have nothing: and the people of the prince that shall come shall destroy the city and the sanctuary; and the end thereof shall be with a flood, and even unto the end shall be war; desolations are determined.

—Daniel 9:25–26

Prophesy fulfilled: As for the time of Christ's birth Luke writes that He was born while Quirinius was governor of Syria (Luke 2:1–2). Many attempts have been made to learn from Daniel's prophesy the time of Christ's crucifixion. Among these it has been calculated:

That beginning with Artaxerxes' decree on Nisan 1 (March 4, 444 B.C.) that Jerusalem would be rebuilt (Nehemiah 2:5) and ending with the crucifixion of Christ would be "69 sevens" or 476 years + 256 days, ending March 30, A.D. 33 [69 x 7 = 483 years of 360 days = 173,880 days. Since 1 Solar year = 365.24219879 days, therefore 173,880 days = 476.067663 solar years or 476 years + 24.7 days. Adding 476 years + 25.7 days to 444 B.C. brings us to March 30, of A.D. 33 (Gregorian years) when Jesus likely entered Jerusalem (Luke 19:28–40). The Temple of Jerusalem was destroyed later in A.D. 70. Subtracting 33 from 70 it is calculated that Christ could have been "cut off" at the age of ca. A.D. 37.[182]

5. Messiah: His sanctuary is defiled by one who makes desolate.

And he shall make a firm covenant with many for one week: and in the midst of the week he shall cause the sacrifice and the oblation to cease; and upon the wing of abominations shall come one that maketh desolate; and even unto the full end, and that determined, shall wrath be poured out upon the desolate.

—Daniel 9:27

And forces shall stand on his part, and they shall profane the sanctuary, even the fortress, and shall take away the continual burnt-offering, and they shall set up the abomination that maketh desolate.

—Daniel 11:31

---

[182] Anderson, R. Sir (1841–1918). The Coming Prince (Cosimo Classics, 2007)

And from the time that the continual burnt-offering shall be taken away, and the abomination that maketh desolate set up, there shall be a thousand two hundred and ninety days. Blessed is he that waiteth, and cometh to the thousand three hundred and five and thirty days.
—Daniel 12:11–12

Prophesy to be fulfilled: Matthew and Mark, quoting Jesus, write of the signs of the times at the end of the age when the "abomination of desolation" spoken of by the prophet Daniel shall stand in the temple of Jerusalem.

When therefore ye see the abomination of desolation, which was spoken of through Daniel the prophet, standing in the holy place (let him that readeth understand), then let them that are in Judaea flee unto the mountains:
—Matthew 24:15–16

But when ye see the abomination of desolation standing where he ought not (let him that readeth understand), then let them that are in Judaea flee unto the mountains...
—Mark 13:14

Chapter Twenty-Three
PROPHESIES IN HOSEA

1. Messiah: He will be King David in the latter days.

...afterward shall the children of Israel return, and seek Jehovah their God, and David their king, and shall come with fear unto Jehovah and to his goodness in the latter days.

—Hosea 3:5

2. Messiah: He will be resurrected on the third day, and Israel restored.

Come, and let us return unto Jehovah; for he hath torn, and he will heal us; he hath smitten, and he will bind us up. After two days will he revive us: on the third day he will raise us up, and we shall live before him.

—Hosea 6:1–2

Prophesy fulfilled: Matthew, Mark, Luke and Paul write that Jesus would rise the third day:

...and shall deliver him unto the Gentiles to mock, and to scourge, and to crucify: and the third day he shall be raised up.

—Matthew 20:19

For he taught his disciples, and said unto them, The Son of man is delivered up into the hands of men, and they shall kill him; and when he is killed, after three days he shall rise again.

—Mark 9:31

...and they shall mock him, and shall spit upon him, and shall scourge him, and shall kill him; and after three days he shall rise again.
—Mark 10:34

Him God raised up the third day, and gave him to be made manifest, not to all the people, but unto witnesses that were chosen before of God, even to us, who ate and drank with him after he rose from the dead.
—Acts 10:40–41

...and they shall scourge and kill him: and the third day he shall rise again.
—Luke 18:33

He is not here, but is risen: remember how he spake unto you when he was yet in Galilee, saying that the Son of man must be delivered up into the hands of sinful men, and be crucified, and the third day rise again.
—Luke 24:6–7

and he said unto them, Thus it is written, that the Christ should suffer, and rise again from the dead the third day; and that repentance and remission of sins should be preached in his name unto all the nations, beginning from Jerusalem. Ye are witnesses of these things.
—Luke 24:46–48

For I delivered unto you first of all that which also I received: that Christ died for our sins according to the scriptures; and that he was buried; and that he hath been raised on the third day according to the scriptures.
—1 Corinthians 15:3–4

3. Messiah: He was called out of Egypt.

When Israel was a child, then I loved him, and called my son out of Egypt.
—Hosea 11:1

Prophesy fulfilled:

Now when they were departed, behold, an angel of the Lord appeareth to Joseph in a dream, saying, Arise and take the young child and his mother, and flee into Egypt, and be thou there until I tell thee: for Herod will seek the young child to destroy him. And he arose and took the young child and his mother by night, and departed into Egypt; and was there until the death of Herod: that it might be fulfilled which was spoken by the Lord through the prophet, saying, Out of Egypt did I call my son.

—Matthew 2:13–15

4. Messiah: He will ransom from the grave.

I will ransom them from the power of Sheol; I will redeem them from death: O death, where are thy plagues? O Sheol, where is thy destruction? repentance shall be hid from mine eyes.

—Hosea 13:14

Prophesy fulfilled: The words of Hosea are paraphrased by the Apostle Paul who writes:

But when this corruptible shall have put on incorruption, and this mortal shall have put on immortality, then shall come to pass the saying that is written, Death is swallowed up in victory. O death, where is thy victory? O death, where is thy sting? The sting of death is sin; and the power of sin is the law: but thanks be to God, who giveth us the victory through our Lord Jesus Christ.

—1 Corinthians 15:54–57

Chapter Twenty-Four
PROPHESIES OF JOEL

1. Messiah: He will pour out the Holy Spirit on whoever calls.

And it shall come to pass afterward, that I will pour out my Spirit upon all flesh; and your sons and your daughters shall prophesy, your old men shall dream dreams, your young men shall see visions: and also upon the servants and upon the handmaids in those days will I pour out my Spirit… And it shall come to pass, that whosoever shall call on the name of Jehovah shall be delivered; for in mount Zion and in Jerusalem there shall be those that escape, as Jehovah hath said, and among the remnant those whom Jehovah doth call.

—Joel 2:28–29, 32

Prophesy fulfilled: The out-pouring of the Holy Spirit, as prophesied by Joel, is mentioned by the Apostles Luke and John.

And when he had said this, he breathed on them, and saith unto them, Receive ye the Holy Spirit…

—John 20:22

And when the day of Pentecost was now come, they were all together in one place. And suddenly there came from heaven a sound as of the rushing of a mighty wind, and it filled all the house where they were sitting. And there appeared unto them tongues parting asunder, like as of fire; and it sat upon each one of them. And they were all filled with the Holy Spirit, and began to speak with other tongues, as the Spirit gave them utterance.

—Acts 2:1–4

…but this is that which hath been spoken through the prophet Joel: And it shall be in the last days, saith God, I will pour forth of my Spirit upon all flesh: and your

sons and your daughters shall prophesy, and your young men shall see visions, and your old men shall dream dreams: yea and on my servants and on my handmaidens in those days will I pour forth of my Spirit; and they shall prophesy.

—Acts 2:16–18

The Apostle John writes that following the resurrection of Jesus He appeared to the Apostles and breathed on them the Holy Spirit.

Jesus therefore said to them again, Peace be unto you: as the Father hath sent me, even so send I you. And when he had said this, he breathed on them, and saith unto them, Receive ye the Holy Spirit…

—John 20:21–22

Chapter Twenty-Five
PROPHESIES OF AMOS

1. Messiah: Darkness at noon, and mourning for an only son.

And it shall come to pass in that day, saith the Lord Jehovah, that I will cause the sun to go down at noon, and I will darken the earth in the clear day. And I will turn your feasts into mourning, and all your songs into lamentation; and I will bring sackcloth upon all loins, and baldness upon every head; and I will make it as the mourning for an only son, and the end thereof as a bitter day.

—Amos 8:9–10

Prophesy fulfilled: The Apostles Matthew, Mark and Luke all refer to the darkness that accompanied the crucifixion of Jesus from the sixth to the ninth hour.

Now from the sixth hour there was darkness over all the land until the ninth hour. And about the ninth hour Jesus cried with a loud voice, saying, Eli, Eli, lama sabachthani? that is, My God, my God, why hast thou forsaken me?

—Matthew 27:45–46

And when the sixth hour was come, there was darkness over the whole land until the ninth hour.

—Mark 15:33

And it was now about the sixth hour, and a darkness came over the whole land until the ninth hour, the sun's light failing: and the veil of the temple was rent in the midst.

—Luke 23:44–45

Reference is also made to a future post-tribulation darkness:

But immediately after the tribulation of those days the sun shall be darkened, and the moon shall not give her light, and the stars shall fall from heaven, and the powers of the heavens shall be shaken: and then shall appear the sign of the Son of man in heaven...

—Matthew 24:29–30

The sun shall be turned into darkness, and the moon into blood, before the day of the Lord come, that great and notable day: and it shall be, that whosoever shall call on the name of the Lord shall be saved.

—Acts 2:20–21

And I saw when he opened the sixth seal, and there was a great earthquake; and the sun became black as sackcloth of hair, and the whole moon became as blood

—Revelation 6:12

2. Messiah: On that day He will rebuild the Tabernacle of David.

In that day will I raise up the tabernacle of David that is fallen, and close up the breaches thereof; and I will raise up its ruins, and I will build it as in the days of old; that they may possess the remnant of Edom, and all the nations that are called by my name, saith Jehovah that doeth this.

—Amos 9:11–12

Prophesy to be fulfilled: The apostle Luke directs attention to the post-tribulation prophesy of Amos.

And to this agree the words of the prophets; as it is written, After these things I will return, and I will build again the tabernacle of David, which is fallen; and I will build again the ruins thereof, and I will set it up: that the residue of men may seek after the Lord, and all the Gentiles, upon whom my name is called, saith the Lord, who maketh these things known from of old.

—Acts 15:15–17

Chapter Twenty-Six

PROPHESIES IN OBADIAH

1. Messiah: He is the Deliverer.

But in mount Zion there shall be those that escape, and it shall be holy; and the house of Jacob shall possess their possessions. And the house of Jacob shall be a fire, and the house of Joseph a flame, and the house of Esau for stubble, and they shall burn among them, and devour them; and there shall not be any remaining to the house of Esau; for Jehovah hath spoken it.

—Obadiah 1:17–18

Chapter Twenty-Seven

Prophesies in Jonah (Jonas)

1. Messiah: He was in the heart of the earth three days and three nights.

And Jehovah prepared a great fish to swallow up Jonah; and Jonah was in the belly of the fish three days and three nights… Then Jonah prayed unto Jehovah his God out of the fish's belly. And he said, I called by reason of mine affliction unto Jehovah, And he answered me; Out of the belly of Sheol cried I, and thou heardest my voice. For thou didst cast me into the depth, in the heart of the seas, and the flood was round about me; all thy waves and thy billows passed over me. And I said, I am cast out from before thine eyes; yet I will look again toward thy holy temple. The waters compassed me about, even to the soul; the deep was round about me; the weeds were wrapped about my head. I went down to the bottoms of the mountains; the earth with its bars closed upon me for ever: yet hast thou brought up my life from the pit, O Jehovah my God.

—Jonah 1:17; 2:1–6

Prophesy fulfilled: Some of the scribes and Pharisees asked Jesus: "Teacher we want to see a sign from You. Jesus answered and said to the people:

An evil and adulterous generation seeketh after a sign; and there shall no sign be given to it but the sign of Jonah the prophet: for as Jonah was three days and three nights in the belly of the whale; so shall the Son of man be three days and three nights in the heart of the earth. The men of Nineveh shall stand up in the judgment with this generation, and shall condemn it: for they repented at the preaching of Jonah; and behold, a greater than Jonah is here.

—Matthew 12:39–41

Part Three: Prophecies Fulfilled

Ye know how to discern the face of the heaven; but ye cannot discern the signs of the times. An evil and adulterous generation seeketh after a sign; and there shall no sign be given unto it, but the sign of Jonah. And he left them, and departed.

—Matthew 16:3–4

And when the multitudes were gathering together unto him, he began to say, This generation is an evil generation: it seeketh after a sign; and there shall no sign be given to it but the sign of Jonah. For even as Jonah became a sign unto the Ninevites, so shall also the Son of man be to this generation.

—Luke 11:29–30

The Jews therefore answered and said unto him, What sign showest thou unto us, seeing that thou doest these things? Jesus answered and said unto them, Destroy this temple, and in three days I will raise it up. The Jews therefore said, Forty and six years was this temple in building, and wilt thou raise it up in three days? But he spake of the temple of his body. When therefore he was raised from the dead, his disciples remembered that he spake this; and they believed the scripture, and the word which Jesus had said.

—John 2:18–22

Chapter Twenty-Eight

PROPHESIES IN MICAH

1. Messiah: He will gather the remnant of Israel and go ahead of them.

I will surely assemble, O Jacob, all of thee; I will surely gather the remnant of Israel; I will put them together as the sheep of Bozrah, as a flock in the midst of their pasture; they shall make great noise by reason of the multitude of men. The breaker is gone up before them: they have broken forth and passed on to the gate, and are gone out thereat; and their king is passed on before them, and Jehovah at the head of them.

—Micah 2:12–13

2. Messiah: He will teach and judge out of Zion in the latter days.

But in the latter days it shall come to pass, that the mountain of Jehovah's house shall be established on the top of the mountains, and it shall be exalted above the hills; and peoples shall flow unto it. And many nations shall go and say, Come ye, and let us go up to the mountain of Jehovah, and to the house of the God of Jacob; and he will teach us of his ways, and we will walk in his paths. For out of Zion shall go forth the law, and the word of Jehovah from Jerusalem; and he will judge between many peoples, and will decide concerning strong nations afar off: and they shall beat their swords into plowshares, and their spears into pruning-hooks; nation shall not lift up sword against nation, neither shall they learn war any more.

—Micah 4:1–3

Part Three: Prophecies Fulfilled

3. Messiah: He shall come forth from Bethlehem his birth place.

But thou, Beth-lehem Ephrathah, which art little to be among the thousands of Judah, out of thee shall one come forth unto me that is to be ruler in Israel; whose goings forth are from of old, from everlasting.
—Micah 5:2

Prophesy fulfilled:

Now when Jesus was born in Bethlehem of Judaea in the days of Herod the king, behold, Wise-men from the east came to Jerusalem, saying, Where is he that is born King of the Jews? for we saw his star in the east, and are come to worship him. And when Herod the king heard it, he was troubled, and all Jerusalem with him. And gathering together all the chief priests and scribes of the people, he inquired of them where the Christ should be born. And they said unto him, In Bethlehem of Judaea: for thus it is written through the prophet, And thou Bethlehem, land of Judah, art in no wise least among the princes of Judah: for out of thee shall come forth a governor, who shall be shepherd of my people Israel.
—Matthew 2:1–6

And Joseph also went up from Galilee, out of the city of Nazareth, into Judaea, to the city of David, which is called Bethlehem, because he was of the house and family of David; to enrol himself with Mary, who was betrothed to him, being great with child. And it came to pass, while they were there, the days were fulfilled that she should be delivered. And she brought forth her firstborn son; and she wrapped him in swaddling clothes, and laid him in a manger, because there was no room for them in the inn.
—Luke 2:4–7

Some of the multitude therefore, when they heard these words, said, This is of a truth the prophet. Others said, This is the Christ. But some said, What, doth the Christ come out of Galilee? Hath not the scripture said that the Christ cometh of the seed of David, and from Bethlehem, the village where David was?
—John 7:40–42

Chapter Twenty-Nine

PROPHESIES IN NAHUM

1. Messiah: He is a Stronghold in the day of trouble.

Jehovah is good, a stronghold in the day of trouble; and he knoweth them that take refuge in him.

—Nahum 1:7

The Chronicler, as well as David, refer to God as my stronghold:

God, my rock, in him will I take refuge; my shield, and the horn of my salvation, my high tower, and my refuge; my saviour, thou savest me from violence.

—2 Samuel 22:3

Jehovah is my rock, and my fortress, and my deliverer; my God, my rock, in whom I will take refuge; my shield, and the horn of my salvation, my high tower.

—Psalm 18:2

Chapter Thirty
PROPHESIES IN HABAKKUK

1. Messiah: His glory shall fill the earth.

For the earth shall be filled with the knowledge of the glory of Jehovah, as the waters cover the sea.

—Habakkuk 2:14

Prophesy to be fulfilled:

And the city hath no need of the sun, neither of the moon, to shine upon it: for the glory of God did lighten it, and the lamp thereof is the Lamb. And the nations shall walk amidst the light thereof: and the kings of the earth bring their glory into it.

—Revelation 21:23–24

Chapter Thirty-One

PROPHESIES IN ZEPHANIAH

1. Messiah: He is the just Lord and King in their midst.

Jehovah in the midst of her is righteous; he will not do iniquity; every morning doth he bring his justice to light, he faileth not; but the unjust knoweth no shame... Jehovah hath taken away thy judgments, he hath cast out thine enemy: the King of Israel, even Jehovah, is in the midst of thee; thou shalt not fear evil any more.

—Zephaniah 3:5, 15

Chapter Thirty-Two
Prophesies in Haggai

1. Messiah: He will fill the temple with glory.

...and the precious things of all nations shall come; and I will fill this house with glory, saith Jehovah of hosts.

—Haggai 2:7

Chapter Thirty-Three
PROPHESIES IN ZECHARIAH

1. Messiah: He will dwell in the midst of Judah his inheritance.

For I, saith Jehovah, will be unto her a wall of fire round about, and I will be the glory in the midst of her… Sing and rejoice, O daughter of Zion; for, lo, I come, and I will dwell in the midst of thee, saith Jehovah. And many nations shall join themselves to Jehovah in that day, and shall be my people; and I will dwell in the midst of thee, and thou shalt know that Jehovah of hosts hath sent me unto thee. And Jehovah shall inherit Judah as his portion in the holy land, and shall yet choose Jerusalem.

—Zechariah 2:5, 10–12

Prophesy fulfilled: The Apostle John in Revelation writes that Christ, the Lamb, will sit on the throne of David, and that every creature will worship Him:

And every created thing which is in the heaven, and on the earth, and under the earth, and on the sea, and all things that are in them, heard I saying, Unto him that sitteth on the throne, and unto the Lamb, be the blessing, and the honor, and the glory, and the dominion, for ever and ever.

—Revelation 5:13

2. Messiah: The Branch shall build the temple, and rule from His throne.

…for, behold, I will bring forth my servant the Branch.

—Zechariah 3:8

Behold, the man whose name is the Branch: and he shall grow up out of his place; and he shall build the temple of Jehovah; even he shall build the temple of Jehovah;

and he shall bear the glory, and shall sit and rule upon his throne; and he shall be a priest upon his throne; and the counsel of peace shall be between them both.

—Zechariah 6:12–13

3. Messiah: He is coming with all his gathered saints.

Thus saith Jehovah of hosts: Behold, I will save my people from the east country, and from the west country; and I will bring them, and they shall dwell in the midst of Jerusalem; and they shall be my people, and I will be their God, in truth and in righteousness.

—Zechariah 8:7–8

4. Messiah: His feet will stand on the Mount of Olives in the day of the Lord.

For I will gather all nations against Jerusalem to battle; and the city shall be taken, and the houses rifled, and the women ravished; and half of the city shall go forth into captivity, and the residue of the people shall not be cut off from the city. Then shall Jehovah go forth, and fight against those nations, as when he fought in the day of battle. And his feet shall stand in that day upon the mount of Olives, which is before Jerusalem on the east; and the mount of Olives shall be cleft in the midst thereof toward the east and toward the west, and there shall be a very great valley; and half of the mountain shall remove toward the north, and half of it toward the south. And ye shall flee by the valley of my mountains; for the valley of the mountains shall reach unto Azel; yea, ye shall flee, like as ye fled from before the earthquake in the days of Uzziah king of Judah; and Jehovah my God shall come, and all the holy ones with thee.

—Zechariah 14:2–5

Prophesy fulfilled: The Apostles Matthew and Paul refer to the Second Coming of Jesus Christ in the glory of His Father with his angels:

For the Son of man shall come in the glory of his Father with his angels; and then shall he render unto every man according to his deeds.

—Matthew 16:27

But when the Son of man shall come in his glory, and all the angels with him, then shall he sit on the throne of his glory: and before him shall be gathered all the nations: and he shall separate them one from another, as the shepherd separateth the sheep from the goats.

—Matthew 25:31–32

For whosoever shall be ashamed of me and of my words in this adulterous and sinful generation, the Son of man also shall be ashamed of him, when he cometh in the glory of his Father with the holy angels.

—Mark 8:38

For the Lord himself shall descend from heaven, with a shout, with the voice of the archangel, and with the trump of God: and the dead in Christ shall rise first; then we that are alive, that are left, shall together with them be caught up in the clouds, to meet the Lord in the air: and so shall we ever be with the Lord.

—1 Thessalonians 4:16–17

...and to you that are afflicted rest with us, at the revelation of the Lord Jesus from heaven with the angels of his power in flaming fire, rendering vengeance to them that know not God, and to them that obey not the gospel of our Lord Jesus.

—2 Thessalonians 1:7

5. Messiah: He makes a triumphal entry into Jerusalem riding on a donkey.

Rejoice greatly, O daughter of Zion; shout, O daughter of Jerusalem: behold, thy king cometh unto thee; he is just, and having salvation; lowly, and riding upon an ass, even upon a colt the foal of an ass.

—Zechariah 9:9

Prophesy fulfilled:

Now this is come to pass, that it might be fulfilled which was spoken through the prophet, saying, Tell ye the daughter of Zion, Behold, thy King cometh unto thee, meek, and riding upon an ass, and upon a colt the foal of an ass. And the disciples went, and did even as Jesus appointed them, and brought the ass, and the colt, and put on them their garments; and he sat thereon. And the most part of the multitude spread their garments in the way; and others cut branches from the trees, and spread them in the way. And the multitudes that went before him, and that followed, cried, saying, Hosanna to the son of David: Blessed is he that cometh in the name of the Lord; Hosanna in the highest. And when he was come into Jerusalem, all the city was stirred, saying, Who is this? And the multitudes said, This is the prophet, Jesus, from Nazareth of Galilee.

—Matthew 21:4–11

And they that went before, and they that followed, cried, Hosanna; Blessed is he that cometh in the name of the Lord: Blessed is the kingdom that cometh, the kingdom of our father David: Hosanna in the highest.

—Mark 11:9–10

Go your way into the village over against you; in which as ye enter ye shall find a colt tied, whereon no man ever yet sat: loose him, and bring him… And as they were loosing the colt, the owners thereof said unto them, Why loose ye the colt? And they said, The Lord hath need of him. And they brought him to Jesus: and they threw their garments upon the colt, and set Jesus thereon. And as he went, they spread their garments in the way. And as he was now drawing nigh, even at the descent of the mount of Olives, the whole multitude of the disciples began to rejoice and praise God with a loud voice for all the mighty works which they had seen; saying, Blessed is the King that cometh in the name of the Lord: peace in heaven, and glory in the highest.

—Luke 19:30, 33–38

On the morrow a great multitude that had come to the feast, when they heard that Jesus was coming to Jerusalem, took the branches of the palm trees, and went forth to meet him, and cried out, Hosanna: Blessed is he that cometh in the name of the Lord, even the King of Israel. And Jesus, having found a young ass, sat thereon; as it is written, Fear not, daughter of Zion: behold, thy King cometh, sitting on an ass's colt. These things understood not his disciples at the first: but when Jesus was glorified, then remembered they that these things were written of him, and that they had done these things unto him.

—John 12:12–16

6. Messiah: He is betrayed for thirty pieces of silver.

And I said unto them, If ye think good, give me my hire; and if not, forbear. So they weighed for my hire thirty pieces of silver. And Jehovah said unto me, Cast it

Prophesies in Zechariah

unto the potter, the goodly price that I was prized at by them. And I took the thirty pieces of silver, and cast them unto the potter, in the house of Jehovah.

—Zechariah 11:12–13

Prophesy fulfilled:

Then one of the twelve, who was called Judas Iscariot, went unto the chief priests, and said, What are ye willing to give me, and I will deliver him unto you? And they weighed unto him thirty pieces of silver. And from that time he sought opportunity to deliver him unto them.

—Matthew 26:14–16

Then Judas, who betrayed him, when he saw that he was condemned, repented himself, and brought back the thirty pieces of silver to the chief priests and elders, saying, I have sinned in that I betrayed innocent blood. But they said, What is that to us? see thou to it. And he cast down the pieces of silver into the sanctuary, and departed; and he went away and hanged himself. And the chief priests took the pieces of silver, and said, It is not lawful to put them into the treasury, since it is the price of blood. And they took counsel, and bought with them the potter's field, to bury strangers in. Wherefore that field was called, The field of blood, unto this day. Then was fulfilled that which was spoken through Jeremiah the prophet, saying, And they took the thirty pieces of silver, the price of him that was priced, whom certain of the children of Israel did price; and they gave them for the potter's field, as the Lord appointed me.

—Matthew 27:3–10

While I was with them, I kept them in thy name which thou hast given me: and I guarded them, and not one of them perished, but the son of perdition; that the scripture might be fulfilled.

—John 17:12

7. Messiah: His hands are pierced.

And I will pour upon the house of David, and upon the inhabitants of Jerusalem, the spirit of grace and of supplication; and they shall look unto me whom they have pierced; and they shall mourn for him, as one mourneth for his only son, and shall be in bitterness for him, as one that is in bitterness for his first-born.

—Zechariah 12:10

And one shall say unto him, What are these wounds between thine arms? Then he shall answer, Those with which I was wounded in the house of my friends.

—Zechariah 13:6

Prophesy fulfilled:

For these things came to pass, that the scripture might be fulfilled, A bone of him shall not be broken. And again another scripture saith, They shall look on him whom they pierced.

—John 19:36–37

Except I shall see in his hands the print of the nails, and put my finger into the print of the nails, and put my hand into his side, I will not believe.

—John 20:25

Behold, he cometh with the clouds; and every eye shall see him, and they that pierced him; and all the tribes of the earth shall mourn over him. Even so, Amen.

—Revelation 1:7

8. Messiah: He was arrested and his disciples scattered like sheep.

Awake, O sword, against my shepherd, and against the man that is my fellow, saith Jehovah of hosts: smite the shepherd, and the sheep shall be scattered.

—Zechariah 13:7

Prophesy fulfilled:

Then saith Jesus unto them, All ye shall be offended in me this night: for it is written, I will smite the shepherd, and the sheep of the flock shall be scattered abroad.

—Matthew 26:31

But all this is come to pass, that the scriptures of the prophets might be fulfilled. Then all the disciples left him, and fled.

—Matthew 26:56

And Jesus saith unto them, All ye shall be offended: for it is written, I will smite the shepherd, and the sheep shall be scattered abroad... But Peter said unto him, Although all shall be offended, yet will not I. And Jesus saith unto him, Verily I say unto thee, that thou to-day, even this night, before the cock crow twice, shalt deny me thrice.

—Mark 14:27, 29–30

And they all left him, and fled. And a certain young man followed with him, having a linen cloth cast about him, over his naked body: and they lay hold on him; but he left the linen cloth, and fled naked.

—Mark 14:50–52[183]

Jesus answered them, Do ye now believe? Behold, the hour cometh, yea, is come, that ye shall be scattered, every man to his own, and shall leave me alone: and yet I am not alone, because the Father is with me.

—John 16:31–32

9. Messiah: He is King over the whole earth.

And Jehovah shall be King over all the earth: in that day shall Jehovah be one, and his name one.

—Zechariah 14:9

---

[183] The young man may have been Barnabas's cousin John Mark.

Chapter Thirty-Four
Prophesies in Malachi

1. Messiah: His name shall be great among the Gentiles.

For from the rising of the sun even unto the going down of the same my name shall be great among the Gentiles; and in every place incense shall be offered unto my name, and a pure offering: for my name shall be great among the Gentiles, saith Jehovah of hosts.

—Malachi 1:11

2. Messiah: His messenger will precede and prepare the way before Him.

Behold, I send my messenger, and he shall prepare the way before me: and the Lord, whom ye seek, will suddenly come to his temple; and the messenger of the covenant, whom ye desire, behold, he cometh, saith Jehovah of hosts

—Malachi 3:1

Prophesy fulfilled:

For this is he that was spoken of through Isaiah the prophet [Isaiah 40:3], saying, The voice of one crying in the wilderness, make ye ready the way of the Lord, make his paths straight.

—Matthew 3:3

This is he, of whom it is written, Behold, I send my messenger before thy face, who shall prepare thy way before thee.

—Matthew 11:10

Part Three: Prophecies Fulfilled

> *Even as it is written in Isaiah the prophet, Behold, I send my messenger before thy face, who shall prepare thy way.*
>
> —Mark 1:2

> *And he shall go before his face in the spirit and power of Elijah, to turn the hearts of the fathers to the children, and the disobedient to walk in the wisdom of the just; to make ready for the Lord a people prepared for him… Yea and thou, child, shalt be called the prophet of the Most High: for thou shalt go before the face of the Lord to make ready his ways.*
>
> —Luke 1:17, 76

> *This is he of whom it is written, Behold, I send my messenger before thy face, who shall prepare thy way before thee.*
>
> —Luke 7:27

> *He said, I am the voice of one crying in the wilderness, Make straight the way of the Lord, as said Isaiah the prophet.*
>
> —John 1:23

3. Messiah: He shall purge, refine and purify.

> *But who can abide the day of his coming? and who shall stand when he appeareth? for he is like a refiner's fire, and like fullers' soap: and he will sit as a refiner and purifier of silver, and he will purify the sons of Levi, and refine them as gold and silver; and they shall offer unto Jehovah offerings in righteousness.*
>
> —Malachi 3:2–3

Prophesy to be fulfilled:

> *…whose fan is in his hand, thoroughly to cleanse his threshing-floor, and to gather the wheat into his garner; but the chaff he will burn up with unquenchable fire.*
>
> —Luke 3:17

> *For other foundation can no man lay than that which is laid, which is Jesus Christ. But if any man buildeth on the foundation gold, silver, costly stones, wood, hay, stubble; each man's work shall be made manifest: for the day shall declare it, because it is revealed in fire; and the fire itself shall prove each man's work of what sort it is. If any man's work shall abide which he built thereon, he shall receive a*

reward. If any man's work shall be burned, he shall suffer loss: but he himself shall be saved; yet so as through fire.

—1 Corinthians 3:11–15

And out of his mouth proceedeth a sharp sword, that with it he should smite the nations: and he shall rule them with a rod of iron: and he treadeth the winepress of the fierceness of the wrath of God, the Almighty. And he hath on his garment and on his thigh a name written, King of Kings, and Lord of Lords.

—Revelation 19:15–16

4. Messiah: He is the Sun of Righteousness.

But unto you that fear my name shall the sun of righteousness arise with healing in its wings; and ye shall go forth, and gambol as calves of the stall.

—Malachi 4:2

5. Messiah: His messenger will come in the spirit of Elijah.

Behold, I will send you Elijah the prophet before the great and terrible day of Jehovah come. And he shall turn the heart of the fathers to the children, and the heart of the children to their fathers; lest I come and smite the earth with a curse.

—Malachi 4:5–6

Prophesy fulfilled:

For this is he that was spoken of through Isaiah the prophet, saying, The voice of one crying in the wilderness, make ye ready the way of the Lord, make his paths straight.

—Matthew 3:3–2

And as these went their way, Jesus began to say unto the multitudes concerning John, What went ye out into the wilderness to behold? a reed shaken with the wind? But what went ye out to see? a man clothed in soft raiment? Behold, they that wear soft raiment are in kings' houses. But wherefore went ye out? to see a prophet? Yea, I say unto you, and much more than a prophet. This is he, of whom it is written, Behold, I send my messenger before thy face, who shall prepare thy way before thee... And if ye are willing to receive it, this is Elijah, that is to come.

—Matthew 11:7–10, 14

Part Three: Prophecies Fulfilled

And his disciples asked him, saying, Why then say the scribes that Elijah must first come? And he answered and said, Elijah indeed cometh, and shall restore all things: but I say unto you, that Elijah is come already, and they knew him not, but did unto him whatsoever they would. Even so shall the Son of man also suffer of them.

—Matthew 17:10–12

And they asked him, saying, How is it that the scribes say that Elijah must first come? And he said unto them, Elijah indeed cometh first, and restoreth all things: and how is it written of the Son of man, that he should suffer many things and be set at nought? But I say unto you, that Elijah is come, and they have also done unto him whatsoever they would, even as it is written of him.

—Mark 9:11–13

And he shall go before his face in the spirit and power of Elijah, to turn the hearts of the fathers to the children, and the disobedient to walk in the wisdom of the just; to make ready for the Lord a people prepared for him.

—Luke 1:17